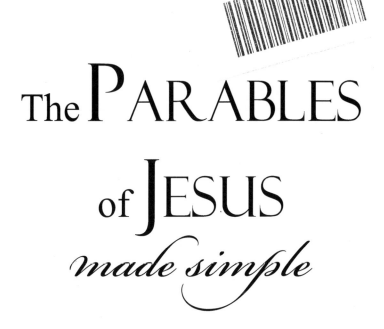

The PARABLES

of JESUS

made simple

MATTHEW ROBERT PAYNE

DEDICATION

This book is dedicated to the Holy Trinity of God and to a personal friend

To Jesus,

Thank you Jesus for being my friend from age 8. You made an impact on my life and started speaking to me and making yourself known through songs and Scripture verses. All my life I have known you and you have been especially close to me through all the years of my addictive sin. As dark as things became and as bad a sinner as I was, you have always been there for me, always forgiven me, always loved me. Thank you very much for being my Savior.

To the Father,

Thank you Father for running to me and embracing me, like the father in the Prodigal Son parable. I first met you in Heaven and you embraced me with your love and showed me that even wicked sinners are allowed into Heaven to be forgiven. I will never forget what you told me there in Heaven in that vision and it has inspired me to go on and do big things.

To the Holy Spirit,

Thank you Holy Spirit for being so humble. You are the last person of the Trinity. I would say that you are the most humble out of the three but I know that you are God. No part of God could be more humble. Thank you especially for giving me the inspiration for what I have shared in this book, because surely many of the words and many of the thoughts that came into my mind were inspired by you. Thank you also for conveying the thoughts and voices of Jesus and God the Father through all my life and thank you also for illuminating the Bible and giving me insight and wisdom into what the Bible says.

And last but not the least,

Thanks to Robbin Moulds, a personal friend and pastor in my life.

Robbin,

Thank you for demonstrating practically what the love of Jesus Christ really is. I think every human being needs a real touchstone — a real point of contact between God's grace and the world. Equally important, you represented Jesus Christ to me and thank you for being my friend.

ACKNOWLEDGMENTS

I wish to thank my mother and father first and foremost for bringing me up and suffering with me as I grew into the person I needed to be to publish this work. Many faithful hours of prayer went into the restoration of this child of God into what he is today and my mother and father were the people on their knees.

I have to once again thank the Trinity for being my guide and my strength. Through the testimony of my life shared in this book and the insights I have been given, readers of this book will come to know that Jesus, God the Father and the God the Holy Spirit are very real entities.

I have to thank my psychiatrists for keeping me out of hospital and keeping my mental illness in check, for without them, and without my medication I would not have been able to accomplish this mammoth task.

I have to thank my pastors, past and present for being there for me, for their un-biased love and support of me and the patience in seeing me develop to this stage in my life where I can accomplish the writing of this book.

I have to thank my siblings, Rodney, Carmen and Tony for loving me as I am and championing me to be all that I could be in life. I have to especially thank Rodney for being my very special friend and listening to me talk over the phone for hundreds of hours.

I have to thank my former wife for once loving me, and I have to thank my son Brandyn for giving me the reason to live.

I have to thank my personal friends, too many to name all of them, but Sarah, Yianni and Phil have to be commended for sticking by me through the years.

For the book's production, I have to thank Odesk.com for their freelance website that allowed me to get labor cheap enough to have this book affordable for me to produce and I personally thank all the people that worked on the book from the transcribers to the editors and the book reviewers, needed for the back cover.

I have to thank "Create Space" publishing for producing this book for me and the Australian Government Social Security for advancing me a loan to do so.

Thanks to Charlotte for the final edit.

And a big thank-you to all the friends of my family who have loved and supported me throughout the years.

TABLE OF CONTENTS

CHAPTER 1

THE PARABLE OF THE ALERT SERVANT
MARK 13:33-37

Mark 13:33-37 Reads:

"Take heed, watch and pray; for you do not know when the time is. It is like a man going out to a far country, who left his house and gave authority to his servants, and to each his work, and commanded the doorkeeper to watch. Watch therefore, for you do not know when the master of the house is coming—in the evening, at midnight, at the crowing of the rooster, or in the morning— lest, coming suddenly, he find you sleeping, and what I say to you, I say to you all: Watch!"

Jesus shared with His followers the signs of the end time. He said that there will be false Christ's and false prophets who will try to deceive people. There will be terrible tribulation; the stars of Heaven will fall and other devastating events will occur.

While reading or listening to these parables, I hope you will fully understand who the Lord Jesus Christ really is and what is truly going on. Jesus often used parables in His teaching, with the topic of His leaving and returning a recurring theme.

I have heard many recent accounts of people who have met either Jesus or the Father in Heaven, and they were told that the end time is very near, for Jesus is coming back very soon. Some of these people had visions and others had experienced near death encounters where they had been aware of leaving their physical body for a short time and then suddenly finding themselves back again on familiar territory.

In this parable, Jesus uses the character of a master going away to a foreign country, to illustrate His ascending to Heaven and leaving earth behind until the Second Coming. At that time, Jesus was still with the people, but today, Jesus has in fact gone to a far country. This is no longer just the topic of a parable. It says in the Scriptures just before this passage, concerning the day of His second coming; that we cannot know exactly when Jesus will return. In Matthew 24:36 Jesus said, "But of that day and hour, no one knows, not even the angels of heaven, but My Father only." The plea of Jesus follows: *"Watch therefore, for you do not know what hour your Lord is coming. Therefore, you*

1

also be ready, for the Son of Man is coming at an hour you do not expect." (Matthew 24:42 and 44)

In several parables, Jesus talks about leaving people in charge. In the "Parable of the Talents" and the "Parable of the Ten Minas," He speaks about going away and leaving us to do something good and faithful while He is gone. In the "Parable of the Five Foolish Virgins," people were waiting for the bridegroom, whose return was delayed. In the "Parable of the Wedding Feast," the king sent out for people to come to his feast, but they all had their excuses! In this parable, Jesus was telling the people that He would be going and then returning some time later, pointing people towards His imminent return.

The early disciples were expecting Jesus' return to happen in their lifetime. So too, down the centuries, His return has been the Christian's hope in every generation. Today, Christ's church can see all the things that have been prophesied in the Old Testament and by the words of Jesus Himself, falling into place in a way that has never occurred before. The church worldwide is excited and expectant that in their generation, Jesus will come for them; suddenly and secretly, like a "thief in the night," the Bible says.

We are told of a time when people who are longing for Jesus to return, will not experience death, but instead, will be suddenly caught up by God to meet Jesus in the air and will be forever with Him. People on earth will speculate why so many millions of people have disappeared all at the exact same moment!There will be devastating disasters all around the world; crashing planes, trains, buses, and cars, surgeons and hospital staff snatched away, families separated and loved ones missing.

"For the Lord Himself will descend from heaven with a shout, with *the voice of an archangel, and with the trumpet of God. And the dead in Christ will rise first. Then we who are alive and remain shall be caught up together with them in the clouds to meet the Lord in the air. And thus we shall always be with the Lord. Therefore comfort one another with these words. (1 Thessalonians 4:16-18)*

1 Corinthians 15:51 says: "Behold, I tell you a mystery: We shall not all sleep, but we shall all be changed – in a moment, in the twinkling of an eye, at the last trumpet. For the trumpet will sound, and the dead will be raised incorruptible, and we shall be changed."

This event is known by believers as the "Rapture" - a term meaning "snatched away" for that is what will happen. It will occur at some stage before Jesus "physically" returns to Israel as Judge and King. Then the nations will be judged. Because Jesus identified with us and suffered in our place, the Father has given Him the power and authority to be the Judge of all the earth. If you have not surrendered your life to Him before then, it will be too late, once Jesus physically returns to the holy land called Jerusalem.

In this particular parable, Jesus is talking about coming back at a time that no one knows. So what is the purpose of leaving us behind – what should we be doing? He has left His church in charge! What should we be doing while we wait for our Master to return? How should we conduct our business?

When I worked for McDonald's Corporation, at four different stores, three of them were privately owned, each by a different franchisee. Each franchisee operated the store as a private owner. He paid McDonald's commissions on all the sales he made; he bought all his food from McDonald's; he paid the lease of his building to them as well, but essentially he owned the local business. These owners treated me like their own son.

There was also a time when I worked for a McDonald's store that was owned by the Corporation. It had a manager in charge, but neither he, nor his team had ownership of the store. In other words, it didn't have a private owner; it was owned by the McDonald's Corporation. This was because it was new and it hadn't made sufficient sales per week to sell the business to a private owner. When its profits grew, it would be sold.

When I worked for the corporate-owned store, McDonald's had a visiting area supervisor who regularly came to check on our store and others, under his authority. Sometimes, another store would tip us off and say, "He has just left us! He's on his way to you." The moment this happened, our managers would panic and throw us into a frantic flurry of activity. They would tell us to clean the cooking area and every other part of the store. We would all be rushing around like mad people trying desperately to make the store shine spic and span.

For a while, I conformed to this, but one day in total frustration, I angrily confronted both the manager on duty and then the store manager. I said, "To put pressure on us, to instantly clean up like this, just because the supervisor is coming is being disrespectful to McDonald's Corporation. The store should be kept clean whether anyone is checking on us or not. People are meant to be doing their jobs *all the time!* The store is meant to function that way. You shouldn't be putting such pressure on the staff and expect them to have it spic and span in ten minutes!" You can only imagine the response I received.

This is similar to what Jesus is saying. As Christians, we should live our lives in such a way, that if Jesus should return tomorrow, He would find us ready for His arrival. This means, that we are to be in union with Him; resting in His love and peace and therefore bearing fruit that remains. In the "Parable of the Five Foolish Virgins," I share that the wise virgins lived a life that consisted of joy in the presence of the Holy Spirit. This was represented by the oil and it is how we should always live.

In other words, there should be no fear of Jesus coming back and finding "hands in the cookie jar." As His children, our lives should reflect His love - there should be none of us stealing or treating people indifferently or no one having a bad attitude. Jesus should not catch you off guard. Instead, you should be feeling joy, living a life of peace, regardless of life's day to day frustrations. You should feel inwardly contented, knowing that you are loved and accepted into God's own family.

Jesus knows first hand that life in this world's system is not easy! It has its hard, difficult times. This parable is certainly not saying that you must be perfect and without any sin in your life, so that if the Master was to return early, He would surprise you and reject you. No! He will never reject one of His children. His shed blood on the cross makes us perfect in His sight! If by faith, we accept this, we will manifest Christ's perfection in our life. On the cross, Jesus took the punishment for our sin and gave us His right standing with His Father. As believers, we are accepted by God totally, even though *we know we fall short.*

One parable tells of the wise and faithful servant who is doing what his master commanded him to do. It also tells of the evil servant who is treating people badly and recklessly drinking too much. Sadly, many Christians live a lifestyle where there is not much difference between them and the non-Christians in the world. This is not the way we should be behaving when the Master returns.

I am not laying down the law and condemning people for drinking or having a life that has sin in it. I readily admit that I have lived a wretched life of sin for many years. I personally lived under an indoctrination of judgment and condemnation, which in turn caused me to sin even more! Therefore having been set free, I no longer condemn others. Also, I no longer pretend to be self-righteous in order to be accepted by God.

Regardless of my own feelings, there is a warning in Jesus' parables that we should be conducting our lives in a holy and righteous manner. That way, we don't give a foot-hole for the devil to attack us. We can be strong and resist temptation because of God's power working in us. Also, because of His presence and grace, we can live holy lives!

Holiness does not come from self-worth. Holiness comes from the power and the enabling of the Holy Spirit through the grace of God, established by the finished work of Jesus Christ on the cross for us. Jesus is saying that we should be living in a manner that is ready for Him to come back at any time. We should be conducting our personal and public life appropriately — in a way that brings honor to the Lord Jesus Christ.

I hope that you will be encouraged. Jesus summarized His Father's commands by saying in John 13:34-35 "A new commandment I give to you that you love one another, as I have loved you, that you also love one another. By this all will know that you are My disciples, if you have love for one another."

One of the signs of the end times is the fact that, "the love of many will grow cold" (Matthew 24: 12). We are living in a society where many people simply do not care for one another because of the self-centeredness in their own life. As Christians, (Christian means, "little Christ") we should imitate Jesus and His way of living: He had a servant's heart; He was always looking for opportunities to show God's love to people and ultimately, He surrendered His own life for mankind.

Therefore, ask God to make you "people-focused,"meaning to consciously look for ways and opportunities to be Jesus to those around you. This will require personal sacrifice and goes against the natural desires of our flesh. If we have a servant heart and rest in God's enabling, then a pattern of good works will be evidenced in our life to His glory.

I am not saying that the Christian life should be sad or anything laborious. Our life should be enjoyed and we need to learn to find our calling and purpose, so that we can live it joyfully. For all of us, our highest calling is simply to enjoy God and to learn to love others in the forgiveness and patience of Christ.

I hope you have enjoyed this parable, I pray that Jesus our Lord will find you *"ready and waiting" when He* returns for you.

CHAPTER 2

THE PARABLE OF THE BARREN FIG TREE
LUKE 13:6-9

Luke 13:6-9 says:

"He also spoke this parable: A certain man had a fig tree planted in his vineyard and he came seeking fruit on it, and found none.

Then he said to the keeper of his vineyard, 'Look, for three years, I have come seeking fruit on this fig tree, and find none; cut it down; why does it use up the ground?'

"But he answered and said to him, 'Sir, let it alone this year also, until I dig around it and fertilize it and if it bears fruit, well; but if not, after that you can cut it down.'"

I feel compelled to share some of my life, which may help illustrate this parable to you.

First of all, on the surface, this parable is talking about a barren fig tree. Normally, a fig tree does not bear fruit for three or four years, but in the parable, the implication is that this particular type of fig tree *should have been* bearing fruit and the owner of the vineyard had unsuccessfully sought it for three years. (Perhaps, if the tree had not been able to bear fruit on its second or third year, it would have been different.) But here, the owner is frustrated and he wants to cut it down immediately.

I find that I need to be able to apply the things that I read in the Bible to my own personal experiences in order to fully appreciate and understand them. I need to be able to relate Scripture to myself. This may seem strange to you, but this is just how I am.

I am forty three years of age. For a period of sixteen years, I genuinely thought I was one of the last two prophets that were called to come and judge the world. I actually believed in my manic state that I was the reincarnation of Elijah, the prophet. You see, I suffer from a mental illness called, "Schizoaffective Disorder," which is a combination of Bipolar Disorder and Schizophrenia. Part of the Bipolar Disorder is a delusional mind-set called, "Visions of Grandeur." I steadfastly believed that both Moses and I were the two Prophets mentioned in the Book of Revelation, chapter

5

eleven. (I was continually expecting to meet up with Moses and actually thought that I had found him on two occasions). I was paranoid that I had to learn how to accomplish my illustrious mission from God; therefore, I spent all those terrible years, searching the Scriptures desperately trying to work out every unfulfilled prophecy in the world. I was not only delusional, but very tense and frustrated. Looking back now, I know that I was extremely judgmental and overbearing, especially towards my brothers and sisters in the Lord. I had even been kicked out of some churches.

I reacted very strongly against all those who believed that we are saved by grace and that all our sins, past, present and future, were forgiven through the shed blood of Jesus Christ. I would not accept the fact that Christians are now not under the commands or the judgments of the law. In those days I would agree with absolutely *none of the teaching on God's grace!* Needless to say, I had no joy and very few "normal" friends accept my own family who of course loved me with God's kind of love.

Since being on medication, an enormous load has lifted but I still remained very legalistic. I have for the past four years, been writing Christian articles on the internet. Also during that time, I have been operating a prophetic website, doing personal prophecies for people, and only recently have I come to the revelation that my past understanding has been totally wrong. I needed to repent and adopt the wonderful inner assurance that the work of redemption has been fully paid for by the Savior. Jesus said, "It is finished!" We are now in the grace of the New Covenant.

There are many articles I wrote that I still believe contain good and solid content, yet there are many articles that I had to take off the internet, because they were entirely false in doctrine.

Today, I know that I am called to be a teacher of the Word of God. I look at my life now and I consider it to be quite fruitful. I know also, that I am called to preach in churches and recently some doors have been opened to do just that.

For so much of my life I had been bound in sin and lived a good-for-nothing existence. I had been living with various addictions: one of which was an insoluble problem with sexual fantasies and actual involvement. In fact, when I look at my earlier life, it looks as though it had been wasted. But I know that God never wastes anything!

When I read this particular parable I recognize that if I hadn't had the mercy and grace of Jesus operating in my life; if I had been under the Law of the Old Covenant, I would not be here today. Instead I would have been cast aside; cut off and thrown into Hell.

This parable makes me wonder about the owner of the vineyard. Do you remember in another parable about a certain landlord, (see Chapter 21) that the owner of the vineyard sent servants and the workers actually killed those servants. So, the owner sent his son and they killed the son, thinking that they would have the rights to the vineyard after his death. I am starting to think now that the owner of this vineyard is God the Father. Also the law, that Old Testament covenant law, was the fact that the tree should be bearing fruit within three years or it should be cut down.

I am thinking that the actual gardener who said, "No, give it one more year. Let me give it some fertilizer," was Jesus Himself saying, "No let me give this person some more of my grace. Let me give them some understanding. Let me give them the power of the Holy Spirit. Let me dig up their life and teach them some new things and give them the ability to overcome. Then, let me see if they bear fruit after that."

See? The message of the New Covenant is that you are forgiven. There is no judgment against you. There is nothing held in your account. The hand of God is not against you. All of your lawless deeds, God remembers no more when you have repented and believed in God's Son.

Now, in my spirit, I feel that God has personally written me a letter. It reads: "Yes, the reason why you have survived all these years in your unfruitful lifestyle Matthew is because you are living in the time of the New Covenant as a believer of God. *Under the Old Covenant, as an adulterer and fornicator, you would have been stoned to death, but because you live under the New Covenant you have received mercy and grace instead of death. Also, under the Old Covenant, you would have been rejected as a priest, a preacher or a minister of the Gospel. But under the New Covenant, you are forgiven, washed clean, set free and made whole in my sight and given My authority and the My ability to preach the Gospel."*

Because of that, this parable is tremendously encouraging. I hope that, you too, can fully capture its meaning. I hope that you can dig deep into the teachings of grace and the finished work of the cross. May you understand the grace of God and allow it to "fertilize" your life so that you may bear good fruit in the coming season. You may feel that your life has been a total failure, but I hope this book on the parables, and particularly this parable, will truly bless your life.

CHAPTER 3

THE PARABLE OF THE BREAD OF LIFE
JOHN 6:31-38

It is important when studying any section of Scripture to first read it in its correct context. Therefore, when you read the four Gospels in their chronological order, you discover that Jesus had been in a state of personal grief when He performed the following act of compassion. He had just received news that His much loved cousin, John the Baptist, had been brutally murdered. He had planned to spend some private time with His Father who would comfort His inner anguish. However a huge crowd had gathered to hear him teach. After many hours of teaching, He knew the people needed to commence their long walk home. It was late, they were hungry and tired. To test His disciple's faith, He asked them: "Where shall we buy bread that these may eat?"(John 6:5b) One young boy had five barley loaves and two fish. With only this small provision, Jesus miraculously fed 5,000 men and their families. (It was usual in those days, to count the number of men only in estimating the size of a crowd.)

Therefore, at least twelve to fifteen thousand hungry people were fed with just one boy's packed lunch. I suspect that as the twelve disciples were actually handing out their allotted portions to each person, God was supernaturally multiplying the food in the disciple's hands. God blesses abundantly; twelve baskets of left-over food were collected by the astonished disciples!

Then, Jesus dismissed the people and asked His disciples to leave and to come back later for Him, so they returned to their boat. Suddenly, they were buffeted by strong winds. Jesus, sensing their fear, walked out on the water toward them and Peter called out, "I hope it's really you Lord. Let me walk to you." So Peter's faith allowed him to walk some hesitant steps then he panicked and Jesus assisted him back into the boat. Jesus boarded the boat and they headed towards the other shore.

Then Jesus began to lead up to our key passage:

When they arrived, the people asked, "How did you get here?" They knew that Jesus hadn't been on the boat when His disciples had left. He answered: "Most assuredly, I say to you, you seek Me, not because you saw the signs, but because you ate of the loaves and were filled. Do not labor for the food which perishes, but *for food which endures to everlasting life, which the Son of Man will give you, because God the Father has set His seal on Him."* (John 6:26-27)

The truth is many of us today still labor for the food that perishes. Many people today are satisfying their soul's appetite with food such as the internet, TV, DVDs, MP3s and all sorts of things that pass away. We all have to have the latest mobile phone and we just spend money, then more money and more money after that. Our desire for all things new is insatiable.

Jesus says, "Do not work for things that perish, but instead set your appetite toward food that results in everlasting life, which is Me." Then they said to Him, "What shall we do, that we may work the works of God?" Jesus answered them, "This is the work of God, that you believe in Him (Jesus) *whom He* (The Father) *sent."* (v.29) Note these words: the only "work" Jesus requires of us, is to believe in Him. When we do that, with all our heart, our faith will be evidenced by good fruit done in His strength.

The disciples then asked Him: "What sign will You perform then, that we may see it and believe You? What work will You do?" (v.30) Now, I don't know about you, but Jesus had just walked on water. He had helped Peter walk on water. He had fed 12,000 to 15,000 people with two fish and some bread rolls. Not only that, His disciples had witnessed Him performing mighty signs such as healing every sick person that had come to Him. Yet despite all this evidence of His supernatural power, they were still looking for some special sign! Can you believe it?

Do you know that nothing has changed today? Some of the most gifted evangelists in the world are constantly being asked for signs. People want a medical doctor's proof of cancer and diseases being healed. If a person is raised from the dead, people want official evidence to say that they had in fact died. When God causes bones to grow etc evidence of x-rays are sought. Someone's testimony of a miracle is not enough! No, people today have not changed at all; they still want signs.

The major passage for this particular parable is this: *Jesus said, "Most assuredly, I say to you, Moses did not give you the bread from Heaven, but My Father gives you the true bread from Heaven. For the bread of God is He who comes down from Heaven and gives life to the world."*

Then they said, "Lord, give us this bread always." Jesus said to them, "I am the bread of life. He who comes to Me shall never hunger, and he who believes in Me shall never thirst, but I said to you that you have seen Me and yet do not believe. All that the Father gives Me will come to Me, and the one who comes to Me I will by no means cast out. For I have come down from Heaven, not to do My own will, but to do the will of Him who sent Me." (vv. 32-38)

Did you understand that incredible promise Jesus just made? He said: *"All that the Father gives Me, and the one who comes to Me, I will by no means cast out."*

Jesus just re-assured all those who have partaken of this bread; who have received Him as their own personal Savior and Lord, that their salvation is eternally secure. We have this blessed assurance from the greatest authority who ever lived on earth. Many Christians believe and even teach others, that certain sins will cause loss of salvation. Does this passage actually mean that if you are a Christian, that Jesus will never cast you out from His Kingdom? YES! I pray that God's extraordinary grace will keep that revelation of assurance deep in your spirit so that your peace will remain steadfast and sure.

In saying "he that comes to me shall never hunger," Jesus is saying that one day you are going to be hungry and the next day the same, and the day after, you will still be hungry. But if you eat the true bread from Heaven, you are not going to be hungry any more. So how does that work out practically in our lives? Often I have sat in churches and heard teaching on the parables of Jesus, but not often in a way that means something to me personally.

For ten years I have been thinking of writing a book on the parables of Jesus and I have been looking into them, simply to answer other people's questions and also my own.

Mental illness has taken me to extremely dark places, but knowing Jesus as my intimate friend has always been my anchor. Feeling His presence, even at my lowest times has been my only reason for living. I have personally experienced His awesome love and this motivates me to stay close to Him.

Without His intervention in my life, I would not be alive today for He sent a total stranger to minister to me, even as I was on my way to end my life in Brisbane. Often I feel that His heart and mine are intertwined. I truly live for Him and perhaps some people may think I am strange! He really is my passion in life! Even from a very young teenager, my desire has never been focused on the riches of this world, but to reach souls for Jesus Christ.

I know that true fulfillment comes from knowing Jesus. Ask Him to put His "love filter" over your eyes so you can actually see people as He sees them. His love and compassion will over-ride your complacency and timidity and you will be compelled to place the needs of others higher than your own. That is my tried and true recipe for the human heart's fulfillment.

Jesus has created our spirits to hunger for Him and His will in our life. When we find His will and embrace it, then we are completely in union with Him and peace will reign in our heart. It is important to realize that what you do with your money and time changes lives and when you have a positive impact on others, you will discover that you will have a totally fulfilled life. People look for a new car, a new house, a new mobile phone, a new digital TV, a new this, a new that, in order to bring fulfillment into their life. Even when you are buying the latest trendy gadget, there is always an associated "high" but it soon fades.

Everyone is looking for that little burst of joy, but what sort of joy really lasts? What is the kind of joy that is like this bread of life Jesus is talking about here? Where can you find the joy that will hang around for years? What can you do in this world that will stop you from feeling drained or empty? Jesus said that He is the bread of life but how can you consume this bread? What is Jesus talking about? Here are some suggestions:

If it cost an evangelist on average, twenty dollars a month to save a lost soul in Africa, you could make a commitment to God to give this amount each month towards this work. Do you realize that in a year your money would save twelve souls? How many souls are you currently saving in a year?

Did you know, you may have problems in your life, but as soon as our Lord Jesus comes into an African person, whose life has been either bound in the Muslim tradition or in witchcraft, that transformation in their life is a joyful experience for them? It is a total revolution in their life, and you, just by giving an easy twenty dollars a month, are their benefactor. You have co-partnered with the evangelist and are jointly responsible for these people going to Heaven. By donating an hour or so of work per month you could be saving one person a month. Imagine that!

Imagine giving twenty dollars to someone who is homeless, or taking a homeless person out for dinner at a club. Your *company* alone to them would make their day. Imagine how far twenty dollars would help a single mother in your church. Imagine buying twenty dollars worth of baby formula for her? There are so many things you can do when your eyes are focused on other people, and on God's priorities. You know God owns the cattle on a thousand hills (Psalm 50:10). God does not need your money, but He delights in involving you in His work on earth. When you have been blessed by Him, as I have been, you will feel compelled to take part in His Kingdom business. You will want to do this, not out of a "works mentality" but out of gratitude for all that He has done for you.

Jesus spent all day every day in ministry to others. When He came out to breakfast after prayer, He would begin to serve others. If He was not healing people and casting out demons, He was teaching them a new way of life. When He was finished speaking, the people flooded Him with questions and He gave a few more hours to answer them. Jesus was always giving, always serving, always making Himself available to all people to meet their spiritual and physical needs. So too, the bread of life can be properly accessed in a life of service and giving.

You see, whenever you are striving for food, whenever you are striving for one new thing after another, you are never going to be satisfied. The reason we put up with television and all the advertisements in between our favorite programs is because we love the advertisements just as much as we love the shows. We enjoy buying new things. We are addicted to the rush of buying. Become addicted to the blast of doing Kingdom business.

Many people live in this life with no real direction and purpose. Few Christians really know the purpose of why they are on earth. Most people are simply living and wandering around aimlessly. It is vital to discover not only God's general will but His personal will for you in His kingdom plan. Only in living in your purpose can you really be fully satisfied. Only by walking in the will of God each day can we really cease to be hungry.

Apparently, a survey in the United States found that only ten percent of Christians knew what their spiritual gifts were. Out of these, only ten percent of them were actually walking in and using their spiritual gifts. That means that ninety nine percent of Christians in the United States are not doing what God has called them to do and sadly, only one percent of Christians in the United States experience full satisfaction in life.

Find out what your spiritual gifts are. Spend your time and money in using those gifts. You will then see what Jesus was talking about: you will see the fundamentals of His Kingdom and how to live in them.

You know that Jesus mostly taught in parables because it made people really think deeply about His words. Have you ever wondered what the bread of life is? Are you a Christian who is not sustained by faith? Are you a Christian living a life of sadness, depression, feeling down, or feeling as though the Christian life is not everything that it was cracked up to be? Are you living with self-condemnation? Is your life steeped in sin? Do you have addictions? Do you have sins that you simply cannot stop doing? There is more to the Christian life than this.

It is not God's will for us to be living in depression or spending time being consumed by the lusts of the world. He wants us to experience joy and godly contentment. We live in the world but we are not meant to be of the world. You can live in the world without lusting for what it offers. The Holy Spirit residing in you is your overcoming strength.

Living God's will for your life is the only place where you will cease from hungering. Ask your friends and those who really know you, what they think your spiritual gifts are and consciously begin to operate in them so that they will fully develop. Then you will discover a joy that cannot be compared to what you have now.

CHAPTER 4

THE PARABLE OF THE BUDDING FIG TREE (MATTHEW 24)

The whole of the chapter refers to End-Times events. I have picked out certain verses:

"Now learn this parable of the fig tree: When it's branches has already become tender and puts out leaves, you know that summer is near: So you also, when you see all these things, know that it is near - at the doors!" (24:32-33)

When spring comes and a fig tree starts to put forth its leaves, then it is time for the figs to come out and be part of the fig tree.

So, Jesus is saying, the signs are the leaves. He said previously *"Take heed that no one deceives you. For many will come in My name, saying, "I am the Christ," and will deceive many."* (24:4b-5) Today, in the world are many false prophets who adamantly claim to be Jesus Christ. There are people of the Hindu faith and there are New Age people who profess to be an incarnation of Christ.

Many people talk about false prophets being within the Christian church, which is something we will discuss later. In a totally separate category, there are thousands of deluded people in mental hospitals who say they are Jesus Christ! These people need medication and love, not condemnation!

Jesus has said that in the last days there will be certain signs to watch for. These signs include: wars and rumors of wars, famines, pestilences and earthquakes. Yet, we are not to be troubled, for all these things must come to pass." *(Matthew 24:5-7) Today, we are seeing these things on TV, radio and the internet.* Countries are continually at war, according to the current media releases: everyday more people are being killed by hate.

The AIDS virus is killing millions of people and you could call this a type of modern pestilence invading the world. There are many famines in Africa and starvation in other developing countries. Farmers are familiar with the locust and mice plagues that devastate their hard work. In recent times, we have heard of increasing earthquakes happening worldwide. Scripture says that these are all the *"beginning of sorrows."*

(v.8) Today's terrible tremors resemble labor pains the earth is suffering, before the great and terrible Day of the Lord is birthed. The tsunamis, earthquakes, famines, diseases and viruses are all the beginnings of sorrows.

They will deliver you up to tribulation and kill you, and you will be hated by all nations for My name's sake. "" (v.9) Record numbers of Christians are being killed for the sake of the Gospel right now in some parts of the world.

The signs include: *"Many will be offended and betray one another and will hate one another,"* (v.10). You only have to preach the true Gospel today to offend people. I know the humiliation of being called a false prophet but God knows my heart. My doctrine was *extremely* off track before medication and even after medication for many years I misunderstood the doctrine of grace, but I have always exalted the Lord Jesus Christ as God's only Savior for the human race.

The one problem with deception is that, when you are deceived, you do not know it. It often takes new knowledge to bring you out of your deception. When you are in a delusion, you are deluded. When you know that you are deluded: you are not deluded anymore. (This is "Matthew" theology!)

Many Christian leaders perform signs, wonders and miracles by the power of the Holy Spirit and yet they are called false prophets by other denominations. I would be careful about which man of God I would call a false prophet.

Some people in the church believe that prophets and apostles no longer exist today, so anyone who claims to be one of these people is called a false prophet! However, Hebrews 13:8 says; *"Jesus is the same yesterday, today and forever."* The ministry of Jesus has never, nor will ever change; not in this life anyway. None of the nine gifts of the Holy Spirit have disappeared from the modern church: they are all still in operation! If Jesus is the same: so too is the Holy Spirit. It's absolutely foolish to think that there could only be false prophets but no true prophets of God today.

On the other hand, there are authors of books, claiming to bring the words of an Archangel, or Jesus Himself or God, in New Age bookshops. These books should be avoided and their readers need to be told the true Gospel: they and the authors are being deceived by the devil. Also, there are people in the New Age Movement claiming to channel Jesus and these deceived people are like false prophets because in their zeal, they lead readers astray. Many New Age books are contrary to Scripture. Therefore, their doctrine is false. These people really believe that they are speaking on behalf of God, but I believe that it is not the God of the Bible, but a false god who inspires them.

One of the end-time signs is that lawlessness will cause the love of many to grow cold. (Matthew 24:12) Let me illustrate this. I know of a Pastor who has a disabled son. One day, his son fell in a small gap between the train and the platform. The people on the station, rather than come to his rescue, just started to step over him and did not even worry if he was still there when the train took off! The Pastor was appalled! He could not get anyone to help him pull his son free. This describes love gone cold.

Another sign is the increasing tribulation on earth. People are generally more selfish and suspicious of others than in times past. Self-centeredness blinds them to the needs of others. This attitude causes increasing hardship. Selfishness is the human key to the world's suffering today. People overseas have died of diseases that safe water and medication could prevent. Clean drinking water, diseases, poverty and starvation could all be solved. The fact that the love of many is growing cold is a real sign today.

"Only by pride comes contention." Proverbs 13:10 (Schofield King James Bible) Self-centeredness is rooted in human pride. Pride is expressed by frustration, anger and *even timidity*. We think that people or situations make us angry but this is not true! Pride makes us angry and causes us to negatively react. Even someone who is super quiet all the time has an issue with pride: they are afraid of being labeled ignorant so they say nothing. Jesus was never self-centered! He didn't take personal offense. When He was angry, it was righteous anger. To stand up for righteousness for others isn't prideful. But most times, our anger is related to a personal offense: not to righteousness. By denying self, as Jesus commanded, we will experience the abundant life. Inner anger and hurt will be defused once you commit to love God and others more than yourself. This requires great humility on our part.

"Many will come in My name, saying, 'I am the Christ,' and will deceive many....then many false prophets will rise up and deceive many.....False christs and false prophets will rise and show great signs and wonders to deceive, if possible, even the elect." (24:4:5, 11 & 24.) Some Christians witness genuine works of miracles, signs and wonders yet assume that something is wrong because of warnings like these. There is a great lack of discernment and love in the Christian world, with brothers pulling down brothers.

The early Apostles walked in signs and wonders and this fact proved the power of God: they validated the message of salvation and thousands were saved. But in the last days certain people will arise who will deceive even Christians through lies and deceptions, being motivated not by the Gospel, but by human pride being gratified by fleshly desires.

Deception must be disclosed by new revelation. Many "false prophet watchers" point a finger in accusation by a condemning spirit. They themselves may be full of fear and unbelief—unbelief in the fact that God is working through these people. Jesus said that a person's lifestyle will determine what fruit they produce. If you listen to someone's teaching with an attitude of pointing the finger, you will find fault in everything.

"Therefore, if they say to you, 'Look, He (Christ) *is in the desert!' do not go out: or 'Look, He is in the inner rooms!' do not believe it."* (24:26.) When Jesus comes to collect His bride at the Rapture, (mentioned in Chapter 1) the whole world is ultimately going to know about it. Their eyes will be blinded to the event itself, but not to its consequences. Almost every family on earth will be affected by this catastrophic event. The unbelievers of the world will be left behind to make their own conclusions, unless God intervenes and sends angelic messengers to minister to them and to lead them to Jesus. You can be sure that the media will have some plausible explanation to suit their own agenda, but it won't be the truth that they will proclaim!

"Immediately after the tribulation of those days, the sun will be darkened and the moon will not give its light; the stars will fall from the heaven, and the powers of the heavens will be shaken. Then the sign of the Son of Man will appear in heaven, and then all the tribes of earth will mourn, and they will see the Son of Man coming on the clouds of heaven with power and great glory. And He will send His angels with a great sound of a trumpet, and they will gather together His elect from the four winds, from one end of heaven to the other."" (24: 29-31.)

Some Christians think that this passage refers to the time of the Rapture, but I'm not one of them. I may be in error, but I believe it is referring to an event that will occur some time after the Rapture on a Day that only the Father knows. My reason being is that at the Rapture, Jesus doesn't set foot on earth but He will be in the clouds, when He snatches up His saints from the earth! (1 Thessalonians 4:16-18 see Chapter One.)

Therefore these verses must refer to the great and terrible Day of the Lord, when Jesus physically comes and sets His feet down in Jerusalem. His coming then, will be as the awesome and frightening Judge and Supreme King, to execute the wrath of God against all unbelievers and ungodliness, at an unknown date at the end of the seven year tribulation period. This return of Jesus is certainly not going to be simple, silent or secret. The whole world will know that He has come. He will first protect those who have believed in Him since the Rapture and then He will turn his attention to the great mass of fearful unbelievers on earth, who will be trembling in terror at His coming.

It's wonderful to have Jesus as your very close friend in these last perilous days? Rejoice continually that believers have a bright future and let others know what is ahead.

"Now learn this parable from the fig tree: when its branch has already become tender and puts forth leaves, you know that summer is near. So you also, when you see all these things, know that it is near - at the doors," (24:.32-33).

Because all of these things are happening in the world today, I am confident that Jesus is certainly at the door. Keep your eyes focused on Him and this will motivate you to share His love with others.

CHAPTER 5

THE PARABLE OF THE CHILDREN IN THE MARKET-PLACE. (MATTHEW 11:16-19)

Jesus shared this parable in Matthew 11:16-19:

But to what shall I liken this generation? It is like children sitting in the market-places and calling to their companions and saying

'We played the flute for you,

And you did not dance;

We mourned to you,

And you did not lament.'

For John came neither eating nor drinking and they say, 'He has a demon.' The Son of Man came eating and drinking and they say, 'Look, a glutton and a winebibber, a friend of tax collectors and sinners!' But wisdom is justified by her children.

Okay, let us have a look at this. Elsewhere, Jesus had good things to say about children. He said, "Assuredly, I say to you, whoever does not receive the Kingdom of God as a little child will by no means enter in." (Mark 10:15) Yet here, He is using the ways of children as a rebuke. Why?

Well, let me tell you what child-like faith is: this faith is a simple readiness to trust, to believe something as being the truth without questioning or suspicion. Most children have no experience of being deceived or having their trust abused. However, as a child becomes an adult, he realizes that not everyone can be trusted; that there are people who would hurt them and abuse their trust. Because of life's experiences, adults can have a jaded and cynical view of the world and they may take much convincing to believe in things, especially if it requires faith. Jesus wants us to have the simple faith of a young child. He doesn't want us to be cynical or suspicious, but instead to have an innocent view towards God and His promises.

Another thing - a child is normally totally dependent on his parents. A child whose parents do not provide for him will starve. Most children are reliant upon their parents providing them with food, shelter and clothing. Essentially, if left by themselves children would be in serious trouble and sadly many are in this unfortunate predicament.

To have child-like faith, also includes being totally dependent on God and to let Him rule in our life. It's true, when an adult comes to God in humility, he becomes child-like.

However, in this parable, "child-like" is really meaning "childish"—a child who wants their own way: a rebellious, stubborn sort of child. Children are very good at getting their own way! They can be all happy and nice when it comes to wanting to receive a treat. But, if the treat does not eventuate, they can throw a tantrum on the floor. This is the sort of child that Jesus is talking about.

"We played a flute for you,

And you did not dance." (v. 17a)

If you wanted to please someone, it shouldn't matter if they danced or not. If you wanted to play a flute for Jesus, you should be happy that He would listen. He need not dance!

"We mourned to you and you did not lament." (v. 17b)

To expect others to mourn for you is selfish and immature. Scripture says: *"When I was a child, I spoke as a child, I understood as a child, I thought as a child, but when I became a man, I put away childish things."* I Corinthians 13: 11

It is like Jesus was saying to the Pharisees or even to some of the leaders and people in this generation: "Stop being immature, grow up! John has come in the spirit of Elijah. He doesn't drink because God called him to take a Nazirite vow not to drink! Because of this, you say he has a demon. I come along and I am not a Nazirite and yes, I drink with my friends. Because I do this, you call Me a drunk! No, I don't fast all the time, so you call Me a glutton! You class Me as some kind of pervert because I prefer to hang out with My tax collector friends and sinners. This you would never do, because you piously consider it to be offensive and undignified, for it may scar your precious reputation. You have far too high an opinion about yourselves!"

Jesus may be known as a gentle, meek and mild person, but He is also the sort of person I respect. I like someone who does not speak about me to other people in a derogatory manner, knowing full well it will get back to me through other people. I would rather that a person who has a problem with me, to come and lay their cards on the table, face to face, rather than go behind my back. I do not like confrontation, but I enjoy hearing someone's opinion of me. Even if it does initially hurt, I would rather hear it face to face.

Earlier, Jesus had been talking about John the Baptist and this is what led Him to this passage. He was first describing John and then He was talking about the leaders and also this current generation. John was said to be greater than all the other Old Testament prophets. Yet, Jesus said that even the least in His kingdom was greater than John. What does He mean by that? I believe that we are greater because we have the testimony of our conversion experience. John never had a testimony like us. John had the Holy Spirit already in him at his birth. Therefore, he had never been separated from God like we had before our conversion: before we repented of our sin and received Jesus into our heart.

Today, people reject Jesus for various reasons. One main reason why people reject Him is that they maintain that Jesus had an ego problem! Actually, they renounce the fact that He is the *only way to the Father*. Jesus said in John 14:6 "I am the way, the truth and the life; no one comes to the Father except through Me." These words upset people!

But if Jesus was *not the only way to the Father*, He would not have had to die on the cross. Jesus pleaded with His Father, *"O My Father, if it is possible, let this cup pass from Me; nevertheless, not as I will, but as You will."* (Matthew 26: 39) By the silence that followed, Jesus knew His Father was in fact saying "No Son, there is no other way! You have to die." Jesus submitted to His Father's will because it was the only way that man could be saved from their sin problem and receive life eternal. Love conquers fear!

According to John 17:3, eternal life is to know the Father and His Son Jesus Christ! Those who invite Him into their life have eternal life living inside them, because Jesus is that life! Therefore, we enter into eternity at the moment of salvation, not at our death!

The Pharisees had a problem with Jesus because He was not interested in keeping their rigid laws. It was not so much the laws of Moses that Jesus was disobeying, it was all the added laws that the Pharisees had made up in their wrongful interpretation of the Law. Jesus fulfilled the Law because He only ever operated in the "spirit" behind the law - this means that we are to have a godly *attitude and motive for observing the law*. Some people do the "right" thing and yet they are absolutely wrong in the "spirit" of why they do it. There is a huge difference and people do not readily understand this concept.

"Man looks at the outward appearance, but the Lord looks at the heart." 1 Samuel 16:7b. This verse totally sums up what I am trying to point out here. The prophet Elijah had said that before the coming of the Messiah, (this word means the "anointed One") God would rise up a special messenger among the Jewish people, who would prepare the people's heart to welcome the Savior. Four hundred years later, John the Baptist did this preparation work. He was not Elijah himself, but John operated in the "spirit" of Elijah.

Jesus operated out of love and mercy and this compelled Him to heal even on the Sabbath when it was forbidden by law to do any work. God is love and full of compassion – wholeness is more important to Him than the legalistic outward observance of the law.

The Pharisees were agitated that Jesus healed sinners and chose to spend time with them. They reasoned that if He was so righteous why didn't He choose them to be his closest friends? They were totally blind to their own pride and hypocrisy.

There was a law that said you became unclean if you touched a leper. Compassion over-ruled this law when Jesus touched the leper and made him well. What some people would consider breaking the law, Jesus considered as showing love. Love trumps everything.

Jesus, the night before his death met with His disciples and spoke of a New Covenant for us to live under, but in reality He Himself had always been operating in this New Covenant of grace towards others at the expense of the Law.

This parable of the children in the market-place is really a warning to people who are stubborn against Jesus and rebel at His teaching. It is also a warning to all of us that we should not be little children demanding things from Jesus. We should not be sitting down giving Him commands and then getting stubborn and upset because He didn't jump to our commands or answer our prayers in the way we wanted.

Some Christians pray stupid prayers, just like children at times ask for stupid things. While God is a generous God, He will only give us things that are good for us. Some people fluctuate between not feeling loved by God and silently despising Him. The Pharisees were different, because they despised Jesus all the time!

Yet, God has not cast off the Jews: they still remain His covenant people and therefore hold a very special place in His heart. He had first selected them to be His chosen people and promised to always be their God. God is faithful to His Word. He will never go back on any promise He has made. The Bible says that the whole world came into existence through the spoken word of God and it is held together by the power of His spoken word. I seriously believe that if God were ever to break a promise, *any promise* He has made, the whole world would disintegrate! It would no longer be held together!

Today, people are suspicious of the way to salvation, wondering why it should be so easy to be forgiven for all of their sins just by accepting Jesus into their lives. But bear in mind – it wasn't easy for God to see Jesus hanging on the cross! Nor was it easy for Jesus to die in our place with the weight of every sickness, disease, deformity, every sin ever committed or ever yet to be committed by the whole of mankind – all bearing down on Him so that for the first time ever, His Father could not even look at Him and turned His face from Him. Jesus was in anguish, "My God, why have you forsaken Me?" (Matthew 27:46) Don't ever call God's grace easy! It is wonderful for us but *it cost God everything!*

Others think the Christian life is too hard and too restrictive – that it's only made up of silly out of date rules. People don't want to give up the things that they love doing. This is like a fisherman eating the bait instead of catching the fish. Unbelievers do not know how exciting God is and they settle for mediocrity.

The Pharisees believed John had a demon because he seemed, "too way out." They said he was possessed. At another time they said that Jesus was filled with Beelzebub. (The devil) They rejected Him because He was hanging around with the wrong crowd! They hated His popularity, His works and His teaching and saw Him as a threat to their livelihood and success.

The best way to imitate Jesus is to befriend hurting people and to show compassion to them. If Jesus physically showed up in our town where would He first go? Would He go to the pubs, the brothels and the homeless on the streets at night? Or would he first go to church where His brothers and sister gathered? It's right that we fellowship at church regularly and worship as a collective body of believers but not at the expense of overlooking people who desperately need Jesus. We have God's grace to draw on and the Holy Spirit to guide us, so we can minister in the overflow of what we have.

This parable is a warning to us not to be like little stubborn, sad, rebellious children. Instead, we are to have child-like faith and we are not to hold grudges. God is a good Father and Jesus wants us to respond to the love of His Dad. Jesus wants us to be like a child who trusts their heavenly daddy to care for them.

CHAPTER 6

THE PARABLE OF THE CHRISTIAN LIGHT
MATTHEW 5:14-16

Matthew 5:14-16 says:

"You are the light of the world. A city that is set on a hill cannot be hidden. Nor do they light a lamp and put it under a basket but on a lamp-stand and it gives light to all who are in the house. Let your light so shine before men, that they may see your good works and glorify your Father in heaven."

I was listening to a much anointed preacher, Pastor Joseph Prince, speaking on the grace of God. He was preaching in Israel. He was describing his location and it was clear from his description that it was the same place where the telling of this parable took place. At the time when Pastor Prince was talking, there was a hill from which he could see the city lights. He believed that perhaps it was the very hill where Jesus had been. If Jesus had of been preaching from the same spot, He would have seen the hill and the lights of the city.

Therefore when Jesus said: "A city set on a hill cannot be hidden," He was talking about a literal town that was on a hill. The people knew that the city glowed at night. It could not be hidden.

Have you traveled through dense bush country and came out of a valley to see bright lights up on a hill? The world is steeped in darkness and needs light, especially the wonderful light of Jesus that will never burn out. Have you been to a city where there is light all over the place? That is an example of a city on a hill that cannot be hidden.

I believe that I have the gift of exhortation or encouragement and in order to illustrate this parable I will share some things in my every day life with you.

Once leaving my unit my daily routine begins by walking towards the suburb where the train station is. I first pass by a real estate office on the right-hand side and I wave my hand to those at the reception desk. I come across a hairdresser and give her a smile and a slight wave. If she is outside having a smoke, I have a short conversation with her. I come to a Lebanese chicken shop and I pop in and say hello to the people there.

At the video store, I actually go inside to have a two to three-minute conversation with a very gentle salesman who appreciates my friendship.

Arriving at the train station, I greet the man who owns the newsagent kiosk. Then I head for the ticket office and have a conversation to my friends there, depending on how soon my train is due and how busy they are. On the train I make it a point to have eye contact with the passengers and if the person next to me is not reading, I greet them with a few words. Depending how they respond I usually enter into a conversation with them.

Everywhere I go, I say, "Hello," to everyone, encouraging them to have a happy day. Nearly all the people I meet every day are well aware that I am a practicing Christian.

Why do I do that? About thirty years ago, when I was about fourteen years of age, I heard a testimony from a visiting Pastor about being the light of Jesus. This story happened to him when he was at a supermarket checkout in a local shopping center. The woman in front of him didn't have sufficient money for her goods that day and began asking the cashier to deduct certain items from her shopping to suit her budget. The pastor felt her embarrassment as she nervously began to eliminate everyday essential items, including washing powder, toilet rolls and basic household needs.

This Pastor noted that her trolley was full of things she obviously needed. Her shopping comprised of essential items as there were no luxury items that he could see. The Pastor casually said to the cashier, "I will pay for her bill. Put all her things through the register. I want her to have them all."

The woman profusely said, "No, you can't do that sir!"

The Pastor said, "But I want to do it!" So he paid her whole bill and then he further told the woman, "Go and get another trolley and fill it up. Makes sure you put in a few luxury items as well this time. I am more than happy to pay for them."

The lady left and came back three times, embarrassed with a quarter of a trolley, half a trolley, and three-quarters of a trolley, respectively. Three times, he sent her back to the aisles until she filled the whole trolley. Despite her objections and embarrassment, he paid the bill and helped her load them into her car. The lady said her name was Betty.

This Pastor was a loveable guy with good communication skills. As he was sharing his story, the whole church was listening with anticipation. Then he said, "I know what all of you are waiting for. You want me to share with you how I told Betty that I was a Christian, or how she broke down in tears and became a Christian too. But no, I didn't say anything about that to her. I didn't even tell her that I was a Christian. But do you know something? That day Betty met Jesus."

He continued: "All Christians need to do, is to go out each day with the attitude that they are going to be Jesus to the world. Maybe then one day, someone else will be sharing the Gospel with Betty and the Holy Spirit will cause that obedient believer to describe the love and compassion of Jesus to her by innocently illustrating it with the exact kind of scenario that had happened to her so long ago in my presence. Don't ever under estimate the power of the Holy Spirit and the way His love and memory works.

I believe that it would suddenly dawn on Betty that it had indeed been God who was at work helping her that day with her purchases and that it wasn't just the result of the generosity of a kind stranger at all: it was God's gift to her because He loved her. She may even break down in tears and say, "A total stranger did that for me one day!"

As I left the church service that night, I was so challenged. I realized that all I needed to do was to be Jesus to people. Even now, every day I still try to do this everywhere I go. One time, one of the people I have made it my business to befriend, asked me to pray for him when he was in a bit of a crisis situation. Do you know that when people are really desperate and searching for answers, if they know that you are genuinely interested in them, they will come to you when they have problems? Always remember that God's number one priority is all about developing good relationships with others. God is always reaching out to people and He wants us to do the same.

Many people criticize the "mega" churches. These churches are growing exponentially; they are filled almost beyond their capacity. It is said that they have loud music and all they are doing is "dulling" down their sermons and creating loud worship music to be popular. It is also said that there is no "meat of the Word" in these churches, but you know what? Every time I go to one of those so-called mega churches here in Sydney, people are being saved. Every single service! The sermons I've heard are not "wishy washy" – they are great!

I have sat in a church that taught basic theology for two years or more, but no one was saved during that whole time. People say that they want the "meat" of the Word but what about saving people? Churches must be relevant to today's culture. What worked in the past is not going to cut it today. I know that the Word of God never changes but fresh ways of application must be appropriated to the age and type of person in the congregation. I realize that this is a hobby horse of mine, but I am positive God approves of it whole heartedly.

For example, a Pentecostal church in Sydney produces many Christian worship songs that are known throughout the whole world. I truly believe that they are an excellent example of a city set on a hill. Their light shines so brightly that people all around the world worship God with the music that God creates through this much criticized church.

The Pastor of this church is a man with a vision to impact this generation and the whole world with the love and saving power of Jesus. I believe that preachers like him have been raised up for such a time as this.

The opposite of being Jesus to someone, would be to deliberately hide your light or to be so full of your own agenda that you take no notice of those who pass you by.

What shines out to others in your life? Is it the love of Jesus? Or are your conversations always based on negative situations all around you? Be consciously aware of the things that shine out to other people through you. Will these things bring them closer to the Savior or will they lead them further away from Him? Despite what is going on around us, our mission is to always shine our light for Jesus. Don't be side-tracked by the negativity of the world and of the flesh.

Most people like to be noticed: they light up to a non-threatening remark. We all need to find answers in Jesus. We all need to undergo spiritual healing. We all need to find a purpose in life. No one is meant to be an island all by themselves!

Now, one way of being happy is by being friendly to everyone you meet. Smile! Do you know it is amazing how smiling can even cheer you up? You do not even have to be happy. Just know enough people; walk down the road and acknowledge people with a genuine smile and a brief "Hello" or some other applicable comment. By doing so, you will have people smiling back and waving at you. Suddenly, you are feeling good. It is amazing how being friendly can really lighten your mood. I quite often suffer from depression and I know first hand how a stranger's smile can pick me up!

"Let your light shine before men that they may see your good works and glorify the Father in Heaven." *Matthew 5:16.* Good works are to be done with the right attitude.

Nearly all of the people I chat with on the way to the station ask me what I am doing that day. They probably all know by now the type of things I do on a regular basis and have a good idea of my day to day life. It's so easy to chat to them. I will briefly share with them my immediate plans.

They all know what I do. I make videos. I write articles and do all kinds of Christian research. They all respond to my friendliness and are jovial with me. None of them ever say to me: "You need to go and get yourself a real job Matthew!" No, they know I am busy doing ministry and doing other worthwhile things. They are all happy and they are all my friends.

My wonderful Pastor came to see me one day and we bought a pizza for ten dollars that would normally have cost twenty three dollars. I was given the discount because of my relationship with the owners of the gourmet pizza store. She reported back to everyone at church. "You should see Matthew. You should see how cheap he buys his pizza for. He knows all the staff by name. I think he must know everyone in his suburb by now. Everyone says hello to him." She was pleased to boast on my behalf and I was hearing it from everyone that they want to come to my place for pizza. That to me is all part of being a light in the world.

Because I am happy doing what I do, I smile a lot in my parable video series. I don't smile just to do a better presentation. My life is fulfilled and Christ-centered. I feel the presence of God. He watches out for me and leads me in all my conversations. I enjoy peace because I live with kingdom purpose. I have no personal financial needs. I know Jesus and He is my constant friend and He knows the things that I need.

We live in a very dark world today. The good thing is that light penetrates the dark even brighter in such a time as this. The light of Christ is noticed more because people are used to the darkness surrounding them. Many people won't or cannot read the Bible. If they do, they may not understand it, but they can very easily read *you!* You can be their living Bible! To many people, you are perhaps the only Bible that they will come across. Be aware of that. Stand out from the crowd. God freely gives us the power to go the extra mile with people and be kind to them. Through this, you will be a light to all men and a city on a hill in times of need.

CHAPTER 7

THE PARABLE OF THE DINNER GUESTS
(LUKE 14:16-24)

"A certain man gave a great supper and invited many; sending his servant at supper time to say to those who were invited, 'Come, for all things are now ready.' But they all with one accord began to make excuses. The first said to him, 'I have bought a piece of ground, I must go and see it; I ask you to have me excused.' And another said, 'I bought five yoke of oxen and I am going to test them; I ask you to have me excused too.' Another said, 'I have married a wife and therefore I cannot come.' So the servant came and reported these things to his master and the master of the house being angry, said to his servant, 'Go out quickly into the streets and the lanes of the city and bring here the poor and the maimed and the lame and the blind.' And the servant said, 'Master, it is done as you have commanded and still there is room.' The master said to the servant, 'Go out in the highways and the hedges and compel them to come in, that my house may be filled. For I say to you, that none of those men, who were invited, shall taste my supper." (Luke 14:15-24)

Jesus had said a few verses earlier in Luke 14:11, *"For whoever exalts himself will be humbled, and he who humbles himself will be exalted."* This is the subject matter in the Parable of the Humbled Guest, in Chapter 18 of this book.

Now to this parable: It was still the Sabbath day and Jesus was still at the home of the same Pharisee. He had already pointed out the folly of selecting the best seat at a feast, by pointing out that it would be more prudent to allow the master of the feast to exalt you, for in doing so, you would be happy to receive glory from the master himself.

Jesus now goes on to give another word of advice to the dinner guests present. He told them the secret of hosting a successful feast. Rather than inviting their relatives, their rich neighbors, or their personal friends and acquaintances all of whom could easily repay them, to do the very opposite. Invite instead, the people who could never repay them, such as the crippled, the blind, the poor and the hurting people: those overlooked by society and find life very hard. By this they will be repaid in the resurrection after-life.

He was saying to the Pharisees: first of all, not to sit in the most exalted places. Secondly, He gives them instructions about how to choose their personal dinner guests and then to top it all, in the middle of the feast, just before He had said these things, He healed a man who had palsy. He came into the house and healed him right in front of them.

In the parable, Jesus is talking about a man whose dinner guests resembled the ones that a normal Pharisee would choose as his own guests and yet all the invited people came up with their own various excuses why they could not accept his invitation.

Therefore, Jesus suggested that the Pharisees should command their servants to bypass the usual guest list and instead to go out into the streets and to invite total strangers: people that they normally would *never* associate themselves with: people who would never imagine receiving such a treat as being invited to a splendid free feast in luxurious surroundings. This type of person would fully appreciate the honor shown to them and would never dream of missing their once in a life time opportunity!

Jesus said that the first group of invited guests who had made so many excuses should have no future opportunity to reject the host. But instead, the second list of people would be compelled to come from their own heart's desire.

In reality, Jesus was subtly directing this message to the enormous pride of the Pharisees at that time. Jesus is really saying: "I am compelling you to come into My Kingdom but none of you are repenting of your evil ways. All I hear from you are your excuses. You are continually trying to trip Me up in the Law, with your pointed questions."

"You are trying to excuse yourself with reasons why I am not your Messiah. You reject Me in any way you can. I'm inviting you to the supper with My Father and you are refusing to come. If you do not watch out, you are not going to come in. I will gather up all the lame, the poor, the blind and the hurting people and invite them to My supper and none of you who have excuses and reasons are going to come to My supper."

Now, let me tell you something: I went through a period of about sixteen years, when I thought I was a prophet - a latter-day prophet. I have mentioned this in other chapters, but it bears repeating. For those sixteen years, I studied the Prophets and was absolutely fanatical about the judgments of God. I believed that God was a very harsh judge. I had all sorts of beliefs that He was a condemning God. So I believed that Christians who were constantly pursuing interests other than Christ, such as their marriage, their job, or their business, were in danger of losing their eternal salvation.

I had read this parable and others and thought anyone who was not totally sold out for Jesus and heavily involved in pursuing Him with all their might, were going to Hell. Praise the Lord; I do not believe that error anymore!

These days, people resist the Gospel for numerous reasons: their own religious beliefs blind them; they are insulted when told their good works don't count; they see that belief in the Gospel is too limiting; they have been offended by people who attend church; they are turned off at the politics of religion; or they maintain that the Gospel is just too easy to be true and say: "You can't just ask Jesus into your life and be accepted by Him." It is an enigma to them! Even as a sincere born-again Christian, I struggled with the full concept of grace for many years.

People have all sorts of excuses why they do not enter the Kingdom of God. They have excuses like: they are happy with their life as it is; they don't want to leave their life of sin behind. (Not that they would say those words!) They are enjoying living with their partner. They enjoy having sex with different people every week. They enjoy drinking every night and wild partying. They enjoy gambling. They enjoy all the so called, "fun," things of the world. These are the type of people who will not enter into the Kingdom, because they find excuses not to!

Other people, who reject Christianity, come from other religions of the world and are therefore not open to the claims or the message of the Gospel. These people are similar to the Pharisees in the days of Jesus. They desperately need salvation and they also need to be set free from the devil's "*performance*" lie, which I had been enslaved to.

If you are a Christian and you have Muslim friends, or New Age friends, I would urge you to lead them to my video series, or better still buy the book because it has more "meat" in it than the short video messages have. You could give it as a friendship gift to someone and say: "Here's what just a simple guy wrote about the parables of Jesus. Have a look at it."

Do you know that most people judge the Christian faith by the Christians that they know? In the previous chapter I spoke about a parable on being the light of the world. Most people see Christians as judgmental and narrow-minded people who believe that they alone are the apple of God's eye. Regardless of this, you must know that a person has until their last breath of life to change and to repent. They have until their last minute of life to turn to Jesus. The problem is that none of us know when that time will be. Some people have absolutely no warning whatsoever. One moment life is sweet; the next moment it is over!

Often in our zeal, our narrow-mindedness and self-centeredness, we try to convince people that Jesus is the only answer, but we do not have the patience or endurance to love the person for who they are for fifteen years first. Generally, people do not want to know how much you know, until they know how much you care.

This is why Jesus impressed upon people to go and have a party and invite the sad and lonely people: the rejected, the misunderstood, or under-privileged people. This is why He wants us to feed the hungry; to give drink to the thirsty; to clothe the naked; to care for the people in the hospitals; to visit the people in prison and take in the homeless. Jesus had a shepherd's heart for the lonely, the lost and the hurting and He had the answers for them. He also said that what we do for others, we are actually doing it for Him. If you love Jesus, then that is a wonderful incentive to put yourself out for others.

Do you know that the people of this world are "blind" to the Kingdom of God? Also, people don't have to be restricted to a wheelchair to be lame! We cannot operate in this world successfully without the peace of God. We cannot be at peace in this world until you know God. Until then, you are "crippled." The world's peace is inferior to God's peace! Many people walk around in life in a shell of a body without satisfaction or meaning in life.

Yes, there are many non-Christians who are successful in life, but if you were at their death bed these same people would be fearful. If you were to ask the rich or famous how much joy they experienced in their busy lifestyle, you would be surprised at their answer. If you really befriended them, you would find out that none of their wealth or fame gave them inner peace. We need to personally know the Peace-maker to experience *His peace*.

You often see reported in the press, that marriages are breaking down in Hollywood and rich people are ruining their lives with drugs, alcohol and promiscuity. Having wealth, doesn't mean you are immune to the temptations and sorrows of the world.

Therefore, to be lame, doesn't necessary mean you need a wheelchair! Everyone has lame or blind friends. We all know people who are blind to the Gospel. You, the reader would have lame and blind friends who do not know Jesus: who are trying to live a life without a connection to God. Give them a jump start: they won't suddenly pick up a Bible or come to church, but they may read this book. It is worth a try!

There are people who are emotionally crippled, emotionally hurt and wounded. They are maimed. They are hurt. They have internal wounds. You cannot see these wounds, but all of these people, when they find out the truth of Jesus Christ, embrace it with both arms. These are the people with whom Jesus commanded us to share the Gospel message with.

The servants in this parable are supposed to be us. When Jesus said: go and get the lame and the crippled and compel them to come in, He was speaking to you and me! That means that it's up to us to physically befriend them. We must earn the right to be able to speak into their lives the answers that they are sub-consciously searching for. It is up to us to find them and bring them to the Master so that they can banquet at His table. Now, where do you find them? You will find them in the shops, in the streets, in the clubs and in the pubs. You find them in hotels, in the sports arena, at your workplace, at the bus stop, sitting in the train, or sitting next to you anywhere.

Once you get the hang of it and your boldness increases, you can extend yourself and find people who need Jesus in the casinos, in the gambling institutions and at the horse races, in gay bars, the strip joints and the brothels. The list is endless. There are needy people everywhere you go in life, they are all around you. God loves every single one of them. All these people are waiting to hear the good news of the Gospel.

So many people wear a face mask that says things are fine, when in reality their life is a mess; some are hurting inside and have no direction. To them, life has no purpose and no joy. You hold the fountain of joy. You hold the answers and you are holding a tool in your hand right now.

Most people these days have the internet, so send them a link to my parable website or direct them to this book. I am not promoting this book for financial gain. The purpose of my book is to glorify God in the lives of other people. That was what Jesus always did!

CHAPTER 8

THE PARABLE OF THE DIVIDED KINGDOM (MATTHEW 12:22-30)

Jesus was always doing His Father's business! Often, in doing this, He had his own way of "rubbing certain people up the wrong way." This is captured in Matthew 12:22-30. It says: *"Then one was brought to Him who was demon-possessed, blind and mute;" v.22.*

The man had demons in him that caused his body to violently react. He was blind and couldn't speak. The Scripture goes on: *"He healed him, so that the blind and mute man both spoke and saw and all the multitudes were amazed and said, 'Could this be the Son of David?'" 12: 22-23.*

This is a way of saying, "Could this be our promised Messiah?"

"Now when the Pharisees heard it, they said, "This fellow does not cast out demons except by Beelzebub, the ruler of the demons." 12:24.

But Jesus knew their thoughts and said to them: *"Every Kingdom divided against itself is brought to desolation and every city or house divided against itself will not stand. If Satan casts out Satan, he is divided against himself. How then will his Kingdom stand? And if I cast out demons by Beelzebub, by whom do your sons cast them out? Therefore they shall be your judges but if I cast out demons by the Spirit of God, surely the Kingdom of God has come upon you. Or how can one enter a strong man's house and plunder his goods, unless he first binds the strong man? And then he will plunder his house. He who is not with Me is against Me and he who does not gather with Me scatters abroad." 12: 25-30*

Now, this is interesting! Do you know that witchdoctors have the power to heal people? Witchdoctors even claim that they can release people from demonic oppression! (That's like the pot calling the kettle black!) While they appear to do a seemingly good thing, they *take* something extremely precious from that person: their need for Jesus Christ.

It seems that other religions have certain "gifted," people who excel at "special spiritual" rites. Obviously, Satan can do these things in his own kingdom, but in fact, he places his clients into greater bondage than they had been in before. By giving glory to the witchdoctor, or some other false god, more power is given to the demons and even to the so called "healer." Satan wins! The devil gets a tighter grip on his victims as they worship a false god instead of the One True God.

Jesus said, *"Every Kingdom divided against itself is brought to desolation and every city or house divided against itself will not stand."* An example of this expression would be: it only takes one spouse to break a marriage. Every house that is divided will not stand.

I heard a story about a man who was continually sick and had to go to the hospital regularly because he couldn't eat. He would be put on a drip and after two months in intensive care, he would come back out. Once again, he would become sick and he couldn't eat again. He had been to the hospital about five times. Then he asked his preacher, to come to his house because he needed help.

As the pastor arrived, he saw a woman leaving the house. After the man described his condition the pastor said, "I don't know any reason for this sickness." Yet, the Holy Spirit had told this man to invite the Pastor to come and see him. His friend said, "Well, the Holy Spirit might have told you, but I don't know the reason. Let us pray."

The pastor started to pray. He was about two sentences into the prayer and the Holy Spirit said to him, "The problem is his mother-in-law: she is always cursing him."

When the pastor finished the prayer, he said, "Who was that leaving? Was that your mother-in-law?"

And he said, "Yes."

The pastor asked, "Does she treat you well?"

He said, "Oh, she's always here, saying I'm no good for her family and she is always cursing me by saying that I will never work and I will always be sick."

The pastor said, "She says all these things and what else does she say?"

The pastor listened to the man relate how his mother-in-law spoke curses of sickness over him.

"You must forbid her to come to your home. You cannot be well and allow her into your home. You will continue to be sick. She is the problem," said the pastor.

So the man did just that! He was healed and stayed healed from that time on.

Now, what am I saying? I am not bringing a charge against mothers-in-laws. I am just saying that a house divided against itself, cannot stand. There are situations where one spouse must choose between parents or the other spouse.

In the Old Testament, in Genesis 2:24 we read: *"A man shall leave his father and mother and be joined to his wife and the two shall become one flesh."*

Many problems in marriages occur because either the man or the woman has not emotionally left their parents. The in-laws are always niggling into their business and giving advice. Parents need to release their grown up children, so that they can become responsible to be able to work out their own lives.

Jesus was using the illustration that even Satan cannot run a divided kingdom. Jesus was casting out demons and healing people: bringing glory to God – there is no way Satan would work through Jesus to do these things because these practices were destroying his kingdom. Jesus was using a logical argument: Satan wouldn't work against himself! To do so, would damage his cause, which is to rob and destroy all of God's creation.

Jesus implied that there were exorcists who existed amongst the Jews. He said to them, *"By whom do your sons cast them out? Therefore they shall be your judges."* 12: 27.

The Jews who were casting demons out of people should be the judges of the Pharisees to see which side *they* were on. These exorcists could judge fairly, because the actual demons left their victims. They would be able to discern whether Jesus was being led by the Spirit of God. It was totally inconceivable to believe that a miracle that glorified God would be initiated by the devil!

Jesus went on to say: *"If I cast out demons by the Spirit of God, surely the Kingdom of God has come upon you."* 12:28.

In a nutshell; the Pharisees were ordered to be judged by their fellow Jews who were casting out demons by faith in God or they would have to acknowledge that Jesus was in fact, casting out demons by the Spirit of God!

Now Jesus goes on to talk about binding the strong man and plundering his goods. He said: *"He who is not with Me is against Me and he who does not gather with Me scatters abroad."* 12: 30.

Jesus was saying in effect, "If you are not for me guys, you are against me. You can't sit on the fence on this issue! You have to accept that I am the Son of God. You have to accept that I am the son of David, as they say I am. Look at the signs and wonders that I am doing and acknowledge: 'Surely this man has the power and authority of God! This man is making blind people see; He is making deaf people hear and casting out demons. He is performing miracles and this prophet claims that he is the Son of God.'"

This is what this parable is talking about. Is Jesus the Son of God to you? Is Jesus the Son of David? Was he descended from David, the King of Israel like the Messiah was supposed to be? Is Jesus really the promised Messiah?

So, what is the practical application? It means that if you can't speak the Gospel, you are mute; if you don't understand the Gospel, you are blind to it; if you are affected by wrong theology or wrong voices are speaking to you, you may be demon- possessed. All these things can be solved through Jesus Christ. The spiritual blindness can be corrected by being led by Jesus into truth. The muteness - the inability to witness or to share the Gospel with your friends - can be corrected by a proper relationship with Jesus and Him giving you the boldness through the Holy Spirit. Life filled with joy and love will also give you confidence. It will produce in others, the living proof that God resides in you.

Many Christians fail to testify of God's truth because they feel insignificant or not confident enough. Often, they feel inhibited from expressing what they fear may be controversial views in today's society. They worry that the Gospel news will offend their friends and acquaintances and therefore keep quiet. They are in fact apathetic because of their own self-centeredness. This renders them ineffective. Then, there are others who do not share their faith with other people because they are just too sad and depressed.

Most Christians never seem to reach their full potential. Less than half of them live in health, vitality or prosperity. A certain pastor teaches about living in your destiny and fulfilling God's calling in your life. When he teaches in various churches and public halls, he always calls for people to come forward for prayer who want to have a deeper walk with God. Over eighty percent of the people come forward. You see, most Christians have no idea what they are here for. Therefore they are not fulfilled.

Are you one of those people? Are you one who doesn't yet know your specific purpose in the kingdom? You need to find out! You need to discover God's purpose and start making steps towards it in His strength. Ask Jesus to reveal these things to you and to give you inspiration and courage to change. Then your blindness and your muteness will go. You are called to live an abundant and righteous life! Christ in us is our hope of glory. Rest in His ability to make you the way you are meant to be. The answers to life are found in Jesus Christ. Reading and understanding His parables is a good start.

CHAPTER 9

THE PARABLE OF THE FEAST INVITATIONS
(LUKE 14:12-14)

Jesus' parable in Luke 14:12-14 says:

"Then Jesus said to him who invited Him, 'When you give a dinner or a supper, do not ask your friends, your brothers, your relatives, nor rich neighbors, lest they also invite you back, and you be repaid. But when you give a feast, invite the poor, the maimed, the lame, and the blind. And you will be blessed, because they cannot repay you; for you shall be repaid at the resurrection of the just.'"

In the verses that precede this, Jesus said that when going to a feast, one should sit at the least important seat until the head of the supper sees you as someone he likes and invites you to a higher place.

There is one school of thought that says that until Jesus had been resurrected after dying on the cross, He was still teaching both grace and the Law and this parable just seems too hard to obey. Imagine having a feast and not inviting any of your relatives, your siblings, your friends, the rich, or the people that you know. But instead, for you to go out into the streets inviting the poor, the sick, the maimed, the homeless and all those sorts of people that you do not know and who cannot repay you.

Jesus is very big on mercy and compassion. If we were to see this parable in its true light, this is a parable reflecting what Jesus Christ did for us. We were poor, we were blind, we were lost in sin when He came and died for us.

We have been invited to the wedding supper of the Lamb. We have been invited into a relationship with the King of Kings and truly there is nothing we can do in return. We have been invited into a lovely relationship with the Creator of the universe. Sometimes, we look at a parable like this and we say that this is all too hard. We talk to ourselves: "If I ignored my friends and just invited strangers, what type of party would that be? I would be a laughing stock and would be looked upon as weird by those who know me. Besides these other strangers would see themselves as a charity case and would be insulted by such a thing. What on earth would I have in common with the outcasts of society? I would be uncomfortable and so would they be. No, it's best to dismiss the whole idea."

I can tell you, three to four times I have sat with homeless people and I felt the actual Spirit of Jesus at the table. I would say something and Jesus seemed to respond through the homeless person. I would comment, He would comment. One conversation went for about half an hour. They were memorable moments. People say all the time, "Would you like to meet Jesus on earth?" I really believe I have in the form of someone else.

I have sat with Christians in churches for many years but I have never had Jesus speak through anyone for ten minutes. I have mixed with the homeless, perhaps a hundred times and Jesus, I am convinced, spoke through them four times.

On many occasions, Jesus spoke through me to other people for ten minutes or even more, with the gift of prophecy. Sometimes on these occasions, I just let the Holy Spirit use my vocal chords to speak His words to a complete stranger. (The words came from my mouth, but were not formed in my mind.)

My experience with homeless people has been tremendous when it comes to fellowshipping with Jesus. Why is it so hard for us to genuinely consider this request of Jesus? Imagine having a twenty first birthday party and going down to a homeless shelter, inviting five of them to your gathering, giving respect and honor to them by showing them a good time.

I think it would be rather difficult for a homeless person to agree to have a wardrobe makeover and general clean-up so as to go to a party with you. You would need to first gain his trust and respect, for him to agree to all the fuss. But if he felt that you really cared for him and he allowed you to tidy him up, he would be thrilled with the result. Maybe he could be convinced that God views his spirit and wants to do an even greater work there!

Do you know any homeless people personally? Do you know any sick or maimed people? Do you know anyone in a wheel-chair? Do you know any poor people—those who could not afford to give you twenty dollars or even ten dollars towards the cost of a party? Don't just dismiss the concept. Jesus would be overjoyed if you really did show His kind of love to His needy people. That is what we are supposed to be doing, isn't it?

Jesus is telling us to show compassion and mercy in this life. Give to people who cannot afford to give back to you; give freely and see how you will be blessed. Jesus gave His twelve disciples an incredible mandate in Matthew 10:8. He then finished this by adding: *"Freely you have received freely give."*

It's amazing to discover how passionate some homeless people are about Jesus. There are only a few times in my life that someone I do not know came up and gave me money. At one time, a homeless person gave me fifty dollars! I have concluded that the homeless and the poor hear God's voice very clearly! Quite often, the more desperate you are, the more you depend on God. The more you suffer hardship, the deeper your relationship can be with God.

Whereas, those who feel satisfied with their life, give no thought to the Savior. But the more grateful we are for our own salvation, the more we feel compelled to reach others less fortunate. He who has been forgiven much will love much. At one time the religious people were hostile toward a sinful woman who was weeping and washing the feet of Jesus with expensive fragrant oil and then wiping His feet with her hair. Jesus answered their scorn: *"Therefore I say to you, her sins which are many are forgiven, for she loved much. But to whom little is forgiven, the same loves little."* Luke 7:47.

Please do not shrug off this parable: this is God's heart cry! You can find homeless people at a soup kitchen. You can find them through the Salvation Army. There are poor people in your church. There is a single mother sitting on your church pew who is having a rough time. There are men and women in your congregation who have too much of the week left - too much of a fortnight left - too much time before the next pay check. They have too many days left without money to buy the essentials. There are people in your church who are poor - invite them round for dinner.

You do not need to have a big party and invite a whole lot of strange, poor or sick people. Just invite one. No one jumps into the deep end of the pool and starts to swim straight away. People gradually get into a stream and go out into the deep end when they feel safe enough to swim. Just start to invite one or two to your parties. You might find it very interesting. I have spent time on the streets. I spent six months in a homeless hostel, officially homeless. You would be surprised how beautiful some homeless people are.

Do not be scared of inviting them into your house. Do not be scared of loving the poor. You cannot be infected by a homeless person. The spirit of homelessness is not going to rub off on you. You are not going to lose your prosperity by having a poor person in your house. Go on, I encourage you; take Jesus at His word. Take the challenge. Reach out with mercy and compassion and touch the broken-hearted today.

CHAPTER 10

THE PARABLE OF THE FRIEND AT MIDNIGHT
(LUKE 11:5-13)

Don't you just love friends that come around at midnight?

I am sitting here with my night-owl friend, who I rang at midnight and invited over. Now he is sitting here watching me record some of my parables during the night hours. Exactly one hundred and eleven minutes worth of memory is left on my video recorder. I feel that this is a much-anointed time to be preaching this.

So, it is midnight...and here we go.

"Which of you shall have a friend and go to him at midnight and say to him, 'Friend, lend me three loaves; for a friend of mine has come to me on his journey and I have nothing to set before him;' and he will answer from within and say, 'Do not trouble me; the door is now shut and my children are with me in bed; I cannot rise and give to you?' I say to you, though he will not rise and give to him because he is his friend, yet because of his persistence he will rise and give him as many as he needs.

"So I say to you, ask and it will be given to you; seek and you will find; knock and it will be opened to you. For everyone who asks receives and he who seeks finds and to him who knocks it will be opened. If a son asks for bread from any father among you, will he give him a stone? Or if he asks for a fish, will he give him a serpent instead of a fish? Or if he asks for an egg, will he offer him a scorpion? If you then, being evil, know how to give good gifts to your children, how much more will your heavenly Father give the Holy Spirit to those who ask Him!"

I always appreciate an illustration. I consider a friend is someone with these two qualifications. A friend is someone who has invited me to their place for a meal and who has accepted my invitation to do likewise. A friend is also someone that I would feel comfortable in asking for a loan of up to three hundred dollars for an emergency flight. This friend would not pester me as to when I would pay them back. Instead, they would be asking me how soon do I need to have the money and into what account should they deposit it. Now, if we haven't been to each others home and if I couldn't see myself asking for such a loan, then I do not see them as a close friend.

I have not asked my friends for that amount, but I know whom I could ask if the need should arise. Many of them have given me some money at times and have displayed a gracious attitude which indicates to me that I could ask them for their help if pressed.

What if you were home, at say 11:30 at night and some people arrive in your city from another state? They had planned to drive through to another state but the driver became too sleepy and he is starting to fall asleep driving. They phone you, because they are not far from your place. Imagine their whole family turns up hungry and you have nothing suitable in your house to feed them. They want to stay for the night as well. You can put them up okay but how are you to feed them at such a late hour?

Do you have a friend who you can wake up at midnight? I am just talking personally now. Do you have a friend who you can wake up at midnight and borrow forty dollars to buy a few pizzas? Or go down to the local all-night convenience store and buy some food? Do you have such a friend who would not be upset with you?

Remember that little boy who gave five small barley loaves to Jesus? Take note, those were not five loaves of bread but five barley buns! They were not wheat, but barley. They were a poor boy's food and they were his lunch; He had five buns and a couple of fish.

In this parable, both the evening and morning meals were needed for a family. This is substantially more than what that little boy had. But Jesus was in control that day and that little lad's lunch stretched to feed five thousand men and their families and still there was plenty left over!

You might go round to an acquaintance's place and knock on the door and he says, "Look, my kids are in bed." Now, I reckon if a person has their children in bed with them, they must be poor. Obviously, they live in a one bedroom house with just one bed in it. Many families live like this. There might be three children in bed plus the parents. Therefore, getting up out of bed, putting the light on and going downstairs could definitely disturb the whole family.

How many friends do you have who you can wake up in the middle of the night, disturb the sleep of the whole family, yet this friend would not be cranky or put-out about having to help you? Come on, count them. Can you think of just one person?

We all have a friend and His name is Jesus Christ. He is awake all the time. He doesn't have a family in bed with Him. This is the friend that the parable is directing us to. We thought that Jesus was talking about a friend down here, but it's actually Him telling us that He is a friend that supplies all our needs and He is never put out by our requests.

I remember one day, I was homeless and I was living in a homeless shelter. I kept on meeting a Christian friend who kept on finding money on the road all the time –not only coins but notes as well. Whenever he saw me, he told me what he had found. I was always giving to the poor. Living in a big city, homeless people would come up to me and ask me for money, so I could never refuse them. (I am extremely mindful that what I do for others, I am doing it for Jesus.) Needless to say, I couldn't keep money in my pocket for long. So even two days after receiving my pension, I would almost be broke. I would have given my money away and I would then be forced to live on free food and accommodation myself, until my next pay day. Anyway, I decided to do as my friend does; I was going to look for some money just for myself.

One time, I really wanted to see a particular movie and buy a pizza, but I had no money. I said to the Lord, "Please Lord, let me just find twenty dollars today. You know I have given all my money away and I really feel like a treat." Then I walked around the whole night, not looking people in the eyes. If you have read my other parables, especially the "Light on the Hill" parable, you will know that I am always talking to people. I always walk up to people saying, "Hello." So, it was very hard for me to spend the whole night looking down at the road for money rather than looking at the people and greeting them in my usual fashion.

I searched for hours for God's hidden twenty dollars but couldn't find it. "Ah well, Jesus doesn't want to give me any money tonight," I said to myself. I had never asked Him for money before. In fact, I hardly ever ask Him for personal treats.

At the end of the night, I saw a homeless friend sitting in a Chinese restaurant. I went in and said:"Hello!" I had been given a loaf of bread from a food van. I sat next to him and asked, "Do you have some wine? I have some bread and we could have Communion together." He removed a bottle of red wine from his bag and collected two glasses from the restaurant. He poured the wine and I broke off some bread. Both of us just sat and gave thanks and said a short prayer each. It was the best Communion I had ever had. We chatted and he offered me some of his meal. I said, "No, I have just eaten."

This man used to live on the streets even when it was raining. We went outside and he said, "Before you go take this!" He reached into his back pocket and pulled out his wallet and gave me a fifty dollar note. I tried to press it back to him but he insisted that I take it because God had told him to give it to me. I walked away crying. I asked Jesus, "Lord, is this the twenty dollars I asked you for?"

Jesus said, "Yes."

I went in to McDonald's and I bought a super-sized Coke for three dollars and fifty cents. On the way out of McDonald's, someone said, "Have you got spare change?" So I gave him my one dollar fifty change..

Then, a girl came up to me and said, "Do you have two dollars sir? "

I felt compassion for her and I said, "How much do you need?"

She said, "I really need twenty dollars." And I gave her my twenty dollar note.

I looked in my wallet and I had twenty five dollars left.This was enough for pizza the next day and to go to the movies as I wanted to. That was one of the three times that I actually asked Jesus for something and you know what? He delivered it through a homeless man, who had just wanted to bless me. When I gave the girl the twenty dollar note, she broke down in tears and hugged me. She hugged me with one of those hugs where you try to let go but the person doesn't want to. Three or four times you try to pull out of the hug but you realize that they are overcome with emotion and they want to keep holding you. Well, we were hugging for perhaps a minute whilst she cried. I was quite emotional by then as well.

"Why would you give me this?" she asked.

I said, "Jesus would give you this. Jesus loves you." That was a testimony.

You know, Jesus loves us. Whilst He does not want to give us our lusts, He does want to give us our heart's desires. However, He says quite clearly in the Gospels, *"Seek first the kingdom of God and all these things will be added unto you." Matthew 6:33.*

Jesus loves us. He loves you. He wants to provide for your needs. Don't be afraid of asking Him. Don't be afraid of seeking His will for your life and pursuing it. Don't be worried about asking Him to provide for your material needs. As He said, "Does a child ask his father for bread and the Father give him a stone?" (Luke 11:11)

Immediately after Jesus was publicly baptized and before He could begin His earthly ministry, the Spirit of God led Him into the wilderness to overcome the devil. During His forty days of temptation, He experienced extreme hunger. The devil tried to tempt Him in His weakness and said, *"If You are the Son of God, command that these stones become bread." Matthew 4:3.* Because Jesus had to fully identify with Adam, He could not use His Divine nature to solve His hunger, so He replied to the devil: *"Man should not live by bread alone, but by every word that proceeds from the mouth of God." (v 4)* The answer Jesus gave to the devil was a direct quotation from the Old Testament.

Here, in our passage today in Luke and in verse 11, Jesus is saying something different to us: *If a son asks for bread from any father among you, will he give him a stone?* The Father loves you. Jesus loves you. One of the best ways I know to prosper in His Kingdom is to read all these parables and apply them in your life.

So often we think that we are annoying God with small requests. So often we think that God is too busy and He is too important to bother with the problems in our life. We think somehow that we are not good enough, not important enough and that we would be giving God a headache with our prayers. Jesus says differently. He says that we are to feel free to come to Him with any request as often as we wish. I pray that you will confidently go to Him with your requests now.

CHAPTER 11

THE PARABLE OF THE GOOD SAMARITAN
(LUKE 10:25-37)

A book on the parables of Jesus would not be complete without a chapter on the Good Samaritan. If you have gone to church for many years, you would have heard this parable preached. I hope that you will enjoy some the fresh revelations from what I have to say.

In Luke 10:25, it says *"and behold, a certain lawyer stood up and tested Him, saying, 'Teacher, what should I do to inherit eternal life?'"*

Obviously this man was testing Jesus to see if He had the right answers.

Jesus answered by asking a question: *'What is written in the law? What is your reading of it?' and so he answered and said, 'You shall love the LORD your God with all your heart, with all your soul, with all your strength, and with all your mind and your neighbor as yourself.' And He said to him, 'You have answered rightly; do this and you will live.' Vs.26-28*

Jesus agreed with this lawyer, who said that in order to gain eternal life we must love God with all our heart, mind and soul and we must also love our neighbor as much as we love ourselves. This would properly fulfill the law. Yes, that's fine. The only problem is - that we just cannot possibly love like this in the natural. We cannot love God with all our mind, heart and soul and strength. Nor can we love our neighbor the way we love ourselves in our own strength. We need the power of the Holy Spirit to enable us to love God's way!

I think this man knew that he was falling short and he was trying to justify himself. He wanted to see if he was in right-standing with God according to this new Rabbi. So he wanted Jesus' interpretation of what it all meant.

For the Jews, a "neighbor" is someone who does good things for you. In their tradition and interpretation of the Law, if someone was your enemy then you would treat him as an enemy. You know, a hit for a hit; a punch for a punch. It was commonly known as the "eye-for-an-eye law." That was the Old Testament law that they had lived under for almost two thousand years. So to this lawyer, his neighbor was someone who was treating him right. This he wanted Jesus to verify. So he asked: *"Who is my neighbor?"*

"Then Jesus replied: *'A certain man went down from Jerusalem to Jericho and fell among thieves, who stripped him of his clothing, wounded him and departed, leaving him half dead. Now by chance a certain priest came down that road and when he saw him, he passed by on the other side. Likewise a Levite, when he arrived at the place, came and looked and passed by on the other side'"* (vv. 30-32).

You notice in the passage that both the priest and the Levite saw the badly beaten man, looked at him and passed by on the other side of the road. In other words, they crossed over to the opposite side so that the poor man would not groan to them and thus obligate them to do something. They both saw that he was in a desperate condition but found a way to escape having to deal with the problem.

"But a certain Samaritan, as he journeyed, came where he was and when he saw him, he had compassion" (v. 33.)

Notice the word compassion; compassion is an act of love; it is mercy in action. If you find compassion in your heart for someone, you find yourself compelled to help them.

"So he went to him and bandaged his wound, pouring on oil and wine; and he set him on his own animal, brought him to an inn, and took care of him. The next day, when he departed, he took out two denarius, gave them to the innkeeper, and said to him 'Take care of him; and whatever more you spend, when I come again, I will repay you.' " (vv. 34-35.)

During that time, this money was equivalent to two days' wages, which is about two to three hundred dollars in Australia. In verse 36 Jesus asked: *'So which of these three do you think was a neighbor to him who fell among the thieves?'*

The lawyer replied: *'He who showed mercy on him.' Then Jesus said to him, 'Go and do likewise."* (v. 37)

The Jews had been set apart by God: He selected them to be His chosen people. In light of this, it would have been especially hard for the lawyer, being a Jew, to admit that in this particular parable, the one to be considered a neighbor was the Samaritan. In their culture, the Jews would not mix with other people and the Samaritans in particular, were seen as the dregs of society; they would not sit down and have a meal with anyone who was not a Jew. They would not have anything to do with the Gentiles (Non-Jews), and so it was a huge step for a Jew to accept that a Gentile—a Samaritan—was his neighbor. Even if this lawyer understood what Jesus said, he would have gone away from there with no intention of applying the parable.

Now, let me make this practical. How many times have you gone down the street and seen someone lying hurt by the side of the road? How many times have you seen someone in a really bad situation? I have only seen this happen twice - people helping someone into a taxi or an ambulance after having a heart attack but apart from those two instances, I have never seen anyone in a bad condition that needed to go to hospital.

So, how do we apply this parable to our own lives? How is this relevant to us today?

I believe that this parable not only talks about negative physical conditions, but emotional and mental conditions that are a tremendous burden to people. Many lives are broken by disappointments and tragedies, or some people may have unsolvable financial problems, or even suffer from mental health issues. Any of these scenarios can result in being homeless. People are trapped in addictions such as alcohol, drugs and habitual gambling. There are all sorts of reasons why people end up on the street. Many of these people have been abused and beaten up by life. These are just some of the people, for whom we are called to have compassion on.

In the parable of the sheep and the goats, we are exhorted to take the homeless into our home, but often people have a family to protect. Unfortunately, compassionate people, after showing love to strangers, have had their assets stolen or even worse! There are all sorts of reasons why taking in a homeless person is not practical these days. You need to have godly discernment, to take a total stranger into the privacy of your home.

However, there is nothing stopping you from buying a homeless person a drink and a hamburger or even taking them to a restaurant to have a steak dinner. There is nothing stopping you from taking such a person to a clothing store and buying them clothes. If you were genuinely interested and really cared about a homeless person with whom you spent enough time, you could perhaps even find a way to get him off the streets. If you are asking where to find injured neighbors, you can definitely consider the homeless people who exist in every town.

You may ask: "Who else, would be my neighbor?" An emotionally injured girl, who spends her time sleeping with numerous men, may be your neighbor! She may be just looking for love and acceptance in the wrong place. She needs to discover the love of Jesus. As Christians we are to love hurting people with the right kind of love. There is a good chance she is acting that way because of low self esteem, perhaps brought about through abuse. She is a person who needs care. She desperately needs to find forgiveness, true support and understanding. How is she ever going to learn to break out from that cycle of abuse, if someone doesn't take her aside, help her and show her what true love is? How would she know how a real man should treat her? She could be your neighbor!

Another neighbor could be the Muslim working at your local coffee shop. Even though he might know you are a Christian, if you treat him respectfully and show him kindness, you may in time gain his interest in your beliefs. You could even lend him this book by saying, "This book explains the parables of Jesus, your prophet. You can borrow it if you like. It is easy to read and I have found it very interesting." So, you can see there are many ways to help your neighbor. There are many people in desperate situations. This parable makes it quite clear that your neighbor is not necessarily someone of the same religion, color or creed, or sex. The word, "neighbor," is not narrowly defined. Your neighbor could be anyone in this world who is going through a hard time. We are called to love anyone and everyone. In this parable, Jesus was saying that the "Samaritan," who helped the injured man, had proved himself to be a good neighbor. To a Jewish mind this was very controversial and even quite threatening.

I have identified the word, "compassion," as the key word in this teaching. We should flow with compassion for everyone: no matter what race, culture, or sexuality. Certain people are stigmatized more than any other group of people in our society. This is the "gay community." These people are really badly treated by the Christian world and homosexuality is often regarded as somehow more sinful than other types of sexual sin. However, God loves the gays and many of them are in search of the truth. If given the opportunity, many would want to become Christians. In fact, in my church, we have a few gay people. We need to embrace them with the love of Jesus and pray that the Holy Spirit would draw them to Himself, so that they can come out of their present lifestyle and live guilt free. Regardless of their particular sin, God does not love them less than any of us. His heart yearns to reach out and totally heal their lives.

That is what the Good Samaritan is all about. In essence, it is about removing all your prejudices against people and treating all people equally with love.

The only people Jesus openly rebuked were those who considered themselves holier or more superior to other people. He called them hypocrites and he considered the religious people in His time as the blind leading the blind. (No wonder most of them hated Him.)

Jesus sees our heart motive and the reasons why we do the things we do. He knows all about the hurting experiences even more than we do and He understands. Jesus Himself was a friend of the prostitutes, tax collectors and publicans. He mixed with them more than He mixed with the religious leaders. Most times, people that are caught up in sin are open and honest about their life, because they are suffering and need answers to their questions. Plus, they are hurting and their sin is often an outward manifestation of that hurt. Only people who think that they are righteous and holy and have everything together have no ears for the message of Jesus.

Jesus said in Matthew 11:28-30 *"Come to Me, all you who labor and are heavy laden, and I will give you rest. Take My yoke upon you and learn from Me, for I am gentle and lowly in heart, and you will find rest in your souls. For My yoke is easy and My burden is light."*

Jesus has invited everyone to come to Him, just as they are. None of us are qualified to enter Heaven by our own goodness, *but Jesus in us, makes us completely qualified!*

CHAPTER 12

THE PARABLE OF THE GOOD SHEPHERD
(JOHN 10:1-18)

Before we look at this parable, we need to first read it in context. See John 9:40-41. *Then some of the Pharisees who were with Him heard these words and said to Him, "Are we blind also?" Jesus said to them, "If you were blind, you would have no sin; but now you say, 'We see.' Therefore your sin remains."*

Jesus was describing a person who is spiritually blind before He went on to speak about the Good Shepherd. *"Most assuredly, I say to you, he who does not enter the sheepfold by the door but climbs up some other way, the same is a thief and a robber but he who enters by the door is the shepherd of the sheep. To him the doorkeeper opens and the sheep hear his voice; and he calls his own sheep by name and leads them out and when he brings out his own sheep, he goes before them; and the sheep follow him, for they know his voice. Yet they will by no means follow a stranger, but will flee from him, for they do not know the voice of strangers." John 10:1-5*

Then in verse 9 Jesus identified Himself as the door for the sheepfold. People have to come through Him to become part of God's sheepfold. This simply means that everyone else who preaches another way to God is wrong, for Jesus says: *"I am the door. If anyone enters by Me, he will be saved and will go in and out and find pasture."*

Let's now concentrate on verse 3 which says, *"To him the doorkeeper opens and the sheep hear his voice; and he calls his own sheep by name and leads them out."*

Jesus knows His family members by name so He can address you by name at the beginning of a sentence. I don't know whether He does this for the rest of His family, but maybe because I have had demonic voices speak to me in my illness, I often hear in my spirit my name being called. I can be walking down the road and then have a thought, "Matthew, I want you to go down to the shops first before you go to church." and because He said "Matthew" at the beginning, I know it's not *my thought* but it's Jesus speaking to me. Essentially, when you start to practice hearing the words of Jesus in an audible sentence *in your spirit*, you can ask Him to address you by name.

45

I have spoken to Pastors, Bible teachers, intercessors and many mature Christians who say that they have only heard Jesus speak in an "audible" voice on a couple of occasions in all their life. So, I'm not talking about that kind of audible voice here, I'm talking about a still quiet voice that you have to train yourself to even hear. That is how God talks to most people in their spirit. If you are filled with your own agenda all the time, you will miss Him. He also talks by giving us sharp promptings in our spirit to do or say something. I feel very blessed because God does speak to me and I have distinguished His voice from those of the enemy. "Lord Jesus in Your name, I ask that you will start to talk to everyone who reads this book and I ask that you might address them by name, just as You do for me. Amen."

John 10:4 says: *"And when he brings out his own sheep, he goes before them; and the sheep follow him, for they know his voice."* Now, if you are a sheep of Jesus, you are His true follower and you will obey His instructions to you. Your life should not be a mish-mash of wrong decisions which are based on your flesh. A true follower of Jesus follows the steps that Jesus gives. Jesus leads your life by showing you the way to do things and what decisions to make according to His perfect will.

This parable has been preached so many times, but very few preachers emphasize the fact that people need to listen to Jesus. Psalm 37:23 says: *"A righteous man's steps are ordered by the Lord."* A believer is already righteous in God's sight. Therefore, a Christian's steps are planned and designed by the Lord.

In John 10:5-6 we read: *"Yet they will by no means follow a stranger, but will flee from him, for they do not know the voice of strangers. Jesus used this illustration, but they did not understand the things which He spoke to them."*

As we become familiar with Scripture and the small quiet voice of the Holy Spirit, we will then be able to recognize false teaching by someone who is misinformed or is led by a wrong spirit. You may hear someone else, or even yourself start to speak, and you will be aware that your "spiritual alarm" has started to ring out. Heed this alarm: for what you have begun to listen to, is not really God's message. Know that you are protected when you recognize the voice of the Good Shepherd because every child of God has been given an inner "virus protector" known as God's Holy Spirit.

John 10:7 continues, *"Most assuredly, I say to you, I am the door of the sheep."* In other words, there is no other door to Heaven. There is no other way that you can be a follower of Jesus but to follow Jesus Himself. Then verse 8 says: *"All who ever came before Me are thieves and robbers, but the sheep did not hear them."*

Jesus is not talking about the anointed Old Testament prophets. They were all true spokesmen of God but the people He is referring to are the teachers of the Law: the Scribes and the Pharisees who have come before Jesus. He said they were thieves and robbers. They were not preaching the truth of the Word of God. They were teaching in a wrong spirit because they themselves had wrong motives. We are not to allow Satan or his spokesperson to steal God's peace or to deceive us from the truth of God's Word.

Verse 9 "I am the door. If anyone enters by Me, he will be saved and will go in and out and find pasture" The sheep receive nourishment from the pasture. If you give your life to Jesus Christ, you will be nourished by Him on the things that are good. So if you are not a Christian and you are reading this book, the Lord Jesus Christ really is the answer you have been looking for.

It goes on in verse 10, *"the thief does not come except to steal and kill and destroy. I have come that they may have life and that they may have it more abundantly."* The Christian life is not a life where one simply exists; it is not only getting by week by week, but having such abundance in your provisions that you can give and freely share with others. You should not be aimless, wondering what the will of God is, or if you will ever find true peace. (Satan and his demons offer false peace and other counterfeit goodies to trip us up!) The Christian life is an abundance of all good things. I am sure that you have received that message as you have been reading this book.

Verse 11 "I am the good shepherd. The good shepherd gives His life for the sheep." Jesus Christ laid down his life and was willingly crucified for our sins. He is our Creator and as such He truly loves every single person.

Verses 12-13 "But a hireling, he who is not the shepherd, one who does not own the sheep sees the wolf coming and leaves the sheep and flees; and the wolf catches the sheep and scatters them. The hireling flees because he is a hireling and does not care about the sheep." A hireling can be likened to a pastor who doesn't take the time to go out and help a member of his congregation who is in need.

In the last ten years, I personally have not found a pastor who has not loved me and has not been there when I needed him. A true pastor is not just a hireling; He is a genuine servant of God and a good shepherd to his congregation.

Bad shepherds and hirelings do exist. This warning by Jesus would not be needed if they did not exist! If the pastor does not have time or does not really care for your concerns, you need to find a church, small enough where the pastor has a vested interest in your life. My Pastor, (to whom I have dedicated this book), is deeply interested in my life. If I do not connect with her once a week, she would want to know what was wrong. If I missed out visiting our community center for a week, she would ring me at home and ask me what was wrong. That is what a true pastor is.

Verse 14 "I am the good shepherd; and I know My sheep, and am known by My own." A true Christian knows Jesus personally. They enjoy an intimate relationship with Him. Real Christianity consists of more than intellectual *knowledge about Jesus*. You should have an experiential knowledge of Him—knowledge based on experience. You should be able to share some wonderful stories about Jesus—about what He has done, how He saved you from this, how He showed you that, and how your life would not be the same without Him. You should be able to confess to others that your life would be unfulfilled, lost and without meaning if Jesus was not in your life.

Many people profess to know Jesus as their Savior and Lord yet they cannot testify like I do. If you have become a Christian and what I have described does not reflect your inner life, than perhaps you could be in some type of bondage or you are not diligently seeking God like He wants you to. The Christian life is actually supernatural because we have a supernatural God actually residing in us forever! I imagine some people reading this book, may envy the life I have with Jesus. The good news is that you too can have that life! You need to: *"Draw near to God and He will draw near to you." James 4:8*

Verses 15-16 "As the Father knows Me, even so I know the Father; and I lay down My life for the sheep and other sheep I have which are not of this fold; them also I must bring, and they will hear My voice; and there will be one flock and one shepherd."

Jesus was talking to the Jewish people about the Gentiles who will become Christians one day and both the Jewish believers and the Gentile believers will be all one flock. This is still happening now! In Israel and all over the world, thousand of practicing Jews have found their Messiah. They have recognized the Lord Jesus Christ as being the "Anointed One," promised in the Old Testament Scriptures.

It is important to know that there are many Christian denominations in the world, but Jesus sees all the *genuine believers* in these churches as being part of one big family of God. There are also church people who are earnestly seeking answers to life and have not yet become Christians. Plus there are church folk who wrongly believe that they are Christians but they are looking for the praise of man, not salvation. Also, Satan may bring a person to a church to cause disunity: these are prisoners who need to be saved.

Verse 17 "Therefore My Father loves Me, because I lay down My life that I may take it again" Jesus willingly surrendered his life for us. He was crucified on the cross for our sin and was physically resurrected and seen by hundreds of people for forty days.

Verse 18 "No one takes it from Me, but I lay it down of Myself. I have power to lay it down, and I have power to take it again. This command I have received from My Father" At any time Jesus could have called for the angels to rescue Him, but this was his mission in coming to earth in the first place. He died in our place, so that we could live with Him.

A good shepherd will put his life on the line against predators of his sheep. The Jews or Satan didn't kill Jesus: the sin of all humanity nailed Him to the Cross. "So when Jesus received the sour wine, He said, *'It is finished!'* and bowing His head, He gave up His spirit." John 19:30. After a sever whipping and six hours of extreme torture, Jesus just quietly surrendered His life to God in order to rescue us. He is a tremendous shepherd. He can be your Shepherd. Ask Him to be with you and talk to you in a personal way.

CHAPTER 13

THE PARABLE OF THE GREAT PHYSICIAN
(MATTHEW 9:10-13)

I laughed upon seeing the title of this parable on my list. I did not even know what it was. So, I turned my Bible to where the parable was and that has been my sermon preparation.

If you ever wonder how much preparation I have done, it includes many years of walking with Jesus. Most of the teachings I am doing on these parables have been preached with no extra reading or commentary. They are all life-related and come from my personal experiences during a thirty five year relationship with the Lord Jesus Christ. Also they come from endless hours spent meditating on the Old Testament; on the Parables of Jesus and His other teachings as well as the Epistles in the New Testament.

Add to that, the fact that when you deliver a sermon for which you have no preparation, it leaves a lot of room for the Holy Spirit to use you. When people see some of my simple teachings and call them profound, rich and deep, all glory has to go to God, because it's not me that is doing it: I am a simple person. If you find these teachings very deep, that is the Holy Spirit speaking through me onto the page.

I find it interesting sharing the parables of Jesus because they do not give the real meaning right away. You have to search for what it really means as intended by Jesus Christ.

So here we go. Jesus was known as a Jewish Rabbi and yet some of His closest associates and friends were tax collectors and known sinners. The religious leaders were appalled by His choice of company. Now we will start our parable:

Matthew 9:11-12: *"And when the Pharisees saw it, they said to His disciples, 'Why does your Teacher eat with tax collectors and sinners?' When Jesus heard that, He said to them, 'Those who are well have no need of a physician but those who are sick, but go and learn what this means: I desire mercy and not sacrifice. I did not come to call the righteous but sinners, to repentance.'"*

Have you ever had a major decay in your tooth? Some of my teeth, I have to confess, are not there any more. An infection came into my mouth from tooth decay so badly that I couldn't sleep without pain killers. I finally sought a dentist. He said that I needed major root-canal therapy which would cost nine hundred and fifty dollars or an extraction.

At that stage, I was still in my addiction and living on a disability pension in a Housing Commission flat, I opted for the latter. Now, let me ask you this question, when you have a rotten tooth and the pain is unbearable, do you seek out the dentist? If you had the means to pay for the big job in order to save your tooth, would you do it? Or would you go for the cheaper option and be willing to lose your tooth? What about when you have a headache? Do you reach for a pain-killer to stop the headache? What about if you have a migraine? What if you develop a troublesome rash on your skin? Don't you go to someone qualified and buy cream for it?

When we are sick, we seek a doctor. But if we have a solution to our sickness, like cold and flu tablets and basic cough medicines, we don't bother seeking a physician because we already have our answer. If our sickness gets to a stage when we can no longer handle it, we look for a doctor's help. Now, that is hard for some people in America, who don't have medical insurance as medicine and doctors are so expensive. Here, in Australia you can basically receive medical or dental attention for free, if you are desperate enough.

Bearing that in mind, Jesus said: *"Those who are well have no need of a physician but those who are sick." Matthew 9:12b.* The Pharisees were Jews who had studied the Old Testament Law. But then, they also had hundreds of other rules in a separate book which listed *their added on* requirements and interpretations. But the Pharisees wrote those rules and conditions in such a way that it was almost impossible to obey them. They were man ordained not God ordained!

The Pharisees took pride in their self-righteousness. They fasted, they tithed and they sacrificed. They always uttered pious public prayers and proudly wore their long robes and their phylacteries on their arm or forehead. These "phylacteries" were portions of Scripture in little leather cases. These were attached to the wearer by small leather straps.

Essentially, they saw themselves as more important, more holy, more respectable and more loved by God. Because they never polluted themselves with sinners, they felt that they were perfectly acceptable to God. They were very self satisfied and opinionated. After all, they were, "good," people who always kept the Law!

For Jesus, holy Rabbi no less, to sit with a real sinner, someone who is blatantly sinning—the scum of the earth—was just an offense to them. It was a stench in their nostrils. It really annoyed them. So much so, that even in Jesus' presence they complained of His choice of companions. John, a disciple of Jesus, records:

"Now it happened, as Jesus sat at the table in the house, that behold, many tax collectors and sinners came and sat down with Him and His disciples" (v.10). Jesus had walked into this house, and right away he had a whole bunch of tax collectors and sinners come and sit down to eat a meal with Him and to enjoy His wonderful company.

To put this in a modern setting: Imagine Jesus was with us today in person and He went and sat down in a certain house. Then many politicians, drug dealers, pimps, prostitutes and pedophiles came in and sat down with Jesus and started to break bread, have dinner with him and tell jokes. Do you think this would offend people today?

What if I came round to your house? For example, you are having an open-air barbecue. I have just sat down. Imagine that I am an international public speaker of the Gospel. I have a busy speaking schedule organized and I am in your city. I have been invited to your house for a barbecue to meet you and to spend some time with you. When I arrive there, all the local pimps, prostitutes, homosexuals, drug addicts, drug lords, child sex offenders and slave traders arrive to greet me and join me for your barbeque. They all gate-crash the party and sit down and say, "Hey Matthew, we have seen you on You-Tube. You are so cool, man. We want to join you guys for lunch."

What if they gate crashed your party? How would you feel? Maybe you are not like the Pharisees. Maybe you are a beautiful Christian. In your daily life, you are mixing with people from all walks of life and you can handle these sorts of people at your party.

I live in a community. My church is actually a community of people like that. These are not offensive people to me. In fact, it's hard for me to relate very well with some goodie-goodie Christians at times. I find it much easier to mix with sinners at my "street-level" church in inner Sydney. Jesus was the same way.

Imagine if Jesus had said to the proud Pharisees that day, "These people are sick. They have a "spiritual" toothache. They need a "root-canal" or they will lose their teeth. Why are you getting on my case? These people are the ones that need attention. You don't even care! You write them off as sinners and tax collectors. They are the scum of the earth to you. You will not lift a finger to help them with their sin, or make them more righteous or help them obey the Law. You just reject them outright. I am not going to reject someone who needs help. They have a toothache, can't you see? They are messed up. They need some answers. You are the guys with all the answers: you obey the Law! You see yourself as healthy, but these people need urgent care."

"Go and discover what this means: I desire mercy not sacrifice. I do not want your type of fasting two days a week. I do not want you to throw your coins into the poor-box and make a big loud ring so the people know how generous you are!"

The poor-box had a large opening in the top of it so that you could place your hand down into it and quietly drop some coins in. Or, you could throw your coin in and it would make a big noisy clang! The Pharisees would choose this way.

Most of these so-called righteous and religious leaders of that day were bound up with self-righteousness. They constantly wanted to impress others. Therefore, they preferred to throw their coins into the poor-box so that everyone would turn around and say, "Oh, he just gave some money to the poor!"

Jesus said, "When you give your alms, do not sound the trumpet." Do not make that big clang that was called, "sounding the trumpet." Do not do that. Do not let your right arm know what your left arm is doing.

So the Pharisees used to sacrifice their money. They even used to sacrifice one tenth of their herbs almost down to the last leaf. They used to give their animal sacrifices to the priests. Also, they made their first fruits offerings. They used to do everything perfectly. But all these things they were doing to be righteous, Jesus classed as works of the flesh.

Jesus had said: *"I desire mercy not sacrifice."* v. 13. (The fruit of mercy is compassion!)

You see, dear reader, most people in Australia would pass by a heroin addict—someone who is putting a needle in their arm—and have no mercy on them. Do you know that approximately eighty two percent of Australians who have heroin addiction have been sexually abused as a child? They need help. I am not sure you understand what it feels like to be molested by someone twenty years older than you. I understand what that is like and I can assure you, it seriously messes with your head.

When you are living with any of the following, it seriously messes your head up: promiscuous relationships; addiction to prostitutes; addiction to pornography; or addiction to alcohol.

It has taken me heaps of work, help, counseling and much genuine understanding, to become healed to where I am today. I still have pain and hurt that needs to be healed, but I am well on the way to full restoration and I know God's forgiveness and His peace.

Jesus says we should have mercy on people like these. Don't condemn these people and write them off as someone who could never be saved by Jesus. This is the first time I have been so frank in this collection of parables, but it serves this parable well for you to know that, in my past, I used the services of prostitutes for twenty years. How many times did I sin then? I have slept with men, I have done all sorts of wicked things and here I am, sharing that I am free of those horrible addictions.

Yet God is still using me because He is a God of mercy and love. He loves all the hurting and broken people in the world. He wants us to show the same love to others. He does not want us to bring further condemnation onto the devil's victims.

We criticize the Pharisees for condemning Jesus and yet, if we are honest—truly honest with ourselves—we do not think that people practicing addictions and sexual sins should be allowed to fellowship with all of the "clean and righteous," church people.

We spend time in the Bible; at church; at Bible studies and we spend our money giving to Lord's work. We make all these sacrifices and we think we please God, but if these things are not done in the right spirit, they are worthless! God calls all of them acts of self-righteousness. (Actually, the Bible calls them, "filthy rags.") The only "work," that we can do to please God, is to live by faith in the Son of God.

Jesus wants us to show mercy to the broken and hurting. He wants us to sacrifice in the proper way, which is led by the Spirit of God and not ego! He wants us to exercise His wisdom and to be doctors to the people who have pain and suffering and to heal their emotional and spiritual lives through the power of the Holy Spirit. Be blessed!

CHAPTER 14

THE PARABLE OF THE GROOM'S ATTENDANTS (MATTHEW 9:14-17)

Then the disciples of John came to him saying, "Why do we and the Pharisees fast often but your disciples do not fast?" Jesus said to them, "Can the friends of the bridegroom mourn as long as the bridegroom is with them? But the days will come when the bridegroom will be taken away from them and then they will fast. No one puts a piece of unshrunk cloth on an old garment; for the patch pulls away from the garment and the tear is made worse. Nor do they put new wine into old wineskins, or else the wineskins break, the wine is spilled, and the wineskins are ruined. But they put new wine into new wineskins, and both are preserved." (vv. 14-17).

I have covered much of this passage in Chapters 28 and 29, where I have dug a little deeper. But it is a very important subject so it bears some repetition. The Pharisees and John were acting under the Old Covenant. Part of that law was to fast. Fasting was a religious duty, as a way of being faithful to God and showing that you were obedient and subservient to Him. In those days, many people fasted to show that they were more devout in following God. It was considered a religious practice for effective prayers.

When He was questioned about fasting, Jesus implied in verse 15, "Imagine being at a wedding supper with the bridegroom and his attendants are fasting? The groom does not call his special friends to fast when it's a time to be merry!"

I believe Jesus was referring to His parable about the king giving a banquet for his son's wedding. He was trying to point out to the hearers that He was the "Son" who was going to marry the bride and it was all His disciples who were going to be His "bride." However, the problem was that Jesus spoke in parables and not everything He said was understood by the people or His disciples. Even today, the parables remain a mystery to many people and that is the reason for this book.

Many people today think that fasting is a way of twisting God's arm behind His back in order to get what you want. Like putting pressure on God to hurry up and answer your prayers the way you want Him to; so you fast for three days, or whatever! This is a religious fasting; this is exactly the way some Old Covenant people acted.

The book of James says: *"Good and perfect gifts come from the Father of lights"* *James 1:17.* If you want something good and perfect, the Father will not deny you. In the modern day, going into some sort of fast is not going to push the Father's hand for you. Fasting should not be carried out from a religious spirit of self-righteousness. Jesus was having none of it. He knew who He was. He was the Son of God and He did not need to do anything to impress the Father. In fact, from sun up to sundown, all Jesus said and did was the will of His Father in heaven. He would never do anything wrong, so fasting was something that was not needed.

Even before Jesus began His public ministry, when He came out from His baptism by John, it was recorded that the heavens parted and the Holy Spirit descended like a dove and it rested on His shoulder. God then said from Heaven, *"This is My beloved Son, in whom I am well pleased" Matthew 3:17.* Jesus had not done any public ministry at this stage, yet His Father was already pleased with Him.

Parable Application: We don't have to try and impress God! The Father has already been impressed! He was impressed by the blood of Jesus Christ on the cross. This blood covenant that was made has provided the only way for us to be *fully accepted* by the Father. God has been totally satisfied that the law and the condemnation that we deserved was nailed to the cross once for all time. All of our sin was nailed to that cross.

Actually, the disciples of John were trying to make Jesus fit into the Old Covenant and Jesus was having none of it. He was expressing the New Covenant way. However, the actual New Covenant did not really come into being until the resurrection of Jesus Christ. The teaching and commandments of Jesus are shown in red lettering in some Bibles; these are much harder to fulfill, than the original laws in the Old Testament.

The old wineskin represents the Old Covenant Law, while the new wineskin is the New Covenant of Grace established by the cross of Christ and verified by His bodily resurrection. Jesus was explaining what the New Covenant meant; the new wine that was being shed was His blood. This new wine of grace cannot fit into the old wineskins. It just does not fit. The old wineskins were old and should be used for the old wine and the new wine was not to be put into them or the skin would burst. If you try and live under the New Covenant but are still being bound up by the Ten Commandments and the other laws, you will land in big trouble: it's a painful and futile effort!

Laws can be as simple as: you *have* to go to church; you *cannot* forsake the gathering of the brethren; you *have* to pray each day; you *have* to read your Bible daily. Yes, God wants us to do all these things, but our motive must be right. You see, you don't have to follow just the Old Covenant Law to be bound up and become self-righteous! Some people allow themselves to be bound up even in the New Covenant! If you try and mix your own form of law with grace, it's impossible for you to be joyful. Similarly, the New and the Old Covenants were not built to mix together. It is just like putting a new bit of cloth on an old pair of jeans; it will make the old pair of jeans rip! That is what Jesus meant about un-shrunk cloth.

Mixing the New Covenant with the Old Covenant is a recipe for disaster. I lived in that condemnation, guilt and shame. The load that was on my shoulders was so heavy, I felt deeply depressed. I thought I was going to Hell because I was stuck in some habitual sins.

Until I received teaching that said the Law has passed away and as a New Covenant believer I was not under its judgment anymore, that *I was able to get free from my habitual sins!* There are so many Scriptures in Romans, Galatians, Corinthians and Hebrews that blew me away in this learning process. When I was convinced that I was forgiven of my past, present and future sins, then I was able to move out from the shame and condemnation that the Law had put on me. *The more I felt bad about my sin, the more I sinned!* I Corinthians 15:56 says that the strength of sin is the law. That is so true!

Are you like I was? Are you mixing a bit of law with God's grace? Are you someone like John, saying that the way of Jesus was all too easy? Is grace too easy for you? Do you have to do your penance? Is there a form of sacrifice that you have to do to be worthy of God? Do you fast some of your TV time or some of your meals? Do you give up precious time with your personal family to do things for God? Are you busy running around serving God and doing things in self-righteousness? Are you one of John's disciples who were still under the bondage of the Law?

Trying to remain free and forgiven by Jesus whilst also believing you have to fulfill all the requirements of the Law: is like mixing bitter drink with the sweet. If you mix them together, all will taste bitter. When the Law was given it was meant to be bitter. The Law was meant to show us that we need Jesus and then when we have accepted Jesus we are meant to obey the leading of the Holy Spirit and not the outward performance of law.

Are you like the Pharisees or are you one of Jesus' disciples—just happy to spend time with Him? If you have Jesus as Lord of your life, are you convinced that you are forgiven, righteous, loved, blessed and seated in the Heavenly places with Christ even now, without doing anything? Can you handle going to Heaven for what Jesus has done, or are you still adamant that you have to earn your way to Heaven? We must fully understand what Jesus has done. Otherwise, thinking that you have to be good, totally slaps God and Jesus across the face. It is like saying, "Yes Jesus, you died for me, but it wasn't good enough!"

I am sure this teaching can be shared many times and be still misunderstood. I guess, like salvation itself, it has to be personally revealed by the Holy Spirit. I believe that the Lord, through the Holy Spirit and through Jesus, has given me a divine insight into these parables. I am responsible for wrong decisions in life, but in hindsight God used my trials and weakness to make me the person I am today. In the process He has never once left me and I am extremely thankful for that. God Bless you.

CHAPTER 15

THE PARABLE OF THE GROWING SEED
(MARK 4:26-29)

The parable of the Growing Seed in Mark 4:26-29 reads:

And He said, *"The kingdom of God is as if a man should scatter seed on the ground and should sleep by night and rise by day and the seed should sprout and grow, he himself does not know how. For the earth yields crops by itself: first the blade, then the head, after that the full grain in the head. But when the grain ripens, immediately he puts in the sickle, because the harvest has come."*

I heard Andrew Wommack teach on this principle. He shared an illustration which was interesting and bears repeating here. There was a man who had come to his Bible College who had never been employed in his life. He was a simple, uneducated man who had many struggles understanding English or comprehending most things, but he had a definite call of God on his life.

This man went to the Bible College to learn basic doctrine and theology. Because he had never earned an income, he lived his entire life on welfare. One day, he went to Andrew with plans to renovate a city building which was going to cost three million dollars. He had some grand plans for making apartments and leasing them back to the government with assured rents at a profit. He told Andrew that he felt God wanted him to do it!

Andrew told him that it all looked very good on paper and seemed as though it would work. However, this man's Pastor carefully explained to Andrew that the man had never held down a job in his life. He did not know what it was like to work, let alone, become a manager of such a large project. He had never had a huge amount of money in his hand, so how could he handle large sums of money for this project? He had never gone to work and had never managed other people. Andrew then shared with the man that, although the plan was a good one, it was not God's will for him to do it. Andrew finished off the story by saying that the man is now working as a manager at a service station and is still going on with God's teaching.

This is what the parable of the seed really means. It means that a seed bears fruit after its own. A person who has never worked, never handled large sums of money and never managed other people can not go on to deliver a project that needs superior skills. Andrew explained that we only build trust with God with big projects when we have been faithful with similar medium ones.

Let us take a look at this parable. *"The Kingdom of God is as if a man should scatter seed on the ground and should sleep by night and rise by day and the seed should sprout and grow, he himself does not know how." Mark 4:26-27*

Certain ministries teach that a Word of God is a "seed" and when you donate money to a Christian ministry to the lost, it is an act of sowing "seed" into God's kingdom. It is being equated to seed because the money is used to spread the Gospel. Now this is true. When Paul was having disputes with the apostles as to who was greater, he said that some sow the seeds, some water them, but God gives the increase (I Corinthians 3:6).

We know that God is love; so when love is sung about in the right way, it can touch someone's heart and bring healing to their lives. There is a song about "tears" in Heaven, for instance: would we cry tears in Heaven? There is another song that says "When I am in Heaven will you remember me there?" Certain songs that mention Biblical things sow seed in the hearts of people. It's not up to us to understand how God grows the seed and brings in the harvest.

I, for instance, have been writing articles for four years. These are published on an article database site and are found on Google searches. I initially started writing articles in order to bring a personal prophecy website high up on Google searches. This web blog that I was subscribed to told me how I could have my website better recognized in search engines. It said a new way of having a site recognized was to write a number of articles with a URL at the bottom linking them to your website. They said if you would write enough articles, your website would slowly climb in the rankings and be found on the first page of Google, Yahoo and Bing.

So, I initially started the articles, not so much to teach people Christian things, but to increase the position of my ministry website. When I started to write ten or twenty articles about my Christian faith, I really enjoyed expressing myself. I have a database that tells how many people have read the articles and have given comments and their rating. Soon, I became carried away with a love for writing.

I have been doing that consistently for four years now. As the inspiration would come to me, I would write articles of various lengths. The earlier ones were rather long but later I could condense my message to fewer lines, but they were all seed. All of the articles are about the Gospel and expounding Biblical truths that are reaching people.

It's not up to us to wonder how God multiplies seed. The fact of the matter is that if you sow seed in good ground, the seed will sprout and grow a crop that will rise out of the ground. First, the blade will come, then the head, then the full grain. When the crop has ripened, then it is time to harvest.

For non-Christians, the harvest is the time when they actually make a decision for Christ. Everyone who has shared the Gospel with a person, either by words or actions, showed a practical demonstration of Jesus Christ to that person. All of these things contribute to the ripening of the crop until it is time to harvest—when the person finally decides to give their life to Jesus Christ.

Seeds are "Truth" words e.g. Jesus not only died for our sin, but He also died for all our sicknesses. Psalm 103:1-3 says: *"Bless the Lord, O my soul; and all that is within me, bless His holy name! Bless the Lord, O my soul, and forget not all His benefits; Who forgives all your iniquities, Who heals all your diseases."* The psalmist linked forgiveness with healing because that is exactly what Jesus did for us. He suffered our sicknesses, deformities and diseases by the severe whipping prior to the agony of the cross where our sins were dealt with.

The Book of Psalms is part of the Old Testament, but there are many healing verses in the New Testament, example: I Peter 2:24. This verse confirms that by the stripes of Jesus we are healed. It is linked to Isaiah 53:5, in the Old Testament. Jesus silently undertook terrible disfigurement in this whipping as full payment for all of our sicknesses: physical, mental and emotional.

Pastor Andrew Wommack teaches on how to claim our healing? I will share this with you. Mark 11:23-24 is a wonderful passage: Jesus said *"For assuredly, I say to you, whoever says to this mountain, 'Be removed and be cast into the sea,' and does not doubt in his heart, but believes that those things he says will be done, he will have whatever he says. Therefore I say to you, whatever things you ask when you pray believe that you receive them and you will have them."*

"The mountain" is any problem you have that does not line up with the Word of God. "Whatever things" are things that we know God wants us to have.

The believing prayer of faith is settled in Heaven when we pray, but the physical evidence to you is a process. Don't nag God to do what He has told YOU to do. We are to speak to the situation (the mountain) out loud and command it to go in Jesus' name. Keep doing this every day. Ignore the outward appearance but keep focused on the fact that God has heard! The situation will change in God's due time.

Tell the devil out loud "By the stripes of Jesus I have been healed." This is Scriptural and he knows it. Tell him to go in the name of Jesus and he has to go! So many times we talk to God about our problems instead of talking to our problems about God.

These are godly principals: they work! We need in depth teaching of what the Bible says. It takes time to learn the right principles of healing and your divine rights through the blood of Jesus Christ. Many Christians cannot say that the harvest has come straight away but you need to plant the seed in your heart and it will bring its fruit in season. A book I strongly recommend on healing is called "Healing the Sick" by T.L. and Daisy Osborn.

Maybe someone prayed for you in a church meeting and you received instant healing – this is called a miracle. Healings are happening all over the world by the power of the name of Jesus Christ. People are being radically healed of blindness, deafness, quadriplegia and life threatening diseases—through faith in God. So, healing verses are good seed that can be planted, watered, nurtured and harvested in our life.

Anything wonderful can manifest with enough of the right Word of God and the right nourishment by the Holy Spirit. God can accomplish anything.

We go to sleep, as it were in the parable, and wake up and see the thing that has sprouted and we wonder, "How did that happen? How did that person go from being such a bad sinner, such an angry, swearing, rebellious, hypocritical person into such a loving and compassionate person, full of mercy? What happened there?" Someone has done a lot of claiming God's promises and has had faith in God's awesome power.

The seed of God matures and bears its fruit. It is the Word of God, the Holy Spirit, the work of His holy angels and His saints, nurturing a person from a place of despair to a place of full healing and full nourishment in the proper things of God. They go from a place of tragedy to a point of blessing, where their attitudes, their behaviors and everything else have all been changed.

So, I hope my sharing here has given some explanation on how the seed principle works.

CHAPTER 16

THE PARABLE OF THE HIDDEN TREASURE
(MATTHEW 13:44)

The Parable reads: "The Kingdom of Heaven is like treasure hidden in a field, which a man found and hid; and for joy over it he goes and sells all that he has and buys that field." Matthew 13:44

This scripture is very special and deeply emotional for me. I will share with you why, by giving you some of my own personal testimony. Hopefully by the end of my illustrations and the testimony, you will have a grasp of what Jesus was saying here.

At one stage, I used to walk to a nursing home to do a dish-washing job. From the moment I arrived at 8.30am until I left at 4.30pm, I was flat out washing dishes, pots, pans and everything else. Around noon, I had to assist the chef in laying out the lunches and serving them on what looked like a conveyor belt. We served packed lunches for one hundred and twenty people in a span of twenty minutes.

At that time, there was so much havoc in my life. I was living in sin with my addiction keeping me financially poor. Also, I didn't do well in my job because I absolutely hated the work– it was a thankless job which gave me no incentive, but I needed the work to pay for my addiction. I was deeply ashamed of my secret degrading lifestyle. Addictions leave a person empty, powerless and totally destitute. Alcohol had become a way out of my depression, so I thought.

But now I praise God because He has changed all that! He has turned me into an enthusiastic writer and teacher of the Word of God. I still have a special love for the women I had wrongly used: they are victims of the devil, just as I allowed myself to be all those horrible years. *I could have been free* because the Holy Spirit lived in me, but these girls don't really understand that Jesus loves them.

So there I was, walking towards the nursing home to do my unfulfilling job. On my way, I walked past a house that was for sale. The sign out the front caught my attention; it said *"Hidden Treasure."* I had written many articles on the internet, so I had made it my business to work out the best attention grabbing headlines. The way this sign was designed and the actual words on it certainly caused me to stop and take a serious look.

True to the sign, the house was set behind a really large hedge and unless you went onto the driveway, you would not see its hidden beauty. I wondered why people hide their treasures from others and figured that privacy was the issue.

I felt compelled to go up and inspect the Real Estate sign more carefully. It had numerous interior shots of the house. I saw that inside, it was like a log cabin made of exposed wooden beams which were highly polished. Despite the old-style charm of the external structure it was a beautiful modern-designed home. The sign said it all! It was rightfully called a *"Hidden Treasure."* The name itself is such a compelling name – it demanded a closer inspection. I felt drawn to study the snap shots of the interior once again.

Reluctantly, I turned away thinking any prospective buyer would be tempted to inspect that home. Everyone would want to own a "treasured" property. All this made me think of my former wife and my little boy. I recently discovered that He is all grown up and married. I have not seen him or my wife for years and years. My wife was fed up with me and I don't blame her. I did my best, but I really needed help and I didn't know it.

Back then, when I was married, no one knew I had a mental illness and neither did I. To be crippled mentally is so debilitating. You lose friends! It causes you to lose the best things in life. But Jesus knew what was ahead for me from my birth and He has always compensated me with his love, even when I was so sinful. I was feeling really sad as I trudged up the hill. As I continued walking to work, Jesus said to me, "Do you know Matthew - that is who you are to me?"

And I said, "What?"

Jesus said, "You are my hidden treasure."

I asked, "What do you mean?"

"You are very valuable and special to Me. You are My hidden treasure. I am going to use you in the future. No one knows you now: you are hidden. Not many people know your talents but I know them and you are hidden for a reason. A time will come one day when people will know who you are."

I started crying. I just couldn't walk towards my work anymore. I had been so taken with the sign itself and by the beautiful wording "Hidden Treasure" and yet, *Jesus had just called me of all people,* "His Hidden Treasure!"

I had also seen the house of my dreams. It was just like the house I wanted to own one day. It was all too much. The thought of going to work in that sweaty kitchen with frustrated staff constantly yelling orders to me all day, was just too much at that time.

About six months later, I was at my parents' house for the Christmas holidays. We went to church and the preacher's sermon was taken from a passage in Matthew. As I was turning to that page, my eyes went to Matthew 13:44, *"The kingdom of heaven is like treasure hidden in a field, which a man found and hid; and for joy over it he goes and sells all that he has and buys that field."*

A burst of joy overwhelmed me and my eyes became moist remembering what Jesus had said when I was walking to that job—how that I was His hidden treasure. I felt very humbled and emotional at that moment.

Let me illustrate: Imagine yourself cutting across someone's land. This land is very barren and is hardly used. The small farm has an inexpensive house on it, plus a few sheep and cattle. The owner is probably doing it tough. While walking, you suddenly trip over and with your feet you dislodge a rather big rock. When you pull your foot out from under the rock, you find that there is black oil all over your boot. You strongly suspect that there is oil on the property which the owner is totally ignorant of. Now, what would you do? You would obviously need to verify your suspicion. And if it was true, you would need to convince the present owner to sell his property. You would then set about to raise enough finances to be able to sell everything you own. You would approach the owner and say, "I love the remoteness of this land and I really want to buy it. I know the soil is not good, but that's okay. I like the solitude and the serenity of the place. I could do something with it and it will give me satisfaction. Is there any chance that you would sell it to me?"

He would most likely see your offer as a way out of the drudgery of trying to farm unprofitable land and would gladly take you up on your offer to buy. As soon as it was all legally settled you'd ring your brothers and father and say: "Come and give me a hand! We need to get an oil rig on this land. We may have to put second mortgages on our homes! I reckon we have a hidden treasure here and we are going to strike it rich!"

However, the hidden treasure in this parable if far more valuable than any earthly treasure we could imagine! In Heaven Jesus is called the Great Morning Star, the King of all Kings, and the Lord of all Lords! He is the Almighty Redeemer! He is Heaven's hero! What an incredible "treasure" He is to those who believe.

When a fashion conscious young lady buys an expensive dress for a special occasion, she doesn't stop there. She immediately goes looking for suitable accessories such as handbag, ankle flattering shoes and perhaps some expensive jewelry or an exquisite hair comb to adorn her head. All of those extras are accessories. Sadly, I see many church goers treating Jesus Christ, the Darling of Heaven, as an added accessory to their religious persona.

Instead of developing a healthy relationship with Him by allowing Him to be their focus in life, many church goers live totally self-centered lives, focusing on temporal things and not eternal things that count. The opinions of others take priority over the opinion of God. Sometimes, we tend to place wrong values on people. Instead of seeing others as precious in the sight of God, we see their outward success and esteem them for the wrong reasons.

Many people see Jesus as some sort of heavenly slave boy, who runs around answering all our prayers and is forever pleading to His Father for us to be continually blessed. They forever take; while He just gives and gives. There is something radically wrong with this theology. No wonder the Christian message is so grossly misunderstood in society today.

The parable of the Hidden Treasure depicts Jesus very differently. Figuratively, He said you should sell all you have - you should gladly give away everything that you own just to possess Christ. If some of you could give a couple of thousand dollars for joy, peace, satisfaction and fulfillment in life, would you gladly do it? Contentment with joy is a rare commodity. If you could bottle it, you would make a fortune. That life is absolutely possible if you are willing to give everything away to possess it. The Christian life is totally opposite to a worldly life and its ongoing rewards continually confirm that fact.

We have to remember that often, Jesus was speaking to the so called experts in the Jewish faith. The Pharisees were often listening to Him. They assumed, by their rigid law-keeping, that they already possessed the kingdom of God. We are to see Jesus as the hidden treasure that you can possess. To do this, surrender your will for His will!

Most of us go to the movies for entertainment. If you were to have dinner with one of the world's most famous actors and he shared with you about his career, you might be surprised with what he went through. Everyone looks fine from a distance: famous people all look like they have had an easy life on their road to success. Yet, if one of them really opened up to you, then you might discover just how hard it was for them to gain success and then how hard it is to keep it.

In the same way, Jesus wants us to know that the abundant Christian life comes with a personal cost. Every Christian is saved through the perfect sacrifice that Jesus paid on the cross. I am not advocating that through works we become more loved by God. No, God forbid! Good works will never earn anyone salvation, because salvation is a gift. Rather, good works are the natural fruit of salvation. Constant good fruit should be clearly evidenced by others and act as a light to draw them to the Lord.

Now, think of yourself as one who has studied acting and has had minor parts in a few movies. Imagine that you had dinner with this famous actor. Because you share a similar dream, you would have more in common with him. He would fully identify with your struggles and sacrifices. The same is true with the Christian life. The more that you are prepared to sacrifice to serve Jesus, the richer the relationship you will have with Him.

This is the meaning of this parable. The more you give to Jesus and the more you give up to possess Him, the more of Him you will possess.

CHAPTER 17

THE PARABLE OF THE HOUSEHOLDER
(MATTHEW 13:52)

Background to Parable: Scribes were people in the Old Testament who wrote down the laws to preserve them. They also interpreted them for the people to follow. They were quite like the Pharisees of the New Testament who taught the laws and kept them up to date. The trouble was: that while God originally gave His prophet Moses the Ten Commandments and other laws, the religious leaders placed more emphasis on their Books of Interpretation of the Laws, than the actual words spoken to Moses by God. This is what angered Jesus the most about the religious leaders. They set hard rules for the common people but broke these same rules themselves. Jesus publicly called them hypocrites: the blind leading the blind!

Now to the parable: Jesus said to them, *"Therefore every scribe instructed concerning the kingdom of Heaven is like a householder who brings out of his treasure things new and old." Matthew 13:52*

Essentially, a scribe was to bring new truth into the Word of God to make things relevant and applicable to the current generation. Scribes brought modern-day application to something that was old. They had to carefully and painstakingly copy all the Scriptures slowly by hand with total accuracy. Otherwise, they needed to start all over again. There were certainly not any modern computers to delete or add things, or to easily change the size and type of font. It was an extremely specialized and arduous occupation but the authority that it generated among the people was worth the associated stress and pain.

If they were to bring something new that was not based on the written Law, or that couldn't be found in what was already written: the scribe would be called a heretic and his reputation ruined as an expert Bible scholar. But if his comment was based on something Jesus taught, then the new application and insight would bring life to the teaching. So the proper teacher of the Word, the real Christian today, should be able to know the Word of God and apply it according to what is currently going on around them, similar to what their Master did on earth.

Since then two thousand years have passed. During that time the printing press was invented which forever changed the way that Scripture was presented and preserved. In fact, every day technology and modern science is developing at an alarming rate and will continue to escalate. Not all change is for the better. Over a hundred years ago, people's teeth rarely rotted or had infections but today, we have sugar added to nearly everything we eat and subsequently our teeth rot. We have all sorts of antibiotics now but decades ago, they did not have them and people just died. Things change, people change, technology changes.

Praise God, Scripture assures us that God's Word will never change, nor will Jesus Christ ever change, His Father, or the Holy Spirit! Today, we can receive a new physical heart by clever surgery. Even more miraculous is the fact that every unbeliever is able to receive a new spiritual heart from Jesus. We know this because God's salvation plan will never be outdated or improved on. However, some human characteristics, like selfishness, do not change in people. Jeremiah 17:9 says that man's heart is deceitfully wicked. But see, we do not have to continue with the old heart of man. As I said, Jesus can give us a new heart.

Life has changed; the way we do things has changed. You and I as Christians are to bring modern applications to something that was taught in the Bible by the Prophets, the Apostles and Jesus Himself. The people today need to understand and apply God's Word in order to gain some sustenance for their day to day life.

I guess that is why I am teaching this series on the parables. For years, I have searched the bookshops for a good book that explained the parables of Jesus. Once, I saw one with glossy pictures and descriptions of the parables, but it contained only the most popular ones. I didn't want to buy deep theological editions that I couldn't understand. I have never seen a book with all the parables in it. For years, I have been studying the words of Jesus and trying to understand the parables and their profound message.

In the same way, I was moving closer in obedience to the prompting of the Holy Spirit. I have been trying to dig deep and get to the heart of what Jesus was saying, but for years that book I was looking for was elusive. So I decided that perhaps the reason I could not find such a book was because I needed to find the answers and write the book myself.

The principles behind the parables do work! Jesus said He is like a householder who brings out his treasure—things old and new. There are certain things which are old, but have modern things mixed into them. An example would be a sixteenth century ring with a stone in it that is fashionable today and deemed "modern". You can imagine this old craftsmanship as something fabulous and admirable—a modern stone in an old gold ring.

Antique furniture and modern silverware and table settings complement each other. A householder brings out the very best of what he has to make a guest feel special. So too, the modern disciple needs a teacher of the Word of God, who is able to apply Biblical truth to our world today. Like the householder in this parable, I want to bring new and fresh meaning to the Scriptures: making the revelation of the "saying of old" relevant enough for the "Facebook Age."

We live in a world that is always on the move. If we did not change or if the world did not constantly need new things, we would continue to be happy with old things, but technology changes and we all want the latest gadgets we see advertised.

Hebrews 13:8 says: *"Jesus Christ is the same yesterday, today, and forever."* The words of Jesus are true. Jesus does not change yet He likes His truth to be relevant and contemporary, which is what this parable is all about. There is great wisdom in keeping some of the old truths in the parables, but there is a great need for modern understanding. Jesus is always up to date. He is relevant. If He were here on earth today, He would be using parables that were talking about things we know and do today. He would engage in Facebook and YouTube: He would communicate in a way we could relate to.

Jesus said that a good scribe is able to do this, just like a proud mother or wife presents a meal with the best of her plates and dishes. She may serve a meal on antique plates that were given to her by her great grandmother but when she serves the food, you can be sure it will not be a hundred years old.

I have tried to explain these parables and have given illustrations to them as simply and as best as I could. I did what a modern householder would do. I have tried to do what Jesus said— to mix His age-old stories with modern day applications.

Many people frown upon "The Message" translation of the Bible, saying that it is not a literal translation and therefore not accurate. However, if more people understand Jesus' teachings and the character of God through this book than the more literal translation, then it serves its purpose and does a lot of good. It is not a "dulled down" version of the Bible because I hear many intelligent and popular spirit filled preachers quoting from its pages. God uses modern books that are easy to understand.

I pray that this has helped you.

CHAPTER 18

THE PARABLE OF THE HUMBLED GUEST (LUKE 14:7-11)

The parable of the humbled guest in Luke 14:7-11 relates:

"So He told a parable to those who were invited, when He noted how they chose the best places, saying to them: "When you are invited by anyone to a wedding feast, do not sit down in the best place, lest one more honorable than you be invited by him; and he who invited you and him come and say to you, 'Give place to this man,' and then you begin with shame to take the lowest place. But when you are invited, go and sit down at the lowest place, so that when he who invited you comes he may say to you, 'Friend, go up higher.' Then you will have glory in the presence of those who sit at the table with you. For whoever exalts himself will be humbled, and whoever humbles himself will be exalted."

I am not sure if I remember ever hearing this being preached. Also, I don't think I have been to a place where one seat is higher exalted than another. At a wedding, yes, there are seats up front, closest to the bridal table, but at modern weddings we have name places and the seating arrangements have already been worked out. It is the same with official functions. So let us talk about the parable in the context of where Jesus was and then we can move on from there.

We read in the passage that the people Jesus was talking about were just taking upon themselves to go and sit in the best seats. Jesus told them not to sit in the special seats because they may be asked to vacate them when the special people arrived, but instead He advised them to sit in the least places and wait until the party host asked them to move to the high places.

I remember a twelve day mission trip in India my parents took me on, where up to one hundred and fifty pastors and their wives attended. There was a dinner served which was hosted by an Indian apostle called Brother James who was the head Pastor over four hundred and fifty churches and also head of a Bible School.

The food was served on banana leaves, which was typical of Indian meals when special people were to be served. There were four long tables. I was about to sit on one of the chairs, when Brother James gestured to me and said, "Come and sit here with me."

It was amazing! I could not believe it. I was seated on the right side of the apostle who ran a huge denomination of churches! A few times, during the meal, he turned to me and asked me questions. It was amazing to be sitting next to this mighty man of God. The reason I was so interested in him was that it was the first time I had met anyone who had such an incredible testimony and had so much authority over such a lot of people.

Indians are my favorite race of people. Before meeting with him I had read his life story. As an unbeliever, he had been diligently searching for the one true God. He had been very disenchanted with the three hundred and thirty million "gods" of the Hindu faith, which all his family and friends adhered to. Not one of these gods had ever answered any of his prayers or had helped him in any way! He had just lived with condemnation and guilt no matter how hard he tried to be a good person. He felt empty and powerless to be able to change his lifestyle and felt that there had to be something more to life. His uncle had told him if he wanted to find truth he was to isolate himself somewhere, pray and fast and he would find the answers he was looking for.

There was a hill not too far from where he lived, actually the village folk call it a mountain, but I visited it after meeting this man and it really is only a hill. James climbed this hill and set up a make-shift home for himself in a cave. There was a fresh water hole nearby that the ladies of the village came to each day to fill their water pots. Brother James had decided to stay at his "retreat" until he received the answers he was wanting.

He had heard about Jesus and was curious to know more. He had been impressed with the testimony of one of his close friends about the Christian God. As he was deep in prayer, he heard his name being called and he opened his eyes to see a man coming toward him. It was Jesus in the flesh! For three awesome hours James and Jesus talked just like we would talk to our brother. Jesus fully explained the full Gospel message and then appointed James to establish and overseer fifteen hundred churches in India. When we were in India in 2005 this man had almost one third of his mission completed.

Not long after this supernatural encounter with the Lord in the flesh, his younger brother died and Jesus told James not to leave his side as He was going to raise him from the dead. This was to be a testimony to the Hindu people that resurrection power comes by belief in Jesus Christ. Despite pleas from the village people he would not leave the side of his dead brother, telling them that his brother would soon rise from the dead. It is the Hindu custom to burn a corpse as soon as possible and it was an offense to their faith to have this body in plain sight; their gods would be angry and the people would suffer.

Then it happened - on the fourth day, his brother rose, stood up and said he was hungry. Hundreds of people converted to Christianity in the following weeks. My family and I later shook hands and spoke to the once dead man. He is now married with a family and pastors a church. The only physical difference to Pastor John now, is that he has a slight twitch in his face from time to time, but in every other respect he is absolutely normal.

This day at the Pastors Meeting, I was excited to meet a real Apostle who had been so used by the Lord, but I was even more impressed to hear all about that wonderful encounter. I felt so highly privileged to have the honor of sitting next to him. This was what Jesus was talking about. When we came into that dinner after the conference, I wasn't sure how the people should be seated. The next thing I knew, Brother James caught my eye and said he had saved me a seat next to him. It was a wonderful day.

In certain churches, the front seat is taken by older pastors or the most important people in the church. I always like to be close to the front at my own church; I feel closer to God at the front. In sports and in entertainment, the closer you are to the front, the closer you are to the action. So imagine that if you are invited to an official function, taking the most important seat or the seat right up in front, near someone you do not know very well, could be a little bit of an insult. How embarrassing to be told in front of everyone to move to a lesser seat – wouldn't you rather be told to move to a better seat? Using this example, Jesus was saying to these prideful men, that if you exalt yourself, you will be humbled by God, but if you humble yourself, you will be exalted.

Now, at the time I was in India, I was quite a prideful person. I still have elements of pride. So, it was not any of my own humility that had me exalted on that day. It is, however, a perfect illustration of this parable. I feel that, even though I have been prideful in the past, God saw my heart and spoke to the apostle that day and said, "Have Matthew come and sit next to you." It was truly a privilege! Peter also said: *"Humble yourselves under the mighty hand of God, that He may exalt you in due time." 1 Peter 5:6.*

Humility was constantly evidenced in the life of Jesus. Although King of all Kings, He was born in a stable. He lived as a devoted and diligent Servant to His Father and was ultimately stripped naked before men as He hung on the cross. He never took the high seat. Yet, Jesus could have taken the most exalted seat in any function in all Israel for He was their Messiah: instead He chose the humble path.

That is the lesson for all of us in this parable. Jesus was speaking here of humility, of taking a back seat, of not being hungry for recognition. If you are a mature, humble Christian, you really have no need for recognition when you do something for the Lord. You know that the Lord has seen what you've done and will not overlook what is done for Him. If you will not be exalted on earth, you will surely reap your rewards in Heaven.

I hope that this parable has touched your heart.

CHAPTER 19

THE PARABLE OF THE KING'S WAR PLANS (LUKE 14:31-33)

The parable was recorded in Luke 14:31-33:

"Or what king, going to make war against another king, does not sit down first and consider whether he is able with ten thousand to meet him who comes against him with twenty thousand? Or else, while the other is still a great way off, he sends a delegation and asks for conditions of peace. So likewise, whoever of you does not forsake all that he has cannot be My disciple."

Everybody is in a spiritual war. (See Chapter 30) If life is easy for you, it means you are just floating the same way down the stream as Satan himself. I heard Andrew Wommack say: "Even a dead fish can float downstream!" I thought it was funny!

The Christian life is meant to be a swim upstream! A salmon, when it is going to give birth to her eggs begins to swim upstream. Every female salmon finds the river in which they were born. They might be thousands of miles away but the GPS God put into them, tracks them back to the river mouth that they came out of as a baby. They traverse the water falls on the way up to the top of that stream and lay eggs and then the mother dies. A new salmon would not be born unless a mother did that. The babies need a place to mature in safety where there are no predators. That is their natural way of growing and living. So too, the Christian life is a swim upstream. Many church goers live like the people of the world and never think it necessary to swim against the tide.

A survey was done in the United States by Barna Research. They found that the only discernable difference between the Christians and the non-Christians in terms of television viewing or buying habits, was that Christians do less on Sundays because they go to church. In other words, during the week, most Christians spend their money and view the same television programs as the non-Christian does.

When we are at war, we can't afford to think like the world does, The Bible has the winning battle plan to use against our enemy Satan. It's important to know that "people or situations" are never the enemy. It is the spirit working *"behind"* the person; it is the spirit working *"in the situation"* who is the real enemy! The battle is a spiritual one and the weapons we must use are not physical, but spiritual ones such as: 1) Calling on the name of Jesus, 2) Claiming the blood of Jesus and 3) Speaking the Word of God out loud directly to the devil. But praise and worship BEFORE the confrontation is essential.

In the Old Testament, God told His people in times of war, to place all their bold and committed worshippers, singers and musicians way ahead of the contingent of soldiers. This had a dual affect; it made the Israelites aware of God's power and it demoralized the opposition. A mind full of fear is never fruitful in war. Moses was the leader of the Israelites and he knew God's battle principles. He boldly stood on a mountain top overlooking the battle in the valley and raised his hands while claiming victory for the Israelites. When his arms dropped from tiredness, his soldiers began to lose; when his arms were up praising God, the enemy was overcome. Therefore, his two prayer warriors held up the hands of Moses. Ultimately, that conflict was not won by the actions of the soldiers in the valley, but by their leader who by faith lifted his hands to God on the mountaintop. Therefore, fight a spiritual battle with spiritual weapons!

A weak Christian poses no threat to Satan, but a committed one knows the devil's strategies and also God's battle plan. These people are always swimming upstream because they are motivated by their mission just as the mother salmon is. The bears may be waiting at the waterfalls for the salmon to journey past, and Satan is always reared up against a strong Christian: this is the nature of war. Some believers back off when trouble comes because they are ignorant or afraid to use the authority Jesus has given them.The book of James assures us that if we go *through* trials, our faith will be strengthened. The tribulation does not come from God but Satan. Through overcoming trials in His strength, we learn endurance. The more tribulations we go through, the stronger our faith becomes and the greater things we can do. (James 1:2-4).

To further illustrate this parable, I will use the example of North Korea. This country has missile guidance systems capable of delivering nuclear devices to many American cities. The Unites States Government has a good defense system but if North Korea sent numerous missiles simultaneously, an incomprehensible area would be devastated for untold years! Millions of lives would suffer terribly or be annihilated. The question that bothers some people is this: the United States waged war against Iraq and Afghanistan because America suspected that they had weapons of mass destruction, but American troops could never prove this! Why then, didn't America wage war against North Korea, *where these weapons do exist?* Instead, America sent a peace delegation to that country.

If America had taken on North Korea with full force, they themselves would ultimately be the losers. Instead, they went with a peace delegation: they wisely used "diplomatic discussion" to settle the issue, instead of force. To put this in context, Jesus said that anyone who starts to build a tower before estimating the final cost is foolish. If the builder just laid the foundation and stopped because of lack of finance, outsiders would mock him and lose respect for him as a builder. No one building even a house should be foolish enough not to first establish the completed price.

Jesus continued *"or what king would make war against another king but does not sit down first and consider whether he is able with ten thousand men to meet him who comes against him with twenty thousand men" Luke 14:31.*

America is aware that it could never win a nuclear war with North Korea. It simply does not have sufficient power or weapon store. Therefore skillful and experienced negotiators are their only option. New strategies must be applied when the old will no longer work.

Why does one king go to war against another King? This is mainly because one wants what the other has. He wants the resources of that other king's country. What if you only have ten thousand men and the king coming against you has twenty thousand? Rather than declaring war against that king and lose all your men in battle, you need to make a sacrifice and come to a reasonable agreement. You may consider approaching that king and saying, "Okay, we will stop undercutting you on the wheat prices and also we will stop selling our cattle so cheap in the Asian markets. Do not fight against us. Okay? We lose - you win! We will take a thirty percent cut in our foreign exports. Our country will suffer and our people will become poor, but please let us not fight over this."

Jesus also said, *"So likewise, whoever of you who does not forsake all that he has; cannot be My disciple"* (v.33.) What does Jesus mean? Perhaps He is warning us, that to follow Him is going to be a sacrifice because you will be in a very serious war with Satan.

Satan doesn't worry unbelievers very much because they just believe every thought that he drops into their mind: they are easily controlled. But when God's Holy Spirit is in a person, the lies that the devil drops into their mind are easily recognized and cast aside. However, the devil plays dirty: he may not attack you outright but the people you love and the things you hold close to your heart may be his target. That is why believers are to continually claim the blood of Jesus over their loved ones and ask Him to place a hedge of protection around them.

Some people decide it's a whole lot easier to float downstream with the rest of society: that it's way too hard to swim upstream. But if you have read Chapter 16 about "The Hidden Treasure" you will see that the benefits of knowing Jesus far outweigh any sacrifice on our part. Also if you look up Chapter 30 about the Pearl of Great Price, you will be further encouraged to keep making the effort.

Satan has done a good job in causing people to resist the Gospel. Some church goers have contributed to this lie because they have not represented Jesus in the right light. The end part of 2 Peter 3:9 says God: "is *longsuffering toward us, not willing that any should perish but that all should come to repentance.*" Also, 1Timothy 2:4 says: *"God desires all men to be saved and to come to the knowledge of the truth."* Did you notice the words "any" and "all" in these verses? This means you, the reader! God never discriminates. He loves ALL people equally and His death was sufficient for ALL people to be saved and forgiven. His "pleasure" towards us may vary but His love is constant. *Every person on earth* is in various degrees of sin! God has never had anyone "personally" qualified to work with Him yet! (This is another favorite statement Andrew has taught me.)

I have shared this parable as I have, to make the reader aware of the seen and unseen costs involved in being a victorious follower of Jesus. But there is a much higher cost to someone who rejects God's only salvation strategy. The cost of surrendering yourself to Jesus cannot be compared to the cost of continued unbelief! This life is temporal, but the next life is eternal and our destiny is determined by the decisions we make today about Jesus Christ. No one can be certain they will have another tomorrow! 2 Corinthians 6:2 says: *"Behold, now is the accepted time; behold now is the day of salvation."*

Warnings are always a good thing. I remember a time when I was helping a friend of mine speak in prophecy. I said to him "Ask Jesus if He has a message for me." I was then told that I was going to go through a refiner's fire. This meant that I was heading for hard times in order for my character to be refined. I thought: "Well, I guess even a rose bush, hates being pruned, but it sure benefits from the process." Within a year the refining began and it was painful. I was glad that I had been pre-warned! After this, I took positive steps to be more watchful and not be so apathetic to spiritual opposition.

Mostly we get angry at people or situations when things go wrong when really it is the devil who is organizing disharmony and trouble. He works through the pride in all of us and it works: we react! We go into automatic defense mode because we have allowed the "offense bait" Satan throws at us, by way of another person's lips, or by their actions, to control and rule our emotions. The secret is not to react: just let Satan's bait of offence fall to the ground and don't pick it up.

Christian! Jesus is warning us with this parable. If you want to do great things for God and make a lasting difference in the world, it is going to come at a very real cost. If you are happy just to coast along, there will not be much victory or war in your life.

In this parable, an earthly king sends a delegation to make peace. In real life, our Heavenly Father sent His own Son, the King of all Kings and Lord of all Lords to us, so that we could be reconciled to God. Satan is a relentless enemy, but we are on the winning side: we have all the resources of Heaven to help us.

A brief word with the unbeliever: We have each been given a free-will to make either foolish or wise decisions. God will never interfere with our free-will. I pray that you will make the right choices! The Bible warns: *"Choose for yourselves this day who you will serve." Joshua 24:15a.*

I am so pleased that I have made that choice!

CHAPTER 20

THE PARABLE OF THE LABORERS IN THE VINEYARD (MATTHEW 20:1-16)

Before we proceed, allow me to say that doing God's work is the most fulfilling task one can do. Walking in His joy and peace is fantastic. To experience His presence is the most precious thing on earth. It really is fun sitting down and sharing these things.

Most people may be familiar with this parable, but for the sake of our study, let us recap. In short, it says that the Kingdom of Heaven is like a landowner who went out early in the morning to hire laborers to work in his vineyard. After agreeing with the laborers for a denarius a day, he sent them to his vineyard. Let us say, that a denarius is worth one hundred and fifty dollars today for a day's work. The landowner went out in the third hour, which is nine o'clock in the morning. Let us imagine that he saw me standing idle in the marketplace. Then he said, "You go out and work for me too." So I went to work.

At mid-day he went out, then again at three o'clock in the afternoon, being the ninth hour of the day. Both times, he invited laborers to work in his field. At five o'clock in the afternoon, at the eleventh hour, he went out again and he said to some men: "Why are you still standing here?" They reply: "No one hired us." He said: "You also go into the vineyard and whatever is right you will receive." (Matthew 20:6-7)

"So when the evening had come, the owner of the vineyard said to his steward, 'Call the laborers and give them their wages, beginning with the last to the first.' And when those came who were hired about the eleventh hour, they received a denarius. But when the first came, they supposed that they would receive more; and they likewise received each a denarius. And when they received it, they complained against the landowner, saying, 'These last men have worked only one hour and you made them equal to us who have borne the burden and the heat of the day.' But he answered one of them, and said 'Friend, I am doing you no wrong. Did you not agree with me for a denarius? Take what is yours and go your way. I wish to give to this last man the same as to you. Is it not lawful for me to do what I wish with my own things? Or is your eye evil because I am good?' So the last will be first and the first last. For many are called but few chosen." Matthew 20:8-16

74

People do various tasks in a vineyard; they don't only collect and sort fruit, but also they cut off any dead wood and damaged branches. The pickers can then pack useable fruit into tubs, which then have to be checked and packed ready for market. Nothing is wasted! Second grade fruit is used for wine making. It's hot and sweaty work and only good workers keep their jobs! It's dangerous too because the workers are in the hot noonday sun. The heat and the pressure to work quickly would be draining. So these laborers have worked hard all day, but when they see new workers arriving at the eleventh hour, they assume that these people would receive only a small pay.

At the close of the day, when their wages were to be paid, the late arrivals were paid first – a denarius. The other workers were amazed at the generosity of the boss. They would have immediately surmised that they would receive far more than what they had expected. Those who began early calculated silently that they would receive an hourly rate, not a daily rate, of one denarius, but instead they only received the same as those who had only worked one hour. This made them really angry. A denarius was the agreed wage for the day, but in light of the late arrivals, it seemed totally unfair!

In this parable, the full-day workers were angry at the landowner's grace shown to the late workers! But do you realize that many people even today, get angry at God's grace towards sinners? Mostly these people are legalistic believers.

What is the practical application of this parable today? There are two different ways to look at it, but first, we will look at it prophetically. In the last days there is going to be a massive harvest.

I have heard a prophecy from several sources—a person from Western Australia, one from Rick Joyner in America and another from a well known prophet. Also, the Lord has told me personally—that much of the very last move of God is going to be done by unknown people—people with no reputation: they come from nowhere. They just rise up in the last days and have massive ministries. They do amazing work for God and everyone in the ministry will say: "Who are these people? Where did they come from?"

These Christians will move so fast in ministry gifting that they will not even have a reputation: their names will be unfamiliar! They will appear right in the last hour and do tremendous signs and wonders and reap a huge part of the harvest. Well, prophetically speaking, these are the people who were hired in the last hour. It seems that many of these people, who come into the Kingdom, will only be saved a very short time and then they will be ministering in signs and wonders.

These late-hour ministers will be supernaturally touched and then go out and touch other people. Now, the people who have been in ministry for twenty years or more will see someone doing five times the amount of ministry and saving five times the amount of people in a short space of time. Feelings of resentment or jealousy could very easily rob these former faithful people. They had put in the hard years of opposition through every form of media and had far less technological advantages to promote the Gospel than these late arrivals, yet all the glory goes to the new ministers and the former hard slogging workers seem to beforgotten!

You may have been faithfully serving in the local church for many years, with not much fruit for your labor. You have been waiting for the great outpouring of the Lord in the last days where multitudes are saved and the Holy Spirit comes with power. Yet, when the big move comes, you are not the hero of the day. Some unknown and relatively new Christian will receive the associated glory. That is one interpretation: Jesus was speaking prophetically in this parable.

Jesus was also speaking to the Jews in His day. They seemed to be stuck in a rut and were not going anywhere. Yet, unlike the gentiles, the Jews had been God's chosen people since the time of Abraham! They actually received the Ten Commandments by the very finger of God. Yet, Jesus had an amazing effect on both Jews and Gentiles and these new converts were being seen as the great achievers, far more than the religious leaders. It seemed that there was no end to the popularity of this Rabbi Jesus. Judaism was being threatened and the followers of Christ were the new kids on the block. The Jews who had the word of God for so long were outraged and jealous. These last hour Christians were turning the world upside down. Christianity spread through the known world in a very short time. So to the Jews, the parable had already been fulfilled.

Yet, I believe this is a parable for the modern day Christian. We are living in the last days before the return of Jesus. As I have already pointed out: only ten percent of American Spirit-filled Christians know their spiritual gifts. I believe that I am currently using all of my spiritual gifts. Therefore I don't feel frustrated. Yet, in America, most Christians may be feeling unfulfilled or frustrated. Actually only one percent of Americans knows their gifting *and actually minister in that gifting.*

Therefore there is much room for late bloomers to rise to the occasion! So, what is the application? You need to find out what your spiritual gifts are by doing a spiritual gift test. Every one of you reading this can be one of these eleventh hour workers. You can come in. There is still time. While you still breathe, you still have time. You have dreams: you have desires! You have un-birthed talents and gifting rising up within you. Read this whole book and contact me. Do whatever you need to do. Become one of those last days' workers. The true Bride of Christ will not be jealous of you, but you can be one of those last people that become first in the parades of Heaven.

CHAPTER 21

THE PARABLE OF THE LANDOWNER
(MATTHEW 21:33-46)

Matthew 21:33-46 reads:

"Hear another parable: There was a certain landowner who planted a vineyard and set a hedge around it, dug a winepress in it and built a tower and he leased it to vinedressers and went into a far country. Now when vintage-time drew near, he sent his servants to the vinedressers, that they might receive its fruit and the vinedressers took his servants, beat one, killed one and stoned another. Again he sent other servants, more than the first and they did likewise to them. Then last of all he sent his son to them, saying, 'They will respect my son.' But when the vinedressers saw the son, they said among themselves, 'This is the heir. Come, let us kill him and seize his inheritance.' So they took him and cast him out of the vineyard and killed him. "Therefore, when the owner of the vineyard comes, what will he do to those vinedressers?" They said to Him, "He will destroy those wicked men miserably and lease his vineyard to other vinedressers who will render to him the fruits in their seasons." Jesus said to them, "Have you never read in the Scriptures:

> *'The stone which the builders rejected*
>
> *Has become the chief cornerstone.*
>
> *This was the Lord's doing,*
>
> *And it is marvelous in our eyes?'*

"Therefore I say to you, the kingdom of God will be taken from you and given to a nation bearing the fruits of it and whoever falls on this stone will be broken; but on whomever it falls, it will grind him to powder."

Now when the chief priests and Pharisees heard His parables, they perceived that He was speaking of them, but when they sought to lay hands on Him, they feared the multitudes, because they took Him for a prophet."

I have heard many similar sermons of this particular parable. This is a prophecy of Jesus and the New Covenant. God used His prophets to bring His people into correction and also to teach and guide them in His ways. These prophets were God's spokesmen and were endowed with special insight and wisdom by God for this purpose. Therefore, they often brought rebuke against sin in the lives of their leaders and other individuals. By using godly words of correction, the people would turn from their wicked ways. But many times the prophets of God were beaten and killed because their message was hated and consequently rejected. Then finally, Jesus, God's holy Prophet, told this parable about the landowner, which is the Father, who sent His Son. The vinedressers killed the Son so that they could take the inheritance. The Pharisees realized that Jesus was talking about them; it says straight after that they tried to seize him.

The parable was saying, "I know that you want to kill me. I know that this prophecy in the Old Testament is referring to your rejection of Me and actually having Me killed, but I am going to win in the end." Now, essentially, this may take a while for me to unpack because I like to find a modern application of a Bible story: so I ask myself, 'What has this parable to do with me and my life?

The Lord has gifted me with the ability to give personal prophecies to strangers and I do this on a regular basis. But the gifting I love most is to teach the word of God and to evangelize. I believe that correction can be brought on people through the truth of God's Word. Bringing correction is not enjoyable, but it needs to be done. God's word is a deterrent against sin and it is the only conclusive source of wisdom, knowledge and understanding. If something is going off track, a correction is necessary, so that truth prevails. Pilots know the importance of making constant correctional changes: otherwise their passengers would really suffer. It's the same with our spiritual lives, someone needs to steer people back to where God wants them to be. God uses a prophet to be his mouthpiece of correction. Reading the Bible is also a very powerful tool of correction.

2 Timothy 3:16-17 says: *"All Scripture is given by inspiration of God, and is profitable for doctrine, for reproof, for correction, for instruction in righteousness, that the man of God may be complete, thoroughly equipped for every good work."*

There are anointed people who hear from God, who have clear words for the church, but they are shunned. Pastor Andrew Wommack has to hold many of his meetings in public halls simply because many churches leaders will not have him. His profound revelation on the grace of God goes against many of their legalistic doctrines. I know from personal experience that the pride of man is a stumbling block to truth. People are offended by the grace of God and believe that *complete* salvation is up to their own puny effort.

I guess teaching in halls instead of churches, may encourage believers to bring their unsaved friends to hear the word of God. Most Christians are not walking in the liberty that Christ died for: Satan likes to keep it that way! The congregation misses out because those in leadership prefer to have blinkers over their eyes. Jesus said the truth will set you free, but hearing the truth can often offend before it actually heals.

I am overweight: I could lose weight by regular exercise and eating healthier food but I am basically lazy and therefore undisciplined in this area. Sure, there is another reason why I am overweight: I take a certain medication which causes weight gain. We can all stay in our excuses, but if we apply the truth, we can all make positive changes. However, the fleshly nature of man resists change and goes for the comfortable options.

Long ago, God's people wanted to be like the surrounding heathen nations and have their own king. God wanted to be their only King but he gave them their desires. In fact, there were three highly ranking authorities: the prophet, the priest and the king. The office of the prophet was important to keep people safe from the enemy and to teach them God's ways. The Priest would attend to their spiritual needs. But of course, the king was the final earthly authority. If he was open to God's truth all went well, but if he was closed to God's ways, the whole nation would suffer loss.

People have not changed much today. Leaders like all of us, resist change!

Today, there are certain individuals who are in touch with God. They hear from God and meet with the church leadership in order to suggest certain things for God's people. Some of these people are called to be prophets. They might suggest things that maybe are directly opposite to what the church is currently doing. If the pastor takes the correction, he will change the direction of the church. That, I believe is what bringing correction really is: it's turning people in an opposite direction, so that God is glorified.

In Jeremiah 1:9-10, the prophet talks about God's calling on his life.

"Behold, I have put My words in your mouth.

See, I have this day set you over the nations and over the kingdoms,

To root out and to pull down,

To destroy and to throw down,

To build and to plant."

Sometimes a prophet has to destroy something absolutely: he has to pull all the foundations out from within and then rebuild something. Often, that is the only way a problem can be fixed. Pastor Andrew Wommack is not welcome in many churches to do this. Andrew, with God's awesome enabling has built a highly successful daytime teaching segment on a Christian satellite network. People may accidently find him at first, but if they want to press deeper into God, they will search him out on the internet. He has three Bible Colleges, and is a world conferences speaker, plus he maintains a regular radio ministry. The Bride of Christ would benefit from his profound teaching. If he came to Australia, I would make it a priority to go and personally meet him and sit under his ministry, even if it was in another state, far from where I live. Why? Because the Holy Spirit chose this one man to transform my life!

This parable tells of people coming to a vineyard to collect its fruits and then being bashed, abused or killed. What has changed today? God sends His messengers to correct His people and many times they are shunned, just like people shun Andrew.

Yet, this servant of God is so wise: he genuinely wants people to know the word of God. He is not a false prophet! He is not harsh and judgmental. He speaks the truth in love and yet he is hated so much by some people. Why?

This parable is true: the truth really does hurt. Jesus prophesied His death. It happened! Jesus talked about the Old Testament prophets. They came to correct the people in His vineyard and to turn the people back to the fruit of righteousness, but the people refused to do that; they beat up the prophets and killed them and then they eventually killed the Son of the Landowner. Two thousand years ago, it happened just as Jesus said it would.

Now you might be reading this and thinking, "I know the truth. I don't need anyone to come to our church and tell us that we are wrong!" You could be right; you may know the right doctrines and believe in the right application of Scripture, but there are many people who do need to change and this parable is relevant for them today, just as it was when Jesus prophesied His own death.

CHAPTER 22

THE PARABLE OF THE LEAVEN
(MATTHEW 13:33)

This is a teaching taken from Matthew 13:33.

Another parable He spoke to them: *"The kingdom of heaven is like leaven, which a woman took and hid in three measures of meal till it was all leavened."*

The best understanding I have of leaven is that it is like mixing up some yeast and flour. Leaven is actually highly fermented sour dough. You mix it into the dough and give it enough time to fully ferment and expand. Some kind of gas reaction takes place to the point where you can fold the mixture to make bread, cakes and buns. Therefore leaven is actually like yeast.

How is the Kingdom of Heaven like that? How is it that you can get a little bit of yeast and make something very substantial, like a whole loaf of bread?

Well, one little baby was born in Bethlehem; one special Prophet; one special Man in the whole of the history of the world. Yet He was born in a simple stable; there was no vacancy at the Inn for His parents at that time. This Man lived as an ordinary person until the age of thirty and then He began His powerful and supernatural ministry for three years. During that time, He seriously threatened the Jewish faith and the leadership of Israel. He was then nailed to a cross to die. Three days later He rose from the dead and the whole world was changed!

The Jews believed that when a person died, his spirit hovered around for three days before it departed. They believed that a person could possibly come back to life in the first three days, because his spirit was still there. If the person's spirit was destined to Hell, it would be sent there on the fourth day; and if it was destined to go to Paradise and wait for the resurrection of the dead, it would be sent there on the fourth day.

When Jesus heard that Lazarus was sick, He delayed going to him for another two days. Why did he do that? Well, he knew that He was going to raise Lazarus from the dead. He had raised someone from the dead before. Jesus purposely delayed for one reason: Lazarus would be raised on the day when his spirit was supposed to be gone

81

forever and no way, according to the Jewish faith, could his spirit be raised again. In doing so, Jesus just totally blew their beliefs about death away. Jesus did something impossible for their faith to comprehend! It was that day, that the High Priest decided that Jesus should die rather than the Jewish faith to be lost. (John 11:49-51.) Jesus was a little bit of leaven in this world and He actually turned the whole world right side up.

It has been reported that about two billion people in the world confess Christianity as their faith. I'm not sure how many of them are genuine Christians, but the leading faith in the world is Christianity at the moment, although the Muslim faith is growing at an alarming rate. Our growth population in terms of natural birth is very small, compared to the birth rate in the Muslim world. Hence the sudden rise in their faith. So what is the application of this parable for you and me? What can we learn from this?

Even a little bit of Christ in us can make a big change! The flour alone won't make bread: it needs the addition of yeast. The chemical reaction caused by the yeast is the secret. Jesus says that we are to be the "salt" of the earth. We are to preserve the earth from decay and add God's flavor to our area of influence. Jesus also said we are to be the "light on the hill." Therefore, our lives should be burning bright.

Jesus is saying that the Kingdom of God is like a woman who first hid some leaven and three measures of meal and it became leavened. This leaven permeated through the dough and then it could be made into bread, the staple of our lives. When Jesus Christ permeates your life, He can make an enormous change in your home, workplace or school.

You could be moving in the gift of prophecy or dream interpretation and everyone could be coming to you for directions in life and solutions to their problems. You could be giving them supernatural answers from God. You could give people wise counsel. You could make such a tremendous difference in the world just with the gift of prophecy. Prophecy is just one of the nine spiritual gifts which the Holy Spirit can give to a spirit-filled believer. There are also other gifts that Jesus and His Father can give a believer. Therefore, Jesus is saying that even though you are just one person, you can have a positive effect on the lives of people in your personal area of influence.

A speaker going through the United Kingdom shared a story about meeting a man who handed out Gospel tracts in George Street, Sydney Australia. He repeatedly called out: "Do you want to hear about Jesus? The speaker shared about how his life was changed because of an encounter with this passionate Christian. He had become a believer because he had been blessed by a total stranger who loved Jesus.

Someone at the meeting stood up and said, "I've met that guy, his simple tract led me to the Lord!" And wherever this man went around the world, he would share his story and many people would come forward and say that a man in George Street Sydney was the reason they had become a Christian. One of those affected by this humble man handing out tracts was a Chaplain on an army base. He was the head Chaplain over fifteen hundred soldiers and later he planted hundreds of churches. Even leaders of countries had been touched by this one man.

Now, this faithful worker of God, handing out his little tracts had no idea that he had affected thousands of people. No one came back to him to share their testimony. One day this preacher came to Sydney, chased down the now elderly man and told him. You can imagine his joy and the tears that were shed as he was told about all the people who had been blessed simply because he had obeyed the leading of the Holy Spirit. These simple Gospel tracts had explained the sacrificial love of the Father, in sending His Own Son to die in our place. This elderly man had been a "little bit of leaven," that had affected countless numbers of people with his three hour a day ministry.

There is one lady I personally know, who went to the spiritual outpouring at Toronto—known as the Toronto Blessing. She became so anointed by the Holy Spirit that night that she had to be literally carried out of the meeting because her legs wouldn't work. She and her husband had been missionaries in Mozambique for many years and had not seen much success or growth in the Kingdom. But after that blessed time on the floor at Toronto, they have since planted ten thousand churches in Mozambique and the surrounding nations. Also, they have taken up to ten thousand orphans off the streets. They are making a massive impact. Every person she lays hands on is healed from diseases. The deaf suddenly can hear again. Blind eyes have been opened, crippled people have been able to walk and a hundred people have been raised from the dead.

She is just one person who walks with God! Heidi Baker is just another bit of leaven that is having a massive effect in the world. You can be one of those people, if you simply believe the word of God and have a humble seeking heart for the things of God.

See, this parable is about you! You are just one person. You may consider yourself as being insignificant. But with Christ in you, you can make a big difference: you could even change your own environment, your state or your country. Come on! You can do it. It has been prophesied that many people are soon to change this world. These are the last-day workers in the parable of the landowner, who paid people a denarius for just one hour of work. This parable tells about the people who are going to come from nowhere and are going to shake this world. People who are relatively unknown, are going to be major players in the "last-days" revival. God may call you!

God has used me to heal people three times in my life. I do not have much faith for healing, but each time Jesus said: "Do something Matthew." I have done it and people have been healed. God used me to heal a lady who had a migraine, day and night, for seven years and you know what I did to heal her? I just wept to Jesus and said, "Jesus, please take that away from her." I just broke down and wept. I wrote her an email and I said that I have prayed that the pain would decrease. She said that when she opened the email, the presence of God dropped on her so powerfully that her migraine disappeared. It has been years and she has never had another migraine since! I didn't have the faith to heal someone but I had the compassion to weep and beg Jesus to heal her for I knew in my heart that He had heard my cry.

It can be the same with you. You too can do wonderful things. Do not let this book be just another book that you read and say, "That was nice." Let it speak to you and move you into doing something great for God's kingdom.

CHAPTER 23

THE PARABLE OF THE LOST COIN
(LUKE 15:8-10)

Have you ever lost something important? Did you ever lose your wallet and all your personal cards? Was there a time when you wanted to have a cappuccino with a friend but when you looked in your wallet, there was nothing there? You thought you had five dollars, but you forgot that you used it for some milk and bread.

Have you lost your inner joy or peace? When you were first saved, you would have been very excited that Jesus had given His life for you. It felt like He had installed springs in your steps and all things were new and better. Everything looked different: things were vibrant. Moments were joyful. You were so blessed. You felt so happy, excited and safe.

Then, you started attending church. Religion slowly set in. There were rules upon rules and without noticing it, some of the joy left. What happened? Why had things turned sad? You were eager to learn; but the people seemed starchy and unapproachable. At the midweek Bible study you had so many questions but you still felt intimidated: you felt restricted even in a private home where you thought that people would have wanted you to ask questions. You were frustrated and sad. Your joy and your enthusiasm waned.

Let's look at this parable: "What woman having ten silver coins, if she loses one coin does not light *a lamp, sweeps the house, search carefully until she finds it and when she has found it she calls her friends and neighbors together, saying 'Rejoice with me for I found the piece which I lost.' Likewise, I say to you, there is joy in the presence of the angels of God over one sinner who repents"* Luke 15:8-10.

Maybe we look at this particular woman differently. She lost one of her ten silver coins. Maybe we ask, "What is the point of looking for that coin? She still had nine of them."

The fifty four videos of the parables on which this book was based, were transcribed by a couple of ladies in the Philippines for only two dollars and fifty cents per hour?

Here in Australia, a good transcriber charges at least twenty dollars per hour. That is eight times the price. Both these ladies wanted the job. In fact, one of them undercut the other, just so she could win the project, because she desperately needed the money.

Well, going back to the woman in the parable, we might think that losing one of the ten coins would not bankrupt her. We probably do not consider that someone who owns ten coins would actually need all of them, but what if she needed all of them to pay the rent?

Most of us live in a world where we have enough money to buy reasonably small desires, like new technology, books, movie tickets, expensive coffee, hamburgers and fast food. Most Australians can save for things. We do not really mix with the people who do not have enough money, or those who do not have any food in the cupboard.

Your heart may not break if you lost one of your ten dollars as this woman did. But I can assure you that, this woman was desperate! She turned over her whole house, in the hope of finding her lost coin: it was very important to her!

Similarly, this is what Jesus said, that the angels rejoice when one sinner repents. Jesus taught the parables in a series. First, it was the parable of the lost sheep where a man had one hundred sheep and he left the ninety nine to find that one who was lost. Then, He taught this parable about the lost coin. Jesus had a wide audience. He was teaching God fearing people, tax collectors, sinners and the Pharisees. He did three parables in a row, the lost sheep, the lost coin and the prodigal son.

To the Pharisees, Jesus was actually rebuking them, saying: "How dare you say that I am not to mix with tax collectors and sinners. These people know that they are sinners: these are the ones that need to be saved and brought into My flock for they represent the one lost sheep. They represent the lost coin of the ten. They are the prodigal son. How dare you judge me? I have come here for them."

Jesus was righteously angry. Jesus always mixed with the "under dogs" of the world. As He sat down with them, He shared motivational and exciting stories where He made them feel that they were precious to God and their souls were worth saving. Can you imagine what these people must have felt? Jesus was even eating with them. This man, Rabbi Jesus, (who unbeknown to them was their promised Messiah,) was always giving them His attention: they must have felt very important!

I mentioned Heidi Baker in the previous chapter. Once God gave me a prophecy about her and I sent it to her husband. She wrote me four emails, thanking me. You know, I was so touched that someone who is making such a huge impact in the world would even write to me. I went to a conference; she laid hands on my head and prayed that I be healed of my mental illness and I have seen a marked change in myself. Having her write an email meant so much to me. I have her letters framed in my house like a doctor displays his medical qualifications on his office walls. Heidi's letters are a treasure to me.

Well, she is a beautiful person but she is not Jesus! You imagine how precious these tax collectors and sinners felt in the presence of Jesus and here in this parable, He was saying that, "If I lost you guys, I would turn my whole house upside down to try and find you, and when I found you I would call all my neighbors around and we would have a big thanksgiving party because you are so precious to me."

As a Christian, you might think this parable has nothing to do with you because you are already saved. But even "saved" people can indulge in sins that open the door to the devil to rob you of blessings and prevent you from reaching your full potential. To me, this parable has a couple of applications for every Christian as well.

If you are a male Christian who is having problems with lust or pornography, Jesus is going to celebrate when you conquer them. When you come to a place of repentance you will feel so loved and forgiven by God! Jesus will be so happy. When you reach a stage where you totally reject every form of pornography, there is going to be a celebration in Heaven for you. Jesus just wants you released from the associated guilt and shame so that you will experience the abundant life he has planned.

Studies show that forty eight percent of Christian men have problems in this area. Because pornography is so assessable on the Internet, men have huge problems keeping their thoughts pure. The way women dress has the potential of causing any male to have lustful thoughts! These days, even many Christian young ladies dress like the women of the world! It seems that many mothers no longer think it necessary to teach their young daughters to dress modestly. None of us are to cause our brothers or sisters to stumble in any area. Unfortunately, the world's fashion and our media, promote promiscuity!

Jesus celebrates when personal bondages are broken. People need to be free of sins like lust, or lying, or swearing, or gossiping, or complaining or any other habitual sin. Now, my reader, do any of these things apply to you? If so, Jesus wants you to be free of them. Nearly every Christian has a besetting sin. God has forgiven all sin but He wants to set us free so that He can bring us to the place He has destined for us. He wants you to know how much He loves you.

We are not to be like a Pharisee! When we see people in sin—the homosexuals, the drug addicts, the prostitutes, the drunk, the gambler, even the divorced or the people whose marriages are not working out right, the gossipers - even some of the people in your church who seem to "not quite fit" just love them. Talk to them as though they are precious, clean, fresh, holy and righteous, because God loves them and once they fully understand that, then the devil will lose his grip on them.

Do not be like the Pharisees and be angry with Jesus for being compassionate. The fact is that Jesus actually loves these messed up people. You could be the bridge that brings Jesus to them. Reach out to these broken-hearted people. Help them come out of sin.

In closing, if you have a sin that you are struggling to conquer, know that this was written for you. You can overcome sin with the grace of God by the power of the Holy Spirit. There will be great rejoicing in Heaven when you do.

CHAPTER 24

THE PARABLE OF THE LOST SHEEP
(LUKE 15:4-7)

I trust that you will enjoy what I have to say about the Parable of The Lost Sheep. If you have been in church for a while, you would have heard this parable preached many times.

"What man of you, having a hundred sheep, if he loses one of them, does not leave the ninety-nine in the wilderness, and go after the one which is lost until he finds it? And when he has found it, he lays it on his shoulders, rejoicing. And when he comes home, he calls together his friends and neighbors, saying to them, 'Rejoice with me, for I have found my sheep which was lost!' I say to you that likewise there will be more joy in heaven over one sinner who repents than over ninety-nine just persons who need no repentance." Luke 15:4-7.

In the Gospel of John Chapter 10 Jesus identifies Himself as the Good Shepherd. He also said that He is the door to the sheepfold and that believers in Him are His sheep. As such, we are to know His voice and not follow the voice of a stranger.

Psalm 23 tells us all about the Good Shepherd. It is a wonderful and comforting Psalm that is often read out at funerals, but it is also a Psalm for us to reflect on right now. This Psalm was written nearly a thousand years before Jesus came to earth to be our Savior and Lord. It is Jesus who makes us lie down in green pastures and who leads us to a source of pure water. He corrects us and guides us with His staff and His goodness and mercy are with us forever. He is indeed the Good Shepherd.

Immediately, prior to the telling of this parable we read in Luke 15:1-3 - *"Then all the tax collectors and the sinners drew near to Him. And the Pharisees and scribes complained, saying, "This man receives sinners and eats with them." So He spoke this parable to them."* Why were the religious leaders so upset that Jesus happily mixed with the common people and in particularly those they considered the worst sinners in the district?

Let's move the parable into today's society. Let us imagine that I was a popular teacher and I came to your city to speak about the gift of prophecy and how to develop this particular gift from the Holy Spirit. You were interested in the subject so you came along. However, when you arrive you realize that the conference has not attracted many of your peers but mostly the undesirables in the community. Seated in the auditorium you see some prostitutes and suspected pedophiles, along with known criminals and drug pushers. Also you notice prominent New Age people and right up the front were people who were obviously from the Gay and Lesbian persuasion.

I would give my message but I would not rebuke anyone or condemn them for their chosen lifestyle or particular belief system. I would not tell them to stop being what they were, but I simply spoke to them on the subject matter as a brother.

It is only the Holy Spirit who can lead anyone to repentance. I would just preach Christ to them and leave the rest to God. Perhaps some would respond to the Gospel and be filled with the Holy Spirit. They may even receive the gift of prophecy!

Imagine if you dutifully paid the conference fee and all those "free-loaders" are in there, are taking up my attention and asking questions. You would want one-on-one time with me to learn about prophecy. You are important and you try to do everything right. You have been righteous all your life. You have come to learn to move in signs and wonders and here I am relating to the worst sinners in your city. How would you actually feel?

If the scenario above was true, you might be feeling very put out by me. In fact, you might very well be feeling exactly how the Pharisees were feeling with Jesus. He attracted sinners like bees to a honey-pot. These people in the parable had come to Jesus with very messy lives and yet this Rabbi just wanted to minister God's grace to them.

As I have said before, there was a time when I had an addiction to prostitutes: I used them whenever I had the means. I was constantly blowing a large portion of my money on this debilitating sin. I was under tremendous spiritual condemnation, which caused me to stay outside of church for fifteen years. I am relieved to now know that while the Holy Spirit gently convicts a person, it is the devil that out-rightly condemns us! Eventually, I was able to return to church but for five years I was going to church while still practicing that sin. Today, God has wonderfully healed me and has taken most of the hurt out of my life so that I can walk free from that sin.

I was in the middle of this addiction one day; I was going through King's Cross, the famous red light district of Sydney, when I saw some girls singing Christian choruses on a corner where all the major heroin deals were done. I went up to these seven girls and I said, "You know, this is really amazing. You are in the heaviest place in the city but I want to encourage you that I can see in the Spirit, that there is a canopy over you; it's just like, you know, Maxwell Smart's Cone of Silence over you. This is a supernatural protection all over you; you are entirely safe and you do not have to worry."

And they said "Yeah, we know we don't have to worry."

I said. "Can I pray for you?"

They all said, "Yes," and I prayed for them.

And then one of the girls said "Can we pray for you?"

I said, "Okay." Then the third girl started praying. She said "The Lord says, 'I am going to send you into a dark place, a place where angels fear to tread and I want you to take My joy and love into that place and share it with the people. Tell them that I love them. Give them treats, spend time with them and shine My light."

I felt that Jesus wanted me to go into one of the brothels as His ambassador. I was to see the girls there through His eyes of love. The girls would dance to entice the men to escort them upstairs to pay them prostitution rates. I felt in my spirit that Jesus was telling me to trust him totally and to befriend all the workers there.

To be friendly towards them was not hard for me, but I was scared of doing it, because I was not going to be a client to them. Instead, God was calling me, of all people, to witness His love for these girls. I was also very nervous because I had heard of people being killed in that particular establishment.

So anyway, I was at a church two weeks later and I still had not gone into that brothel. The Pastor said to me, "Stand up young man." And he said exactly the same prophecy. "I am going to send you into a dark place where angels fear to tread."

Well, I went to that brothel and stayed there a whole year! While I was there, I met a practicing prostitute who was into Buddhism and she confessed to me that her parents went to a local church in the country town where I come from. When I went back to my home town, I told the Pastor in that church, that the daughter of one of the men in his church, who had been abused by her father, was now working as a prostitute and was involved in Buddhism in Kings Cross. I had a lot of hurt and pain in my life and I shouted that out in the meeting in anger. It was not the nicest scene and I certainly wasn't exercising the grace of Jesus. I was out of order and was reacting totally in the flesh.

This girl in the brothel who reached out to me became one of my friends, but there I was— lost. I was a lost sheep myself, stuck in my own addictions as I ministered God's love.

Surely, when it comes to this parable, I can relate. Hurting people need other people strong in the Lord and led by His Holy Spirit to minister to them because they are far away from Jesus. Apart from the Great Shepherd, we all need an earthly shepherd. We all need a Christian friend. Some of the church shepherds are just too busy. This broken world needs compassionate people to look for wandering stragglers and to lead them to the sheepfold of Jesus. To me, that is what this parable is all about.

In the midst of my sin, in the darkest part of my life and at a time when I was not even attending church, Jesus sent me to minister to the hardest, most wicked, most violent club in Kings Cross, Australia and He protected me. I used to buy these girls little treats, like a two dollar chocolate and they would be so touched by it and some would even cry.

I was a lost sheep, but I was ministering too. Looking back now, I realize that I was never really lost to God – He had been there with me all the time! In the worst of my depravity, the Good Shepherd was still with me. The only way Jesus did not talk to me was when I told Him I did not want Him to, then months later, He would interrupt me and play me a song in my mind and once again we were talking and I was crying again. I suffered so much pain in those years. The parables of Jesus are very precious to me personally.

I hope that in sharing my story, I have touched you. Not everyone can go into a strip club or a brothel and minister to broken girls. Not everyone would have the ability to do that! Besides, you would definitely need to know that God was leading you to do it!

Lost sheep can be found anywhere? There are people in your workplace, at your gym and at the café that you go to. Many people have been burnt badly by religion. Many others have even walked away from Jesus to do their own thing. God needs people to befriend them and to show by example the love of the Great Shepherd. We need to let people know that "religion" is not what Jesus wants. He wants you to have a deep personal encounter with Him that develops into a wonderful relationship. Actually introducing people to "religion" is directly opposite to the will of God.

Don't be too quick to judge people. Some atheists have spent more time reading the Bible than us and have their own personal reasons why they do not walk with Christ. We all need to be "little-Christ's" to people and to go out and love them where they are at.

I often look at the time I ministered to those girls in the brothel and wonder why God chose me, a self-confessed addict to prostitutes, and all I can come up with is that He knew that I would love them for who they were and by not using them, I could show *His love* to them. I think back to those times and consider it a miracle that even in a time when I was not going to church I was still being used by God to show His love.

I have said it once before, but it bears repeating. People have until their very last breath on earth to accept Jesus and we do not need to rush the Gospel at every person we know, but simply to reach out to them and love them like Jesus loved the sinners in Israel. God can and will use you in His great plan to save people and you do not need to be an evangelist to save them. He will use your testimony or the gifts He has given you to do His work. This little book may even be a tool that He has put in your hands to bless your friend with. I trust that it will be used for God's glory.

CHAPTER 25

THE PARABLE OF THE MARRIAGE FEAST (MATTHEW 22:1-14)

The passage goes this way:

And Jesus answered and spoke to them again by parables and said: "The Kingdom of Heaven is like a certain king who arranged a marriage for his son and sent out his servants to call those who were invited to the wedding; and they were not willing to come. Again, he sent out other servants, saying, 'Tell those who are invited, "See, I have prepared my dinner; my oxen and fattened cattle are killed, and all things are ready. Come to the wedding." But they made light of it and went their ways, one to his own farm, and another to his business. And the rest seized his servants, treated them spitefully, and killed them. But when the king heard about it, he was furious. And he sent out his armies, destroyed those murderers, and burned up their city. Then he said to his servants, 'The wedding is ready, but those who were invited were not worthy. Therefore go into the highways, and as many as you find, invite to the wedding.' So those servants went out into the highways and gathered together all whom they found, both bad and good. And the wedding hall was filled with guests.

"But when the king came in to see the guests, he saw a man there who did not have on a wedding garment. So he said to him, 'Friend, how did you come in here without a wedding garment?' And he was speechless. Then the king said to the servants, 'Bind him hand and foot, take him away, and cast him into outer darkness; there will be weeping and gnashing of teeth.' "For many are called but few are chosen" (Matthew 22:1-14).

This is not a very exciting parable for a few people, especially for those who mistreated the servants—those who murdered the servants and who suffered when their city was burned. It is not a thrilling parable for the man who was found in the wrong garments.

At that time, Jesus was talking to the Jews. He was saying that His Father was going to prepare a supper. Many times in history, God sent out prophets to deliver His message but the people killed the prophets and the servants. Jesus Himself even came and they killed Him too. The Apostles and Prophets, who started the New Testament Acts, were killed too. Eventually, God had the city of Jerusalem taken by siege. The armies of the other countries killed the people.

The feast in this parable was referring to the Wedding Supper of the Lamb. The Son of the King is Jesus Christ. The King said that the people he had originally invited were not worthy and so He sent out messengers to invite the good and the bad. In other words, everybody was invited, but not everybody accepts the invitation. As a Christian, one day you will be a guest at this great occasion in Heaven. There will be a place card, with your name on it, ready to put on the banqueting table, so that you will be seated in your rightful place!

There are certain people who feel that they are justified by the Law. Some people feel that they need to be justified by their works of self-righteousness. This is what was illustrated in the wedding garment. Every person in those days who had a wedding would give all of his guests a garment. This way, the rich and the poor who came to the wedding would not be discriminated against; everyone would be well-dressed and felt worthy to be at the wedding.

Unfortunately, some people would reject the garments and would choose to enter, wearing their own clothes. This speaks of a person who has been offered the righteousness of Christ but expects to be able to inherit salvation through their own works of righteousness.

It says in Scripture that our works of righteousness are as filthy rags (Isaiah 64:6). Two of my favorite Christian speakers have pointed out that the Greek word translated as "filthy rags" in this particular verse actually means "menstrual" rags.

If you came into a wedding supper and any person was not in a clean fresh white robe of Jesus Christ's righteousness, it would be quite easy to see that sort of rag. That sort of garment on a person would stand out. So, too, we stand out when we try to earn our salvation through our own works.

This is a subject I know very well. For many years, I have read the prophets and I have felt that I was called to be one. I spent copious amounts of time in the Old Testament Prophets learning much of the Law. I felt that we still serve God like that. I felt that I had to achieve my own sense of holiness. I thought holiness and righteousness were not assigned or naturally given to me through the death of Jesus Christ. I believed that I had to earn my righteousness. I had to do good works. I was busy making videos, writing articles and running a prophetic ministry website. I was trying to minister to others, in order to have an insurance policy against the possibility that my sin was too much—against the possibility that I was going to have to go to Hell. *I was trying to actually insure myself against Hell.*

Jesus' Gospel—the Gospel that Paul preached says that Jesus Christ's righteousness is enough! It says that His death on the cross was enough for our past, present and future sins. A person who does not believe this is a person who trusts that they can inherit salvation through their own righteousness. Essentially, they believe that all their sins up until when they were saved or born again were forgiven, but from that time on, they had to read the Bible, attend church, pay tithes, be holy and not sin in order to get into Heaven. These works of self-righteousness are filthy rags.

The only thing that passes God's standard, is His own righteousness: the righteousness of His own Son. I used to feel disgusted when I would hear people say that I had the righteousness of Christ. When God looks at me, all He sees is His Son. I used to laugh at that. I used to get angry at that. I knew I was a sinner. I thought that any idea of me inheriting eternal salvation without my works was stupid—was foolishness and folly. I used to think that people who believed in the promises of God in the Old Testament, but did not believe the Law, were people attending a smorgasbord and merely picking the verses that pleased them and ignored the rest.

I spoke to many people about how foolish it was—to think that we are saved by Jesus Christ's death on the cross and His blood alone. I was like the wedding guest who took Jesus' robe of righteousness and salvation, but shed that robe of righteousness and walked into the party thinking I deserved to go there with my own works of righteousness. This is folly. This is something that Jesus—whether you know it or not—was clearly warning us against in this parable. He was saying that you are not going to measure up.

It says in James 2:10, he who is guilty of breaking one of the laws is guilty of breaking them all, for a person who thinks that they can achieve their own righteousness or achieve their own holiness in this life only has to break one law to be guilty of all of them. This is a passage in the Scripture that used to bring me a little bit of conviction but I could not do anything with the conviction because I was so convinced that I had to earn my own salvation through my own works of self-righteousness.

Can you understand that this parable is talking to people who think they are going to measure up? The purpose of the Law was to show you and me that we could never measure up to the standards of God. The Law was something to point us towards a Creator, towards a Savior that would save us from the penalty of sin and give us the power to resist them.

Jesus Christ did not come to earth merely to die on the cross for you, in order for you to then work out your salvation works of righteousness. *Jesus came to be your righteousness*, to clothe you in His righteousness. As you confess that you are the righteousness of Christ in God, as you believe that you are saved by His grace, as you believe your sins are forgiven in the past, present and future, your thoughts and your lifestyle will start to conform to God's way.

What I am saying is not a license for you to go out and sin your life away. It has certainly brought me a lot of joy and peace to know that I am saved by Jesus Christ and His death alone. I do not have to measure up because Jesus Christ already did it for me.

You have been invited to the party. Are you willing to lay off your own works of self-righteousness? Are you willing to lay down your own cross, a cross that you feel that you have to bear? Are you willing to take Jesus' sacrifice and His cross upon your shoulders and come in to the party that you have been invited to by God Himself? Are you willing to come? Because whether you are good or bad, you are invited to the party.

Come on, you Christians who are bound up with legalism and this idea of having to measure up to certain religious standards. Give it away. Stop trying to wear your own robe into the celebration. Put on the robe of Jesus Christ. Look up Joseph Prince and Andrew Wommack on DVD and on the internet. Andrew has a five DVD teaching which he taught in Minneapolis USA on Law and Grace. I think it's even better than the one by Joseph Prince on "Condemnation Kills."

Start to live in the fullness and abundance that the grace of God provides for us.

CHAPTER 26

THE PARABLE OF THE MUSTARD SEED
(MATTHEW 13: 31-32)

Matthew 13:31-32.

"Another parable He put forth to them, saying: 'The Kingdom of Heaven is like a mustard seed, which a man took and sowed in his field, which indeed is the least of all the seeds; but when it is grown it is greater than the herbs and becomes a tree, so that the birds of the air come and nest in its branches.'"

People talk about the mustard seed faith, or what others call "the faith of a mustard seed." But Jesus says the Kingdom of Heaven is like a mustard seed which a man took and sowed in his field. Then the mustard seed became a great tree.

There is another parable involving someone who did something in a field. There was a man who found treasure in a field? He sold all he had and bought the field because this treasure was so precious. The hidden treasure was an image of Jesus Christ. Also we have the parable called the Pearl of Great Price. Here another man sold all that he had in order to possess this pearl. Both of these parable show us how precious our Savior is.

Do you know that we are the seed that was sown in the field and became a great mustard tree? Do you know that the Bible also says that we are to be considered a peculiar people? Do you know that God sees us as His priests? Do you know that because of our union with Christ, we are called the adopted sons of God?

I want to share with you a story; something that my mother shared with me, that I thought was especially precious. Apparently, during the Roman days, when Jesus was on earth, someone who had a son could sell his son to be a slave and when the father had more money, he could redeem his son by paying to get him back out of slavery. Then, when hard times came again, he could sell his son again. When prosperity came yet again, he could buy his son back. Under the Jewish or Roman law, (whatever it was) a man could sell his own son three times and redeem him back three times.

This father is typical of the seasons in life. We all have seasons in life, when we have sufficient money and times of financial hardship, especially if you are in business. My brother is in business and things can change so fast for him. One season he is prosperous and a few months later he is deeply in debt. So it is understandable that in times past, a father might use his son's freedom as collateral.

Because life moves in seasons, I can understand a father selling his son three times into slavery. The son would know he was helping his father so, even when it was difficult, he would still be okay about being a temporary slave.

In those days, a wealthy man was able to go out and find a homeless person or someone he liked that did not have any income and he was able to adopt that person and make him his own son. However, the difference between that son and his natural son was that under this particular law, you were never allowed to sell an adopted child as a slave. You were only allowed to sell your own natural heir as a slave.

This is the special place we find ourselves in the Kingdom of God. When the Scriptures record that we are adopted sons: we are in fact, joint heirs with Jesus! This means we are of this second class of sons—the type that can never be lost or sold back into slavery. I don't know about you, but this really thrills my heart.

Spiritually, Jesus was given up by the Father for our sins. Physically, Jesus was actually sold for thirty pieces of silver, the going price of a slave. Jesus was the Father's own natural son and as His son He was allowed to suffer to achieve something for His Father.

Do you know how important you are to Jesus? You might be surprised about this: but whether you are a Christian or not, He died for you. If you were not as precious to the Father, Jesus would not have laid down His life for you. We are precious. Jesus willingly laid aside His royal status in heaven to become a servant to His Father on earth. He died a vicious death to redeem us, to bring us into fellowship with His Father. At salvation, God adopts us into His own royal family. So many people either refuse to believe in Jesus and what He achieved for them, so they remain outside of God's family. Many people are just ignorant of the truth and they too, are still outside of the kingdom. However, when we respond to the Gospel message, we are to learn about the wonderful privileges we have as adopted sons of God and co-heirs with Jesus Christ.

Back to the parable: Let us consider that the One who sowed the seed in the field is God and the seed is us. Let us also say that the field that we were sown into is this present world. (I am aware that in other parables the seed represents the Word of God.).

If you have been reading this book from the beginning, you will know about my shady past. Along with my addiction, you will know that I was sexually molested. I felt lonely and sad. I was addicted to disgusting sinful behaviors for many years. I felt so overcome by hard things. If anyone felt unworthy to be a preacher, or to talk about righteousness and holiness and living in the Kingdom of God—it was me. I felt undeserving to be called to speak about God's love. If anyone was unqualified to stand in the pulpit, it was me! Yet that is what is so good about the Kingdom of God, because, according to

Scripture I am considered to be a trophy of Christ. *I have Christ living in me and that qualifies me!*

I am no one at the moment but I have big dreams and there have been great prophecies spoken of my life. I have even been to Heaven in wonderful visions. One of these times, I was given Joseph's coat of many colors and I know that it is on me even now. The personal knowledge that I have that coat of favor on my life, and that God allowed his Son to give it to me in Heaven, brings me tremendous comfort. In fearful times, when sleep will not come at night due to mental illness, the knowledge of me possessing that coat brings deep comfort. I believe with all of my heart that although I am nothing now, one day through God's grace and favor, the prophecies on my life will come to pass.

As the seed, we are sown into the world. Therefore, we all have the potential to become a great tree—a great, big mustard tree! We also get to be mustard! This says to me, that we not only have the potential to become great but our stature is useful for something too.

Jesus is saying here that the mustard seed can become something really big! The least of the seeds, the tiniest of all seeds, becomes such a mighty tree! I feel through this parable that Jesus is saying the tinier that you are, the larger you are going to become. The more insignificant you feel you are, the more you can be used. He is saying that if you can receive it, though you might feel you are the littlest seed of all the herbs, you do not just become a little flower bush in the garden that most herbs are—you become a mighty tree.

The Bible says that God has no favorites. If you will allow Him to mold you and to fashion you, He can mold you into something huge. You see, if it were not possible for all of us to grow into a great tree, this short parable would not have been told by Jesus.

Some people have a mistaken view of the sovereignty of God. Many Christians believe that whatever they do, they will receive the same results in life. They believe that God is in control regardless of the decisions they personally make. But God will not over-ride man's will! Many Christians would be shocked to know that there are ninety percent of them not reaching the potential God has set for them.

Most people freely admit that they have no idea of their ultimate life's purpose. They have no vision for great things. They are simply going to church, going to work, paying the bills and hoping—just hoping—that one day, someone, somewhere, will show them what they are called to do on earth. If I suggest to them that God wants them to grow into a huge tree as illustrated in this parable, they will recoil and say that some people are called to be great and famous but they are not one of them. Even though they don't know their purpose, they strenuously assure me that they were not destined to do great things.

Jesus would not have said that the mustard seed was so little but it outgrew all the other herbs of the field, if the very people He died for couldn't also grow and become the best of their species. One thing is certain, dear reader: God can never take you further than you believe you can go. God cannot make you into a great tree that gives life (the mustard) and a place for people to find rest, if you are not willing to receive what He is trying to say to you today. So much hinges on knowing why we are here on earth. So much hinges on what we know of God and the truth that we know about how the Kingdom of God really operates. There is so much riding on these two things; the knowledge of who you are in Christ Jesus, and how the Kingdom really works. If you do not learn these two things, you will never become who you were destined to be.

There are a lot of little people in the world—and do not get me wrong here. Jesus was not saying that little people do not count. Herbs are herbs and they all have a divine purpose for life on earth. As an adopted child of the Kingdom, God has now redeemed you and given you new DNA and you now can, as a little seed, become a great tree that will cause you to fulfill your destiny and also cause you to be a blessing to others. In our parable the tree became a comfort and shelter for the birds of the air.

You may argue: "But I do not want to become someone of great importance," you say. "I do not need to become big. I am happy with my life as it is. I do not need to be anyone that I am not. I just want to be myself." But that is the whole point of what this parable is about! If you could just get a hold of this in your spirit, you will know that God does not want you to become something that you were not created to be. *He wants you to become better at being you!* He wants you to grow to a point that when you look back at your past life, you will be able to exclaim, "Praise God!"

I have wanted to write a book about Jesus' parables for ten years. It has been one of my secret dreams. On September 19th, 2010, the Lord gave me instruction as to how the book was to be done and He also gave me the name of the book. I have spoken about this in other parables. The book was made to be as cheap as it could be. I followed all His instruction and now, you are finally reading the end result.

I know in ten years' time, my knowledge of Jesus and of His Father will have grown and my understanding of the parables will have grown too. Satan keeps on trying to tell me that other people have more knowledge than I do on this subject and that there is no use writing a book on the parables when in ten years I will know more. Yet with careful conversation with the people I love, I have not listened to his taunts. If we wait until we know everything we will be in heaven, not on earth!

Who knows, one day when I am well known, people may be waiting for my next book to be published! One day my mail bag may be full of people thanking me for the little words of wisdom that I have shared and on that day, even though I am a little seed right now in the world-wide scheme of influential Christian writers and speakers, I might be a big tree.

If you feel insignificant and you have a whole bunch of issues and problems which causes you to lose heart, you are the one that is going to be the mustard seed. You are the one that is going to be the big tree. The other herbs of the field do not grow big, yet they began as bigger seeds than the mustard seed. The more insignificant you are, the more God can do with you.

Do you believe it? If this is encouraging, write your comments to me. Write to my email address. I would love to hear from you.

CHAPTER 27

THE PARABLE OF THE NET OF FISH (MATTHEW 13:47-50)

The parable starts in Matthew 13:47 and goes to verse 50.

"Again, the Kingdom of Heaven is like a dragnet that was cast into the sea and gathered some of every kind, which, when it was full, they drew to shore; and they sat down and gathered the good into vessels but threw the bad away. So it will be at the end of the age. The angels will come forth, separate the wicked from among the just, and cast them into the furnace of fire. There will be wailing and gnashing of teeth."

When He was on earth, Jesus said that the Kingdom had come near. He was stressing that the Kingdom of God was not something to be searched out, but that it was close at hand. The Gospel of Jesus is that everyone has an opportunity to participate in God's Kingdom. We are all born into the Kingdom of Satan, and need to be re-born into God's Kingdom. I say more about this in Chapter 30.

In the Gospel of Matthew in Chapter 13, Jesus began a series of teaching about His Kingdom. In this one chapter alone He taught on seven parables. I will list them in order of how they are recorded by the Gospel writer:

The Parable of the Sower, then the Tares in the Field, the Mustard Seed, the Leaven, the Hidden Treasure, the Pearl of Great Price, and lastly the Net of Fish. In the front index, you will see that I have listed the Parables of Jesus alphabetically and not in the same order that they are written in the actual Gospel.

In this parable, the Kingdom of Heaven is likened to a dragnet that was cast into the sea and it gathered some fish of every kind. The Dragnet is the preaching of the Gospel of Christ. You remember when Peter was told to lay down the net on the shore? He laid it down and caught so many fish that it almost broke the net. Jesus was alluding to some greater meaning here. In the Gospel, He said Peter would become a fisher of men. This is what this parable means. The dragnet here is the Gospel going out on TV, on radio, through Christian's lives witnessing to other people. *The dragnet is the Gospel: "the almost too good to be true news," going out to the world.*

The purpose of the dragnet was to catch as much fish as possible. When it was full, they drew to shore. They then began to sort the catch into good or bad fish; the good they kept and the bad were thrown away.

In other words, the Gospel is to be preached to every person. Everyone is to hear the message that Jesus Christ was sent by God to be our Savior. He is the one you need to submit to. There is no purpose in life without Him. Therefore, the Gospel is the dragnet to catch all the fish. Now, the fish who don't transform into any resemblance of the Master; their lives don't reflect any noticeable change whatsoever, they are classified as the bad fish. This means, these hearers of the Word never did surrender to the Master in the first place! So they are discarded as not being worthy of the Kingdom of God.

Jesus is totally fair because He can read a person's heart. Therefore, He is never deceived by outward show. Are you a person who believes that you don't need Jesus because you are totally content with your present situation? You feel that you have found true happiness and just love your comfortable life and you enjoy all the fruits of your labor. That all seems to be good now, but the Bible warns us that to enter Heaven you must be perfect, not just "happy!" Jesus Christ alone is perfect. If you don't have His Spirit in you, then you will not meet the entry requirements, no matter how good or happy you have been on earth!

Jesus warned His hearers about false prophets. These are people who say they are born-again, but they are not! Jesus said in Matthew 7:15-20, *"You will know them by their fruits. Do men gather grapes from thorn bushes or figs from thistles? Even so, every good tree bears good fruit, but a bad tree bears bad fruit. A good tree cannot bear bad fruit, nor can a bad tree bear good fruit. Every tree that does not bear good fruit is cut down and thrown into the fire. Therefore by their fruits you will know them."*

We are not saved because of our good works, but "good works" are the natural fruit of salvation. The Bible points out that God pleasing good works can only come from faith in Jesus. But faith in God, without good works is dead!

Many people claim that they have faith in God! This worldly expression: "faith in God," can mean anything! Ask anyone do they believe in God and they will say: "Of course!" Bear in mind, in James 2:19 we read: *"You believe that there is one God. You do well. Even the demons believe – and tremble."* The devil's belief in God will not save him!

The people who share the Gospel come with the message. "Are you suffering? Are you tired? Do you have a meaningless life? Do you have a life without purpose? Jesus is pleading, "Come to Me, the living Son of God, who came to earth and lived a life of purpose and miraculous power. Come to Me."

Jesus is fair: He wants everyone to understand His message of salvation! Are you caught in sin and despair? "Come to Me!" Jesus says. Are you satisfied in life without Jesus? "You are deceived, come to Me! I am the one who holds your future in My hands. I am the one who knows your deepest fears. I created you and I gave My life for you!" In Matthew 11:28-30 Jesus invites you to come to Him: *"Come to Me, all you who labor and are heavy laden, and I will give you rest. Take My yoke upon you and*

*learn from Me, for I am gentle and lowly in heart, and you will find rest for your souls.
For My yoke is easy and My burden is light."*

So the Gospel goes out to the people: it is God's love message to us called the Good
News. It goes out to all of the people. Some hear the message, but reject it and continue
to live in their sin of unbelief.

There are more people in this world who do good things then those who don't. They
fall in love; they become good parents and members of society. They achieve success
and contribute their time, energy and money into worthwhile causes. Many Christians
are very successful, but in financial matters, people in the world seem to have the
monopoly. Often worldly families can even seem to have better families because often
they can seem to share more love. When Jesus talks about the wicked people here,
He is not about their dreams, or deeds. What Jesus is referring to as wickedness here,
is a person who has been given the opportunity to become Christ-like, but blatantly
refuses to.

So, this casting out of the net and the sorting out the good from the bad is an image of
what is going to happen at the end of the world. When the Father gives the order, the
angels will come forth and separate the wicked from among the just. They will come
and take all the people off the face of the earth. Those who have heard the message
like this and have decided: "No, I am not going to change my lifestyle in order to
submit my life to God" or, "No, I am not going to give away my philosophies and
my other religious ideas in order to embrace the faith of Jesus Christ." Those people
who have been given the opportunity are going to be cast into Hell and that is an
abominable place to end up in! (See Chapter 33 of this book.)

So, what is the application of the parable? It is the job of believers to cast that net out
to the world. It's our job to be a light on a hill. It is our job to be good and faithful to
people, to love others, forgive others and to treat them with integrity and compassion.
It's our job to tell a person the reason why we do such things. When they ask why, it is
our job to say, "It's not me. It is Christ in me. It is the fact that Jesus loves me. I act this
way because Jesus has changed my attitude about life. Do you want to know Jesus? "

It is as simple as that! When you commit yourself to God, His Holy Spirit comes to
live inside of you. He then empowers you to change! If you try to change in your own
strength, then you will fail miserably and will not please God. All you need to do: is to
go out into the world and shine out Jesus to others, as the Holy Spirit leads you. Dare
to be different! Be kind and treat others like you would like them to treat you.

Be the most diligent worker in your job. Be the most conscientious and loyal worker
your boss has ever had! Take the time to help others when they need help. If you can do
a job well, teach others. Help other people become more creative to assist productivity.

Whatever you are good at, help other people with it. Not everyone has to preach the
Gospel to bring salvation. You are part of the dragnet. You are one of the people that
Jesus depends on to help in the task of saving the peoples of this world. We are to be
able to give God's message and to expose the lies of the devil. Will you do it? Many
people are heading for a lost eternity. Love them in Jesus power.

The reason Jesus told this parable is: He needs you to cast that net out into the world. He needs you to be part of that net.

You know, a net is made up of many strings all sewn together. Not a few strings can make a net, but many strings bonded and held together: the bigger the net that goes out, the more fish that can be brought in. In a little African village, they only throw a little net out by hand. They catch a few fish. Out in the ocean, fishermen throw massive nets out into the water and they catch heaps more fish.

You need to be part of that net. You need to go out and share your love. You need to get this article—this chapter—and send it to a friend. Go and do your part. Fulfill this parable. God bless you.

CHAPTER 28

THE PARABLE OF THE NEW CLOTH
(MATTHEW 9:16)

Jesus said in Matthew 9:16

"No one puts a piece of un-shrunk cloth on an old garment; for the patch pulls away from the garment and the tear is made worse."

To place this parable in context, we need to back track a bit!

The disciples of John and also the Pharisees lived a lifestyle based on Old Testament Law. This was a long list of things that every Jewish person had to do in order to have a right relationship with God. The Law was never intended for non-Jews, known as Gentiles, to keep. Part of the Law, which had become a religious tradition, was to fast one or two days a week. The religious leaders, called Pharisees, had enormous power and felt significantly superior to the common people, they were meant to shepherd the Jews but they actually become hard taskmasters and extremely legalistic in their style of leading.

The Pharisees reasoned that going a day or so without food, was something to be honored and respected by others and it was! But, fasting with wrong motives is not honoring to God: it is hypocritical and repugnant to God! This type of fasting had no spiritual sustenance: it had no life because it was not done to glorify God. Although their fast didn't feed their stomach, it did feed their ego!

Earlier, during the Sermon on the Mount recorded in Matthew chapters 5-7, Jesus had instructed the crowd about the right way to fast. He said: *"When you fast, do not be like the hypocrites, with a sad countenance. For they disfigure their faces that they may appear to men to be fasting. Assuredly, I say to you, they have their reward. But you, when you fast, anoint your head and wash your face, so that you do not appear to men to be fasting, but to your Father who is in the secret place; and your Father who sees in secret will reward you openly." Matthew 6:16-18*

Application: Fasting is a private thing between us and God. We are to dress and behave like we normally do so that only God sees our heart motive and we will be rewarded by Him and not by the empty praise of man.

The disciples of John the Baptist were mostly Jews who had been convicted by God of their personal sin. As a sign of this, they were publicly baptized by full immersion in the Jordon River. This custom was called a "Baptism of Repentance."

Because of Jewish tradition, John's disciples used to fast.They were still practicing the Law and it was clear that they saw good things in fasting. However, they had seen that Jesus and His disciples didn't fast and asked Jesus why that was so. He said:

"Can the friends of the bridegroom mourn as long as the bridegroom is with them? But the days will come when the bridegroom will be taken away from them, and then they will fast." Matthew 9:14-15.

Jesus called Himself the disciple's "Bridegroom." This must have puzzled them at the time. He said that because He and His Bride were happy and were enjoying each other's company there was therefore no need to fast and be sorrowful. But one day, when He is taken away, then His people can return to fasting. So, Jesus is not saying that fasting will pass away, but He is suggesting that fasting will be done in a different way, with a different attitude.

I have said all this as a lead up to this parable: *"No one puts a piece of un-shrunk cloth on an old garment; for the patch pulls away from the garment and the tear is made worse"* (Our title verse.)

For years, this was a mystery to me. Being ignorant of "sewing principles" I had no idea that if you tried to use a new un-shrunken piece of cloth, to patch up an old garment, that the patch would soon pull away and the garment would further tear. The same thing happens if you use an old piece of material to patch up a tear on a new garment. The lesson being you can only patch like to like cloth. Otherwise the repair will not last.

How does all this relate to us personally? I only recently discovered what Jesus was talking about here. Naturally, Jesus was not giving the disciple a sewing lesson! He was giving them a much more important lesson. Jesus was talking about the laws of God. You can only add an old principle to an old law. Likewise, you can only add a new principle to a new law. You see, Jesus leaves us clues: the old garment represents the Old Testament Law, based on the Old Covenant. The new garment represents the New Testament Covenant of grace that Jesus was about to establish by His substitution death on the cross for us.

We need to dig a bit deeper here: we need to establish the difference between an agreement and a Covenant. Today, we make all sorts of agreements with people, but an agreement between two or more people can be dissolved, it is not legally binding unless it has been put in writing and signed by both parties. However an agreement becomes a "Covenant" when one of the parties involved is God Himself. Because God must be true to His word, a "Covenant" cannot be dissolved.

The only way God's old Covenant with His people can be replaced by a new Covenant is if the old one was fully met by God Himself and that is what happened! *Jesus, who was God veiled in human flesh totally fulfilled every single part of the old Covenant Law on our behalf.*

Jesus Christ did not inherit Adam's sin nature because He was conceived not by a natural man, but by the Holy Spirit. He was sinless at birth and he made sure that He lived a sinless life on earth. He then willingly submitted His life to suffer the all the *"punishment for sin" that should have been allotted to us!* He bore the full wrath of God, against all sin once forever! Being God, He was the only One who could do that for us, because He had no sin of His own.

His Father in Heaven stamped His seal of approval and satisfaction, by raising Jesus from the dead. Then the New Testament or the Covenant of Grace replaced the Old Covenant Law and the world was forever changed! This new Covenant is no longer based on *"our performance"* but is instead based on *the work of Jesus demonstrated on the cross!*

The apostle Paul wrote about these awesome changes in great detail. Every Christian is to study the anointed epistles written in the New Testament so they will fully understand what Jesus has done for us and then they will be able to live a victorious life.

The written set of laws were engraved in stone by the finger of God and given to Moses in the Old Testament, are known as The Ten Commandments, but there are hundreds of other laws in the Old Testament as well. The Law reflected God character and His standard of holiness: it was holy and good, but it was impossible for anyone on earth to keep! This was because we had all been tainted with a sin nature from Adam. The Law told us what to do, but it had no life: it could not empower us to keep its rigid demands.

Therefore, why then did God give the Law? He gave it to bring us to our knees and call out to Him that we could never reach His holy standard. To tell Him we need His help – we need a Savior to come and save us from our sinful nature.

The problem was: The Israelites just like us today, compared their standard of holiness to those around them and they became prideful when they saw that in some things their behavior was better than others. We tend to do the same today - we compare ourselves with other people and figure that we are okay and God will accept us like we are. The thing that is wrong about that is: we must only compare our goodness to the holiness of God. He is the only yardstick to use!

No one but God Himself can keep the Law. When the time was right God sent His Son to keep the Law for us. Jesus totally fulfilled every single law so that when we believe in Him we are declared totally righteous before God because when God looks at us, He sees Jesus. He no longer sees us as sinners.

The old garment was faulty: it had a tear in it. In other words the old Law was faulty: it was powerless to change people – it couldn't fix the sin disease. It could only reveal sin! No one can patch the old tear with a new Law or a new piece of un-shrunken cloth.

The only workable solution was for the old Law to be done away with and a brand new system to come into place. That system was "the grace of Jesus dying on the cross for us." This alone would fix up the tear, because it would empower people to live a God pleasing life. Going around in life trying to fulfill the Law we will make you a broken person. You will live with guilt, condemnation and shame: you will go from happy to sad every time you do something wrong.

Mixing law and grace is an abomination to Jesus and an insult to the cross! We are not to read the Bible, pray to God, do good works, fast or make sacrifices with any motivation of keeping the old law. This is "religion" and God detests all work done with a religious mind-set. If your heart motive is not activated by the grace of God then what you consider is good is not good at all! We can't make ourselves holy – only by accepting the work of the cross can make us holy! That is why it is imperative that you come to belief in Jesus. God's solution cuts across human ego and that is what God wants it to do.

It is a whole new system! If you are a Christian, obeying Jesus in everything you do, yet you still have a mindset of the Law, you will have this big burden of shame and guilt. The devil will make sure of this! He will even tell you that you are going to go to Hell because you don't measure up to God's standard. If we keep ourselves focused on the Law, we will experience defeat. Scripture tells us that focusing on the Law causes us to sin more! The Apostle Paul wrote in 1 Corinthians 15:56-57 *"The sting of death is sin, and the strength of sin is the law. But thanks be to God, who gives us the victory through our Lord Jesus Christ."*

To live under the law is to strengthen sin. The more sin conscious we are, the more sin defeats us and we move out from grace. Focus instead on the One who fulfilled the Law for us. Focus on Jesus Christ.

Why am I saying all of this? It is because I have felt such a failure. Because I want you to be set free. I want you to understand that you cannot live with a set of religious rules in your Christian life. When you open your Bible, it is because you want to meet with God—you want to learn what He is like and how He wants you to have an abundant life and how you can be a co-worker in your "Daddy's Kingdom Business."

I really hope that I have been some help to you on this matter. This revelation set me free and I just hope that you will be as blessed as I was.

CHAPTER 29

THE PARABLE OF THE NEW WINE
(MATTHEW 9:17)

Jesus told this parable immediately following the New Cloth Parable in Chapter 28. Therefore, to put this message in context, make sure you read the previous chapter. There, He warned His audience about the folly of putting a new patch on an old garment. *Scripture says: "No one puts a piece of un-shrunk cloth on an old garment; for the patch pulls away from the garment and the tear is made worse" (v. 16).*

Essentially, the new cloth represents the fact that you cannot mix the New Covenant of grace and salvation with the Old Covenant Law. If you are a Christian, you should live in freedom and liberty: you should live to follow the desires and directions of the Holy Spirit, which are to be done in love, and not by a set of rules.

The parable of the new wine is found in verse 17 - *"Nor do they put new wine into old wineskins, or else the wineskins break, the wine is spilled, and the wineskins are ruined but they put new wine into new wineskins, and both are preserved."*

It may take a Christian many years before understanding the difference between Law and Grace. If I had received revelation of it years ago, my life would have been very different. To understand this parable, you must be open to its context and the meanings that underscore it.

Now, wine is mentioned in the Bible a number of times. It is spoken of in the life of Jesus. In fact, the first miracle that Jesus performed was to turn the dirty water that many wedding guests had washed themselves with, into fresh wine. He not only turned this polluted water into fresh wine, but the Scripture says that it was the "best" wine! (You can read the full account of this miracle in the Bible - John 2:1-11)

Jesus was a guest at a Jewish wedding. A wedding feast could continue for up to a week in those days, so people expected to drink plenty of wine. The wine eventually ran out and at His mother's request, Jesus performed this miracle, somewhat reluctantly, because He felt His time hadn't come to publicly minister. The embarrassment of the host and his mother's pleas caused Him to rectify the problem in this surprising manner.

107

So, most of the guests at the wedding feast would have been fairly drunk at this stage. When the host of the feast tasted that "special" new wine, he said it was the best wine! He felt that the servants should have presented it to the bridal party and to the guests much earlier, before they had become intoxicated. That was the normal procedure at wedding feasts.

Firstly, as I have already stated, the people were already inebriated when Jesus brought the new wine made from dirty washing water. There is much imagery in this miracle.

Secondly and more importantly: Jesus can take our dirty water—our dirty life—our life full of sin and hopelessness; shame and guilt—and in an instant, He can turn it into a life filled with joy, peace and the love of the Lord. We can bubble up with such a feeling as though we were drunk. Jesus can take our sins, our sadness and all the things that come against us in the normal, day-to-day routine of life. He can take all your inner junk and turn it into the new wine of His Spirit.

Now the passage says: *"Nor do they put new wine into old wineskins, or else the wineskins break, the wine is spilled, and the wineskins are ruined"* (v.17).

Your life is precious to God. He wants you to be whole. He doesn't want your life to be like a ruined wineskin. He does not want your life to burst like the wineskin did in this parable. The only way your life's wineskin is going to burst and be destroyed, is if you mix the new wine, the New Covenant teaching of Jesus, with the Old Covenant Law.

As I said, this parable and the last one go hand in hand: both carry the warning not to mix together the new and the old covenants of God. The old was meant for people living before Jesus died on the cross. Today we live in the new covenant that Jesus established. The Apostle Paul was insistent on this point. The new Christians tried to incorporate circumcision and all the hundreds of rules of the Jewish law, into their faith. They were trying to mix the Old Covenant Law with the new wine of God's grace (Galatians 5:2-6).

Paul who had founded the Church in Galatia was incensed and frustrated: He said in Galatians 1: 6-8 *"I am amazed that you are turning away so soon from God who, in His love and mercy, invited you to share the eternal life He gives through Christ; you are already following a different 'way to heaven' which really doesn't go to heaven at all. For there is no other way than the one we showed you; you are being fooled by those who twist and change the truth concerning Christ. Let God's curses fall on anyone, including myself, who preaches any other way to be saved than the one we told you about; yes, if an angel comes from heaven and preaches any other message, let him be forever cursed."* (Living Bible Translation)

These are forceful and angry words! If Jesus had been physically present He would have responded exactly the same! He would have accused them of trying to put new wine into the old wineskin of the Law. They were trying to mix the two. Jesus is saying in this parable, if you mix the Old Testament Law with His new wine: with the new teaching of His Spirit, you will end up with a disaster. Not only will you be worse off, with your wineskin burst, you will also lose the power, fulfillment and joy of the new wine of the Holy Spirit. The finished work of the cross and the joy of the cross will be lost. The sweetness, essence and the beautiful sensation of being close to Jesus will fade away. The peace and joy of the message of the Gospel will be polluted to the point, that it no longer even represents the true Gospel. For you, your faith would be in vain.

It is so important that you read the chapter on the new cloth because that goes into even more detail about this topic.

Jesus said, *"But they put new wine into new wineskins and both are preserved"* (v. 17b).What is this new wineskin? What is this new wine? How can that happen? Well, first of all, we have to understand that our old life *is our old life!* In 2 Corinthians 5:17 we read: *"Therefore, if anyone is in Christ, he is a new creation; old things have passed away; behold, all things have become new."*

We have to understand that we are a new creation in Christ when we ask Jesus Christ to come into our life as Savior and Lord. No longer are we to be under the bondage of the Law but we under a new master: the risen Christ. You might say "Well I don't want to come under any master!" The fact is since birth up to the point you become a Christian, *you were under a ruthless master, who wanted to deceive, torment and destroy you.* His name is Satan. But Jesus overcame Satan's authority in your life. Now the Holy Spirit of God wants to bring you into the image of your new Master so that you can agree with Paul and declare: "It is no longer I that live, but Christ that lives in me." Galatians 2:20

"But I don't understand," you say. "I am a sinner: I think and do bad things every day! I don't feel Christ in me!" Feelings deceive: God's word is truth! He cannot lie!

You are forgiven – period! You are a child of God, precious in His sight. At salvation, you were declared "justified!" Therefore, God sees me "just-as-if-I'd" never sinned. I only saw myself as a rotten failure but God sees the Holy Spirit living in my human spirit now! Therefore, my human spirit has been made perfectly fit for Heaven. That means that one third of me was made totally holy! The Holy Spirit will then, over my whole lifetime, bring into alignment the way that God sees me as being the way I see myself. In the meantime my sins are not held against me.

"Does that mean I can sin as much as I like?" you may say. That is like a new bride who is confident that her husband loves her and would even die for her, saying "Well, I think I will just go out and sleep with any man I want to now. My husband loves me and would even die for me, so I may as well commit adultery and have some variation in my life." That is stupid thinking: why would anyone so blessed by Almighty God, even want to think about doing that? When you are saved you want to please God; you want to stop sinning. You certainly wouldn't be looking for new ways to sin against God!

 Jesus died on the cross for every sin. Jesus died for all of the sins that you are ever going to do. When you think about it, Jesus died two thousand years ago, therefore all our sin was future sin! If all your sins were not nailed to Jesus on the cross, where are they? And if Jesus died for every sin that you have done this week and every sin that you will ever do, was not His death good enough? The attitude of "having to do religious duties" is "works mentality." Paul was so angry about that attitude, because it belittles the cross of Jesus. Jesus died for all of our sins: that is the Gospel! It's the New Wine!

So, what is the new wineskin? The new wineskin is the fact that every born-again believer is "the righteousness of Christ." You are holy right now. That was the great heavenly exchange that happened at the death of Jesus. 2 Corinthians 5:21 says: *"For He* (The Father) *made Him* (Jesus) *who knew no sin to be sin for us, that we might become the righteousness of God in Him.* (Jesus)" When God looks from Heaven at you: He looks at you through the mercy seat. On the mercy seat is the sprinkled blood of Jesus Christ which is the ultimate perfect sacrifice!

Back in the Old Testament, the people would go to the Temple in Jerusalem and present a certain animal or bird to the priest to be slaughtered so as to reconcile the sinner to God: in God's sight, the spilled blood of the sacrifice covered over their sin. The priest first checked that the "sacrifice" was perfect; he never inspected the sinner who brought the sacrifice! Think about that! Jesus was the Perfect Lamb of God: He was our sacrifice!

God doesn't look for faults in us, He only looks for perfection *in our sacrifice* – that is why He set up the Priestly Office and the Sacrifice System the way He did! This sacrifice system was put into place by God's instructions two thousand years before Jesus came to earth. It was pointing to a time when Jesus was going to die for the whole world's sin.

God doesn't look at the Law and all its regulations anymore: He isn't a God that punishes sin anymore. This is the Gospel of the new wine. He isn't interested in punishing you: He took all His punishment out on Jesus Christ on the cross!

All of His judgment, all of His condemnation and wrath were poured out on Jesus Christ on the cross. God is not angry with America. God is not angry with Australia. God is not judging these countries. He is not losing the fight. God won the fight with sin and Satan when Jesus died on the cross! Unbelievers must come to know this message and become a partaker of the new wine, otherwise Christ died in vain for them. If they reject Jesus as their Savior, then when they die they will have to receive the wrath of God for their own sin. The sin of unbelief is the only sin that sends anyone to Hell.

I want you to walk in the new wine and to understand this new way of living. I was in terrible bondage and I thought I understood the Gospel but I didn't. I had a wrong mindset for so long and it robbed me of enjoying this beautiful new wine. I urge you to check out on the internet Andrew Wommack Ministries so that you can be free indeed as Christ wants you to be. I have mentioned his name so often that some readers may suspect that I am on some sort of commission. I only mention him because he teaches profoundly yet so simple.

Jesus said in John 8:32 *"You shall know the truth, and the truth shall make you free."* There is a catch here: it is only the *truth that we know,* that sets us free! Because I didn't know it: I had not been set free! Unknown truth helps no one! Up until July,

2010, I was of the understanding that I had to work for my salvation. I had to go to church. I had to read my Bible. I had to be holy. I had to pay God ten percent of my money and if I did not do all these things, I thought God was angry at me and I had to repent. I would beat myself up. I would carry this big load of shame and this load of having to measure up to be worthy of Jesus Christ. Then, I was wonderfully set free with the knowledge of the liberating truth of the Gospel message.

Anyway, you need to understand this parable. Never in my life have I understood the parable of the new wine. The new wine can transform your dirty life—your dirty water. What you did today, what you did last night, all the wrong things you have thought, spoken or done, all your dirty water can be turned into beautiful, new, fresh-tasting wine in an instant: the best wine you have ever tasted. If you believe this, you can go from the feeling of shame and condemnation to joy and peace. You can go from feeling worthless to being filled with the joy and peace of the Holy Spirit. You can go from sadness to joy, from mourning to dancing.

It is a wonderful message. It is a wonderful parable. We have a wonderful Savior! I hope that you are blessed by the revelation I have given you today.

CHAPTER 30

THE PARABLE OF THE PEARL OF GREAT PRICE (MATTHEW 13:45-46)

"The Parable of the Pearl of Great Price"- Gospel of Matthew 13: 45-46.

"Again, the Kingdom of Heaven is like a merchant seeking beautiful pearls, who, when he had found one pearl of great price, went and sold all that he had and bought it."

A merchant of fine pearls is seeking beautiful specimens with the one hope of making a handsome profit. He has a well-trained eye to identify any possible flaws in a particular pearl. Once a rare specimen is found, he is careful not to reveal too much enthusiasm in his voice or body language: he would be casual in his approach to the seller. Certainly to do otherwise, would instantly increase the pearl's value to the seller. Therefore, he nonchalantly inquires of its price.

The seller is no novice: He too is a hardened specialist and believes in a certain value for his prized acquisition. The fact that he actually has the pearl for sale suggests that his competence in appreciation of beauty is not to the same degree as the astute trader. The seller hopefully names a price and is amazed that the trader doesn't haggle.

Too late, the seller realizes his price was too low: the trader would have paid more despite his cool demeanor. However the price was set and accepted: the deal was over. The trader would have secured his purchase with a hefty deposit promising to pay the balance within the legal time limit. The trader then left rejoicing in his windfall. He was not even perplexed that in order to honor the remaining purchase agreement, he would have to sell every valuable asset he had. He knew that this exquisite pearl would bring such a handsome return that his future would dramatically change. No longer would he have to rely on his own resources to make ends meet. He could live like a king for the rest of his life! When he found the right buyer *it would be like being born again and living the life of royalty!*

This parable is all about the Lord Jesus Christ. He is both the "Hidden Treasure" and the "Pearl of Great Price." Both parables not only speak of Jesus, but both are all about the kingdom of God. What is a kingdom? A kingdom is an area over which a king rules.

Let me explain: Every person on earth belongs to two worlds simultaneously: a natural world and a spiritual world. The natural world is made up of things we can see, hear, touch, taste and smell. The natural world is visible. But at the same time, every person also lives in a spiritual world that is invisible.

The invisible world has far more influence over us than we realize. The "invisible world" is itself divided into two opposing camps: one is called the Kingdom of God and the other is called the Kingdom of Satan. If we are not a resident of the first kingdom, then we are automatically residents of the second kingdom. Jesus said: *"He who is not with Me is against Me." Matthew 12:30.* Obviously, there is no dual residency possible. In the natural world a person can have dual citizenship, but not so in the spiritual world.

God's Kingdom consists of the Father, the Son and the Holy Spirit, angels of God and every Christian because they have God's Holy Spirit residing in them.

It is vital to understand that every person at their birth is automatically born into the second kingdom. No one at their birth belongs to God's kingdom. There are only two people that I know of who were born into God's kingdom: they were the Lord Jesus and His cousin, John the Baptist who received God's Holy Spirit while in his mother's womb. Even if both of your parents were Christians, that would not cause you to be born into God's kingdom. (We must personally choose to change kingdoms with the help of Jesus.)

No, you like everyone else, were born into Satan's kingdom because way back in time, our common forefather, Adam, passed his sin nature through the human gene pool, into every generation since creation. Jesus is the only One who has the authority to transfer a person from Satan's kingdom to God's kingdom.

Jesus said in John 3.3 *"Most assuredly, I say to you, unless one is born again, he cannot see the kingdom of God."* Jesus is not talking about physical re-birth, but spiritual re-birth! No, you can only be born once naturally. The Bible negates any notion of reincarnation. *"It is appointed for men to die once, but after this the judgment." Hebrews 9:27.* The psalmist, talking about unbelievers, writes: *"God remembered that they were but flesh, a breath that passes away and does not come again." Psalm 78:39.*

It suits Satan's purposes for people to believe that after death they will be reincarnated! He is the master deceiver! Scripture teaches that we are born once, but we need to be "spiritually" re-born. In fact if we are not born-again spiritually, we cannot enter heaven.

It is important to know that God gave us and the angels a personal free will. Satan was originally named "Lucifer" and he was one of the special arch-angels of God, like Michael and Gabriel. But he exalted himself and wanted to be worshiped as God. Because of his ego, God cast him out of heaven and renamed him Satan. One third of his rebellious followers were cast out as well. These fallen angels are now called demons.

Satan's kingdom consists of: Satan who is the devil, his wicked demons and everyone who has not called on the name of Jesus Christ, meaning, every person who rejects the Gospel message. It was Satan who deceived Adam and Eve in the Garden of Eden. This deception therefore resulted in mankind's defiled gene-pool. This is important because it was the reason why Jesus had to give His life for us. *"For this purpose the Son of God was manifested, that He might destroy the works of the devil."* 1 John 3:8.

Satan and his demons have only one agenda and that is to destroy everything that God has created. This includes the earth itself and its people – their relationships, their health, their prosperity, their aspirations, their children, their belief systems, everything, including their eternal destiny! That's why it is so important to change your spiritual kingdom before this present life is over. After death it will be too late.

People wrongly blame God for negative things in their life but God only brings good things. He may not give us everything we want, but neither does any good parent. He has to look after our well being and some things are just not good for us. Satan and our own wrong choices are the cause of heartache and sickness in this present world. Satan wants everyone to remain in his kingdom until physical death. Then he knows that they will end up in the Lake of Fire with him one day and God will be devastated about that.

Most people are oblivious to the spiritual battle that constantly rages between these two kingdoms. The battle between good and evil is very real. Because of their ignorance, evil is claiming ground at an escalating rate. Many things in the world today are becoming extremely dark and frightening and the Bible predicts that it will become far worse in the coming years. Then Jesus Christ will visibly return as Judge and King!

Why does this precious pearl represent the Lord Jesus Christ? This pearl was hidden in an ordinary oyster shell: there was nothing beautiful in its natural outer form that would suggest its inner beauty. The Bible says that there was nothing beautiful about the Savior. *"He had no beauty or majesty to attract us to him, nothing in his appearance that we should desire him."* Isaiah (53:2b NIV translation.)

Jesus left heaven and was supernaturally conceived by the Holy Spirit of God and born to a virgin as an ordinary baby boy. Jesus, the King of Glory, was born in an animal stable to humble parents and lived a simple life, devoid of the luxuries we today take for granted. Yet, according to the Bible, He is the Creator of the universe! *"All things were made through Him, and without Him nothing was made that was made."* (John 1:3)

Even though Jesus is God, He came hidden in human flesh! He lived on earth and died on the cross as a man. Like a spirit-filled Christian today His miracles were brought about by the power of the indwelling Holy Spirit. Unlike us, He was fully surrendered every waking moment to His Father's will and so the Holy Spirit had total rule in His life.

He is the Son of God but came as the Son of Man because on earth He had to identify totally with us. As such, He completely satisfied God's anger against sin on our behalf, so that we would not have to suffer the penalty of sin ourselves when we die. He was fully human for thirty three years. He successfully completed His mission on earth and returned to the Father. He now sits at the right hand of God interceding for us. He represents us in heaven because He knows firsthand what it is like to be a human and how hard life can be on earth. That is why the Father has handed all authority to His Son to judge mankind at the final judgment.

He experienced every trial and temptation that we do! He suffered hunger, pain, tiredness, disappointment, grief, anger, rejection, humiliation, physical, mental and emotional abuse, stress and every other human emotion. He was constantly misunderstood by His accusers, by the religious leaders and even by His own followers. When He was injured, He bled just like us. But His blood poured out on the cross for us, is the most precious thing on earth!

Yet, He never justified or defended Himself, but always chose to forgive His enemies even when He hung on that brutal cross. As hard as it was for Him to endure the pain, He considered an eternal relationship with us humans more precious than His own life.

His desire to please His Father urged Him on, even though He could have, at any time, called for the angels of God to rescue Him. He said to his disciples: *"My Father loves Me, because I lay down My life that I may take it again. No one takes it from Me, but I lay it down of Myself. I have power to lay it down, and I have power to take it again. This command I have received from My Father.* (John 10:17-18.)

This parable and the parable of the Hidden Treasure both stress the incomparable value of Jesus and His kingdom. The most common interpretation of both parables is that a person should be willing to part with everything they own in order to possess Jesus, the "exquisite pearl of infinite price." However, it has been suggested by some theologians, that another interpretation of both parables could be that Jesus is the purchaser who gave His all, in order to gain us. This seems to be plausible when we read that Paul the Apostle urges the pastors to watch over their flock and to be good shepherds of *"the church of God, which He purchased with His own blood."* *Acts 20:28b*

Because the front cover of this book depicts the Pearl of Great Price, I have gone into much detail with this particular parable. I truly pray that God will use this parable to speak to your heart and that He will reveal His awesome love to you. God bless you.

CHAPTER 31

THE PARABLE OF THE PHARISEE AND THE TAX COLLECTOR
(LUKE 18:9-14)

In Luke 18:9-14, we read the Parable of the Pharisee and the Tax Collector.

"Also He spoke this parable to some who trusted in themselves that they were righteous and despised others: "Two men went up to the temple to pray, one a Pharisee and the other a tax collector. The Pharisee stood and prayed thus within himself, 'God, I thank You that I am not like other men—extortionists, unjust, adulterers, or even as this tax collector. I fast twice a week; I give tithes of all that I possess.'"

"And the tax collector, standing afar off, would not so much as raise his eyes to Heaven, but beat his breast, saying, 'God, be merciful to me a sinner!' I tell you, this man went down to his house justified rather than the other; for everyone who exalts himself will be humbled and he who humbles himself will be exalted."

People say that I wear my heart on my sleeve. But I don't like wearing masks: I don't practice being one person to someone and then someone different to others. Anyone who meets me sees the real me. Anyone who hears me speak or reads my articles hears the truth from my heart. I make no pretences. People say that I make myself too open for criticism, but that's how I am. I don't worry about what others think of me. If I have a message—if I have something to say—I say it as clearly as I can. I reach down into my heart and put as much emotion into what I am saying as I can muster. I may seem odd, but I'm not much for thinking about the consequences of what I say.

Many people are busy wondering what others are going to think of them. They go around carefully planning their words in order to get the right responses. I know who I am. I know that I am important to Jesus Christ. I know that He has given me the ability to visit Him in Heaven through visions and the ability to see angels in dreams. I know that I am loved by Jesus and it is this understanding of His love that gives me confidence and boldness to speak truth from my heart without worrying about consequences.

I surprise people because I share the deepest sins and most disgusting deeds of my past in order that I may share the message of salvation—in order that I may illustrate a point. I don't try to sugar-coat my words. Through verbalizing my thoughts, I have offended people and I am sorry. Of course, I don't want to insult or hurt someone. Sometimes there are things I would like to say to someone, but I manage to restrain myself in love.

In this parable Jesus was comparing two different people: the tax collector was mindful of his sin and pleaded for forgiveness, but the Pharisee saw himself as sinless. He looked down on the tax collector as someone extremely inferior. The Pharisee was truly convinced that his self-righteous acts were pleasing to God. He had no idea that he was using a false measuring stick when measuring holiness! God's level of holiness is perfection, which no one in their own strength can ever meet. The Pharisee measured holiness by comparing himself with others. This is wrong theology: the Bible says we all fall short in the holiness race: if we lose by a meter or by a kilometer, we still lose! The Pharisee was a very "religious" man, who was full of his own importance.

There are heaps of people like the Pharisee and some of them sit in church each week. Everybody, when asked if they are a good person, will automatically respond straight away, saying: "Yes, I am a good person!" That's because we compare ourselves to others and not to Jesus Christ, who is God's only measuring rod.

At the risk of sounding prideful, the tax collector in this story is much like me. He beats his breast and he says, "God, be merciful to me a sinner!" You will notice that the tax collector stood "afar off," in this story because he was too ashamed to go close up to the temple. He kept his eyes lowered to the ground because he felt so low and unworthy.

Some people mistakenly think that those who do not know Christ do not understand that they are sinners. But the Bible says different. In Romans Chapter 1, we learn that God has made Himself very clear to unbelievers. He has made His presence understandable, so that every person in this world is without excuse on judgment day. Every person, whether you choose to believe it or not, knows that there is a God, even the ones that deny this fact. Why would they deny a God when in the first place they did not acknowledge that there is a God? They just *choose* to deny God. Everyone knows of their own sins: they know the wrongs they have done. Some people are more honest about their sins and openly confess them. Others are more private.

God has given everyone a personal conscience, but He warns us that if we deliberately keep sinning in a certain area, our conscience will become hardened or seared so that it no longer convicts us. This is a very frightening place to be in, because it is our conscience that assists us to respond to the Holy Spirit's conviction in our life.

This tax collector in our parable was not making a big deal of his sin. He was just pleading to God to be merciful to him. In today's language, it is hard to understand how bad a tax collector was. In the Roman days, tax collectors extorted people. Their bad deeds were known by the public, but even with all the descriptions, it is hard to understand how bad this man was, because we do not have the modern equivalent of a tax collector.

The best way I can describe how a tax collector was loathed in the Jewish society—and shunned for that matter, is to mention the word "pedophile." I think if we replaced the words "tax collector" with the word "pedophile," we would see the significance of this parable; if there was a Pharisee standing in the temple praying and then a known pedophile went to the temple and was beating his breast and saying, 'God, be merciful to me a sinner!'—I think we would have a clearer idea of how controversial this parable was in its day. The word "pedophile" brings with it a feeling of disgust to our mind, especially when you have been abused by one.

The point is: Jesus is saying that this man who beat his breast, walked away justified. God saw what he did and was compassionate to him. He implied: "You are forgiven, totally forgiven, because you have been humble and truthful and I accept your prayer."

The point of the whole parable is in the opening and closing remarks. Verse 9 *"Also He spoke this parable to some who trusted in themselves that they were righteous and despised others:* At the end of our reading, Jesus said: "everyone *who exalts himself will be humbled, and he who humbles himself will be exalted."*

There are Christians who major on the importance of personal holiness. They point out that in order to be saved we have to be holy and righteous before God. They speak of a God who reproves, judges, and disciplines people. They stress that we *have to do* certain things to gain God's approval such as: read the Bible, pray, go to church and tithe. They say that when we do these things we will be close to God and will be accepted by Him.

I once fully agreed with this, but now I disagree. I am accepted by God for one reason: I have placed my faith in His Son Jesus Christ and now, spiritually Ephesians 2:5-6 says that I am seated in the heavenly places with Christ Jesus my Savior and Lord. In John 19:20 Jesus on the cross uttered these final words: *"It is finished!"* and then gave up His spirit to God. I cannot add to His work! My spirit is just as holy as God's Spirit and God has promised to work on my soul and body until I die to bring them in line with His will.

Some verses robbed me of joy, but not anymore! Verses like James 2:10: *"For whoever shall keep the whole law and yet stumble in one point, he is guilty of all."* James wasn't trying to be legalistic, he was pointing out that no one can live a perfect life without God.

So, how righteous are you, reader? Have you sinned once in the past month? Many people think that they are sinless; that they have totally conquered sin and they are not sinning anymore. I was like one of these people, except that I had an addiction which I could not rid myself of. I would have some successes three months here and four months there. I would have certain breaks in my addiction. I would conquer it for a while through repentance and right living, but then it would come back again. In retrospect, I think I was trying to place my "addiction" into some different box to "sin!" All I know is that it was always a stumbling block to me when I thought I was just so holy and righteous.

I also had a tendency to gossip and *I knew that was a sin!* So, although I paraded myself around as more holy, more devout, more righteous, more zealous for the things of God than most people, I was failing in two points at least! I was stumbling in two areas and James says that from breaking just one Law, *I was guilty of breaking all of them.*

When you think you are righteous, you go around judging other people. You are comparing yourself with other people. The apostle Paul says it is not healthy to compare yourself with others. The righteousness that Jesus won for us on the cross is the only righteousness we are to glory in! If we boast and take glory in our own self works—we are filthy, Scripture says. If you think you are personally righteous, you are wrong: you are not! You are full of pride and Jesus says that if you exalt yourself, you will be humbled. I have had a lot of humbling over the years, I can assure you.

No one regardless of how hard they try can deserve salvation. It is only by faith in Jesus Christ that we can be saved. These following Scriptures are important to understand:

But God who is rich in mercy, because of His great love with which He loved us, EVEN, when we were dead in trespasses, made us alive together with Christ (by grace you have been saved) and raised us up together, and made us sit together in the heavenly places in Christ Jesus, that in the ages to come He might show the exceeding riches of His grace in His kindness toward us in Christ Jesus. For by grace you have been saved through faith, and that not of yourselves; it is the gift of God, not of works, lest anyone should boast." Ephesians 2:4-9.

"Therefore, having been justified by faith, we have peace with God through our Lord Jesus Christ, through whom also we have access by faith into this grace, in which we stand, and rejoice in hope of the glory of God." Romans 5:1-2.

Imagine you have a farm and your dam is empty. There is a creek nearby with fresh running water. If you place a hose in the creek and pump water to your property tap, you can access this water for your crops. Let's rename the hose and call it "faith in Jesus." Also, let's rename the creek water and call it "God's grace." We can now paraphrase these Scriptures: *"We are not saved by any self-righteous works that we have ever done, but we are only saved by the righteous works that Jesus did on our behalf. When we place our faith in Jesus, then God's grace waters our life, so that the works we do, are done in the power of His strength and not from any strength or ability of our own."*

Faith in Jesus is the carrier of God's grace. It is God's grace that gives us the power to resist sin and even when we fall, it is still God's grace that forgives us. The tax collector's sins were forgiven by grace: the Pharisee came away from his praying exactly the same as he was before he opened his mouth! I pray that I have brought some understanding to you in this parable.

CHAPTER 32

THE PARABLE OF THE PRODIGAL SON
(LUKE 15:11-32)

Despite familiarity, don't overlook this parable. It may have an important message for you. I have recorded the whole passage, so let's begin - Luke 15:11-32.

Then He said: *"A certain man had two sons. And the younger of them said to his father, 'Father, give me the portion of goods that falls to me.' So he divided to them his livelihood. And not many days after, the younger son gathered all together, journeyed to a far country and there wasted his possessions with prodigal living. But when he had spent all, there arose a severe famine in that land and he began to be in want. Then he went and joined himself to a citizen of that country and he sent him into his fields to feed swine. And he would gladly have filled his stomach with the pods that the swine ate and no one gave him anything.*

But when he came to himself, he said, "How many of my father's hired servants have bread enough and to spare and I perish with hunger! I will arise and go to my father and will say to him, 'Father, I have sinned against heaven and before you, and I am no longer worthy to be called your son. Make me like one of your hired servants.'"

"And he arose and came to his father. But when he was still a great way off, his father saw him and had compassion and ran and fell on his neck and kissed him. And the son said to him, 'Father, I have sinned against heaven and in your sight, and am no longer worthy to be called your son.'

"But the father said to his servants, 'Bring out the best robe and put it on him and put a ring on his hand and sandals on his feet and bring the fattened calf here and kill it and let us eat and be merry; for this my son was dead and is alive again; he was lost and is found.' And they began to be merry.

"Now his older son was in the field. And as he came and drew near to the house, he heard music and dancing. So he called one of the servants and asked what these things meant. And he said to him, 'Your brother has come and because he has received him safe and sound, your father has killed the fattened calf.'

"But he was angry and would not go in. Therefore his father came out and pleaded with him. So he answered and said to his father, 'Lo, these many years I have been serving you; I never transgressed your commandment at any time; and yet you never gave me a young goat that I might make merry with my friends. But as soon as this son of yours came, who has devoured your livelihood with harlots; you killed the fattened calf for him.'

"And he said to him, 'Son, you are always with me and all that I have is yours. It was right that we should make merry and be glad, for your brother was dead and is alive again and was lost and is found.'"

You will see that the younger son repented of his foolishness in leaving home. He wasn't just sad about it: he actually *did something* about it! Repentance causes positive action - to no longer go in the wrong direction but to turn and go in the right direction. When we turn from God and do our own thing, we land in trouble! Pride prevents us from true repentance and putting things in order. The Father has compassion; he will not make you a slave. He will restore you to full son-ship with Him. God longs for us to come to Him.

This parable used to upset me because it was only recently that I really received revelation on it. Sarah, a good friend of mine, lent me a book on the Prodigal Son. The book spoke about pride in the older brother. He felt he was righteous and his younger brother was not. Because of his good works, He believed he deserved his father's love more than his younger brother who went away and lived a prodigal life.

Sarah gave me a paragraph to read in her book and it deeply convicted my spirit. The older brother's thoughts and actions were like mine! It made me really sad because it revealed my own disgusting attitude. That repentance began the process of change in my life. I knew that I was not living the life that God wanted for me. You have to be sad to change! You have to know that there is a need for change before it can take place in your life. This book clearly did that for me. It dawned on me that, like the brother, I was actually living a "self-righteous" life! I was striving to be holy by my own works.

In July 2010, I discovered the teachings of Joseph Prince and Andrew Wommack. My life changed because my theology had taken an "about turn." The ideas that I had zealously clung to for sixteen years were proved to be totally wrong. My concept of personal holiness, righteousness and sanctification was not Biblical. I had seriously mistaken beliefs about God. In fact, I was wrong about most of my "Christian ideas!" That is the contextual backdrop for what I have to say as we look at this parable.

The second son had insisted that his father give him his inheritance right away so that he could enjoy life! In the Old Testament, Deuteronomy 21:18-21 it speaks about a rebellious child: if a child was rebellious once, he should be warned. If he was rebellious a second time, he should be brought before the elders of the city and then stoned to death. I am so thankful that we live in a time of grace now!

The Jewish audience, who were listening to Jesus, would have readily picked up that there was something quite different about this parable. Jesus was talking about a rebellious son and yet His story did not have the son stoned. In fact, the father willingly gave in to his rebellious son's demands. Also, for a son to demand early payment of his inheritance was akin to him saying, "Dad, I want you dead!"

Instead of rebuking the son, the father may have had to sell some of his land, or his sheep, to give the son one third of his worth, leaving two-thirds to the older brother, who was his first-born son. The oldest son had responsibilities and privileges that other siblings didn't have in those days.

Let's say, that in Sydney today, a third of an average house would be worth about two hundred thousand dollars. If this house had with it, full time servants, we can assume that the younger son was given up to the equivalent of a third of a million dollars at least.

The lad then went and squandered his whole inheritance with drinking and wild living. There was a famine. Jobs were scarce so he ended up feeding pigs! Because pigs were considered "unclean" this young Jewish lad knew he had reached rock bottom! He had now finally come to his senses and thought about his father's servants. They were treated far better and were in a much healthier situation than he was. He decided to go home.

Christian, have you really been home to see the Father? Spiritually, we are seated in Heavenly places with God. Are you a person who has felt the Father's embrace? Do you accept that you are seated in Heavenly places and are holy and righteous? Or do you feel like a wretched sinner? Do you fall in sin and cannot seem to erase its memory from your mind? Do you have trouble staying clean and righteous? Does it seem as though your life resembles a pig pen? Do you long for a way where you could feel forgiven? Do you need the power to stop all the sin in your life? Or like I was, are you in denial? Even though I related to some of the above things yet I also identified with the older brother who I saw as being faithful and obedient. I had sins in my life, but I used to try to excuse them.

Back to the parable: The prodigal returned. The father saw him a long way off and ran to him. I have been told that in the Jewish custom of that day, fathers did not run towards their children. They were to be honored and respected and would expect their children to come to them. The father in this parable illustrates the sheer joy that God the Father has when a prodigal child returns. Rather than wait for them to get to Him, He will run towards them, longing to welcome them home. So once again, a parable of Jesus breaks the Jewish traditional customs. You see, the message of grace breaks all customs! The idea that we can be sinners and still be embraced by God is scandalous.

One time, in the midst of my addiction, I was taken in a vision to Heaven where Jesus wanted me to go into the throne room and meet His Father. As a sinner, I was petrified to meet our holy God, but Jesus urged me and told me not to fear and then He took me inside. The Father embraced me with His love, yet I was a filthy sinner! Four days before this visit to Heaven I had been in the arms of a prostitute.

The father in this parable is a true representation of our Father in Heaven. He hushed his son's excuses and his carefully rehearsed speech and excitedly called to his servants:

"Bring out the best robe and put it on him and put a ring on his hand and sandals on his feet and bring the fattened calf here and kill it and let us eat and be merry; for this my son was dead and is alive again; he was lost and is found."

The robe signified the robe of righteousness that Jesus has given to all believers. Whether we can handle it or not, we are righteous in God's sight if we are born again. You may protest about being righteous but you would be just like I was for those sixteen long years, believing wrong theology.

A ring was placed on his finger, symbolizing an official sign of authority. It could be used as a seal or as a stamp for official documents. It represented all kinds of financial duties. The New Testament writings teach that we also have been given authority in God's kingdom. We, as co-heirs "with Christ" have spiritual power and authority to do great things. Yet without knowledge of this power and authority, we are ineffective.

The son's ambition was to become a servant for his father. Servants had no shoes but now he was given sandals for his feet to protect him from the dusty roads. This reminds me of Jesus washing His disciples' feet, showing that walking in this world will mean that our feet will get dirty, but we can be washed daily by Him. In the Book of Ephesians, it says that we are clad with the shoes of the Gospel of peace.

This son had a wonderful testimony of his father's love and compassion. Every Christian has a unique testimony of our heavenly Father's love. Many of us believe that our personal story is not exciting enough to share with others. Always remember that your story is unique: you are unique! Whatever your story, it still demonstrates God's love and power on earth today! You should never feel that your story is not worthy of being shared. I remember when I was only about ten years old I heard an exciting testimony by a motor bike-rider, who had lived a life or crime and drug taking. That night I asked God to give me a strong testimony of Hi overcoming love and power so that I could share it with others one day. (On reflection, maybe that was an unwise prayer!)

A ring was placed on his son's finger. This brings to my mind a personal testimony. One time in another vision I had once. I went to Heaven and met the Father. Jesus put a robe around me, a crown on my head and a ring on my finger.

Now what about the older brother? The father had organized a huge celebration feast for his once lost son. This angered the brother and he blatantly refused to attend the party.

It is easy for a Christian who is doing all the "good" *Christian* things, to begin to think that they are better than others. When you feel you have a good relationship with Jesus; you are very zealous with the things of God and you are always trying to learn more about the Kingdom. But you might become quite proud of yourself! I certainly did!

If you met an unbeliever who is gay you might be quite friendly to them as a way of helping them see the love of Jesus. But if you saw a gay man holding his boyfriend's hand while praising God at church, your attitude may totally change! You might suddenly rise up in judgment and comment to others that they should not be allowed to come to church as a practicing gay couple. You might forget that once you were an unwashed sinner! You may forget the thousands of times that you have been forgiven. You just think about how they should be told to stop coming to church if they will not change.

There might be a man in your church who has a gambling problem and every time he sees you, he wants to borrow money. You know he has a gambling problem and now you will not even treat him like a human. You tell others: "I'm not going to give him my money! How could he be in such a mess and still call himself a Christian?"

How quickly we forget that being conformed to the likeness of Christ in our soul and body takes an entire lifetime! God has started a work in us and has promised to complete it. (Philippians 1:6) In the meantime we should rejoice that the Holy Spirit is bringing wounded people to us, so that we can love them as Jesus does. They will at least hear the Word of God being taught. When they are convicted by the Holy Spirit they will change. In the meantime their faith will develop.

Like the older son. You might be full of self works, self-righteousness and pride and you might need to change. Or, you may resemble the son who was lost in sin. Either way, there is good news for you. God knows all about both of these sons and He has answers for both situations. Why don't you run to Him?

The Father's arms are continually outstretched toward you.

CHAPTER 33

THE PARABLE OF THE RICH MAN AND LAZARUS (LUKE 16:19-31)

Luke 16:19-31 reads:

"There was a certain rich man who was clothed in purple and fine linen, and fed sumptuously every day, but there was a certain beggar named Lazarus, full of sores, who was laid at his gate, desiring to be fed with the crumbs which fell from the rich man's table. Moreover, the dogs came and licked his sores.

"So it was that the beggar died and was carried by the angels to Abraham's bosom. The rich man also died, was buried. And being in the torments of Hades, he lifted up his eyes and saw Abraham afar off and Lazarus in his bosom. Then he cried and said, 'Father Abraham, have mercy on me and send Lazarus that he may dip the tip of his finger in water and cool my tongue, for I am tormented in this flame.'

"But Abraham said, 'Son, remember that in your lifetime, you received your good things and likewise Lazarus evil things, but now he is comforted and you are tormented. And besides all this, between us and you there is a great gulf fixed, so that those who want to pass from here to you cannot, nor can those from there, pass to us.'

"Then he said, 'I beg you therefore, father, that you would send him to my father's house for I have five brothers; that he may testify to them, lest they also come to this place of torment.'

"Abraham said to him, 'They have Moses and the prophets; let them hear them.' And he said, 'No Father Abraham; but if one goes to them from the dead, they will repent.'

"But he said to him, 'If they do not hear Moses and the prophets, neither will they be persuaded though one rise from the dead."

Jesus, in other parables, talks of "certain" people. He may refer to their profession, but He doesn't name them. Here, the beggar is named "Lazarus." I truly believe that this is not a true parable but because others think it is, I include it here in my book.

I had listed the parables alphabetically and when I found that I was up to this one, my heart sunk and I went to bed. I was going to sleep, but the Lord urged me to get up and begin work despite my lack of enthusiasm for I didn't care for the subject matter. I came to Christ at age eight and I am now forty three years old. In all that time, I have never come to grips with the concept of Hell. Not that I don't believe in it, because Jesus spoke more about Hell, than Heaven. Also, I have heard and read much teaching on the subject and I've heard "near death" testimonies that send chills up my spine. I have no personal fear, but I have a hard time accepting the consequences that are ahead for people who do not give their lives to Jesus and follow Him.

The story centers on a "certain" rich man and a beggar "named Lazarus." Jesus said in Matthew 19:24: *"It is easier for a camel to go through the eye of a needle than for a rich man to enter the kingdom of God."* People say that there was a "Needle Gate" in Jerusalem and for a camel to enter that gate; it had to drop to its knees and be relieved of its load, before entering. It took humility and self-control for a camel to do this.

Other people reject the idea of a gate but suggest Jesus was talking about a little sewing needle and it was near impossible to put anything through the tiny hole. So, whatever your school of thought, Jesus stated that it was extremely hard for a rich person to go to Heaven. The man in this story was very rich!

An abundance of resources, can rob us of a personal need of God. This is confirmed by statistics. Generally, an upturn in prosperity can lead to a downturn in spirituality. In India, there is a cast system that operates, where the lower cast is far more open to the things of God than those in the higher cast system.

I have met an Indian apostle who visits his country often. He is an exception to this rule. He had been very wealthy but empty spiritually, but He then found Jesus. He said that the Christians are quite successful at converting the lower cast: the poor, the beggars, the working class servants and people who have a hunger for answers and are willing to convert to Christianity, but it is near impossible to reach the rich. Do not misunderstand what I say. To be rich is not wrong or evil in God's sight. Money itself is neither good nor bad; the Lord wants to bless His children. It is just that when your needs can be easily solved by money, then the rich will not look to God for help.

Lazarus was outside the gate begging for "crumbs" while the dogs licked his wounds. Perhaps the servants of the rich man would come to the gate each day and leave him with the household food scraps. (I guess you could call him their living garbage bin.)

In Mark 7:24-30 A Gentile woman, (a non-Jew) asked Jesus to heal her distraught daughter, He replied: "It isn't right to take the children's bread and toss it to the dogs" This sounds rude and hard but Jesus was saying that His ministry was meant for the Jews and not the Gentiles. (The Jews nicknamed any Gentile a "dog") To the woman's credit she didn't appear to be offended, such was her desire to see her child healed. She graciously replied: "Even the dogs under the table eat the children's crumbs." She was saying that she'd gladly take the crumbs of Jesus' ministry that were left behind after the Jews had taken their fill. Jesus saw her great faith and healed her daughter.

In the rubbish heaps in the Philippines, hundreds of people struggle to exist. People may say: "Well, the rich are so selfish!" But really, you and I make up the rich. Even a Government pension in the West is a fortune to them. People who are poor in the West are very rich, so when you listen to a parable like this, do not consider yourself poor.

This particular rich man went to Hell, and being in the torment of Hades, he lifted up his eyes and saw Abraham far off and Lazarus in his bosom. Many Jehovah's Witnesses and Seventh Day Adventists say there is no Hell, but those of us who are born again know there is a Hell and it really is a place in which you do not want to end up. Seventh Day Adventists will say that there is such a thing as "soul-sleep." They say that after death, you stay in this soul-sleep until the resurrection of the dead.

This parable is saying that there was a Paradise like a pre-Jesus' resurrection, and there was a Hell where people were actually burning. The slightest hint of soothing water was longed for and appreciated. It says in verse 24, *"that he may dip the tip of his finger in the water and cool my tongue."*

Before the resurrection of Jesus, it is believed that there was a place in the lowest parts of the earth called "Hades," which had two distinct and separate compartments. One part was the temporary hell called "Sheol." The other compartment, though visible to those in Sheol, was separated by a huge chasm that no one could cross. This beautiful place was called "Paradise." You might remember that on the cross, Jesus told the believing thief that He would see Him in Paradise that very day. Lazarus was in Paradise, along with all the other believers from the time of Adam to the time of the resurrection of Christ. The most honored place in Paradise was a place called "Abraham's Bosom" which was reserved for the very closest friends of God. In this story Lazarus was resting here while the rich man was in agony in Sheol.

The Bible infers in 1 Peter, Ephesians 4 and in other places, that when Jesus died, He descended to Hades to release all the spirits and souls of the believers waiting in Paradise. (Our physical body returns to dust as it's only a temporary shell that houses the real person!) Jesus also visited Sheol where He proclaimed total victory over the devil. His victory over death validated the Father's full satisfaction of the Atonement demonstrated on the cross. (God's wrath against sin had been vindicated!)

Generally speaking, the world has no idea how wonderful the Gospel is. Unbelievers are totally ignorant that their sins have already been punished and forgiven by God and that they only have to call out to God for mercy.

Let me illustrate this to you: Imagine a rich uncle left you a million dollars and his lawyer rang and asked you for your bank details so that he could deposit your inheritance. And you angrily replied: "I hate him and never wanted anything to do with him and he knew it! You must have the wrong person." Then slammed the phone down and totally ignored the incident. That is what unbelievers do: they refuse to accept their inheritance!

There are countless people heading for a lost eternity in Hell when they need not be. Jesus Christ completed a legal transaction on the cross for everyone to avail themselves of. Yet, we can read in the funeral notices every week the words "Rest in Peace" or see on graves in the cemetery "R.I.P." even if the deceased had been the most anti-Jesus person on earth and would certainly not now be enjoying God's peace!

Be assured: there is such a place as Hell for the people who reject Jesus Christ, and essentially, this book of parables—Christ's message—is that we have to be the light to the world. I do not want to bear you down with guilt, shame and condemnation, but many of the people you know—friends, relatives and workmates—many of them are counting on you and your witness to lead them to salvation. There are people in every Christian's life heading for Hell, because the Christians they came across failed to share the Gospel.

There is another sobering message for me to share: Jesus left the "physical" part of salvation to the sheep. While it's a fact that no one can come to God unless the Holy Spirit draws them, believers have a big part to play in telling the message of salvation. Many people rely on their pastor or an evangelist to share salvation to people. Pastors do not give birth to pastors. However, sheep give birth to sheep! That is God's natural order of multiplication. It is natural for sheep to give birth to sheep, and it is natural for sheep to share rich pasture with their sheep friend. That's just how it is!

The rich man wanted Abraham to send Lazarus to his brothers on earth. Obviously, now he did have mercy and compassion! Note also that his memory was retained even while in Hell. Some people say we have no memory of our life, but this rich man was fully aware that he had brothers who were destined for Hell too, and he wanted to save them. It is even more surprising to me, that Abraham replied in verse 31, *"But if they do not heed Moses and the prophets, neither will they be persuaded though one rises from the dead."*

That's true! Jesus physically rose from the dead, yet most people do not believe Him or His message. Multitudes of people have been raised from the dead around the world. In the East, in Africa, in India and even in America,—when people are raised from the dead, massive conversions take place. I actually met and spoke to a man who had been dead for four days and I share these details in Chapter 18 of this book.

Andrew Wommack raised someone from the dead in a church, and the church attendance went from fourteen people to one hundred people in a town with a population of one hundred and fifty. Raising people from the dead is possible and it always causes revival.

I have written this book as an outreach to people who perhaps would never attend a church or those who are ignorant of the true Gospel message. People "choose to believe" or they "choose not to believe," but they must be told! Perhaps someone you love and pray for may read my book and in the process, the Holy Spirit may do a wonderful work! Jesus is God's gift to us, but an unwrapped or a rejected gift is not used: It doesn't benefit anyone even though the giver may have sacrificed everything they had in order to purchase and present it to us. God sacrificed His most precious possession for us. We all have unsaved relatives and friends. I really urge you to keep them in prayer.

This parable would certainly not have been spoken for our entertainment. Also, we know that it is God's will for all people to be saved. May you be led by the Holy Spirit.

CHAPTER 34

THE PARABLE OF THE RICH FOOL
(LUKE 12:16-21)

If you are not reading these parables in sequence, you might do well to first read the previous one "The Rich Man and Lazarus." There, I share about a rich man in Hell.

Once again, this parable is rather scary. In Luke 12:16-21 Jesus said: *"The ground of a certain rich man yielded plentifully. And he thought within himself, saying, 'What shall I do, since I have no room to store my crops?' So he said, 'I will do this: I will pull down my barns and build greater, and there I will store all my crops and my goods. And I will say to my soul, "Soul, you have many goods laid up for many years; take your ease; eat, drink, and be merry."' But God said to him, 'Fool! This night your soul will be required of you; then whose will those things be which you have provided?' So is he who lays up treasure for himself, and is not rich toward God"*

We have the summary of this parable in the last sentence: *"So is he who lays up treasure for himself, and is not rich toward God"* (Luke 12:21).

In the Gospel of Matthew 6:19-20, Jesus told His listeners not to lay up treasure on earth where moth or rust can destroy it, or where thieves can break in and steal it. Instead, we are to store up treasure in heaven where we will not lose it. What is the treasure in Heaven that is better than earthly treasures?

Treasure in Heaven is having an intimate relationship with God, allowing Him to work in and through us to further His Kingdom purpose on earth through the blessings, talents and gifting He has given us. This kind of treasure lasts forever and brings us rewards.

One way to help someone discover this treasure might be to buy them a copy of this book. Definitely, laying up treasure in Heaven includes giving to the poor or responding to the Holy Spirit when He prompts you to speak to someone about Jesus. Jesus said by laying up treasure for yourself, you will not be rich towards God.

The Bible has much to say about money. Many people have a problem with giving their money to God. It is a fact that most people spend more on entertainment each week than they give to God. Some Christians spend about four times more on Christian resources for their own use than they give to God towards the Gospel. They come to church with just change in their pockets for the offering plate. If they knew God's book-keeping principles, they would want to give God as much as they could! But this is a lesson that God teaches only when we give by faith in His goodness!

This parable is pretty simple: it doesn't need much explanation. Some people say that this parable is about someone who lived two thousand years ago, who harvested a bumper crop and stored it up. He then just planned to eat, drink and be merry from then on. But God changed all that very suddenly! This parable is still relevant today.

That is the lifestyle of many people in this world. They work during the week and party the weekends. They wrongly assume that this is what life is all about. It says in Scripture that in the "last days," people will be partying and being married just like they were before the judgment came in Noah's day. Life will be going on just as it has always done! But then quite suddenly, all that will change, just like it did back then!

There is nothing wrong with sensible drinking and partying. I don't feel that Jesus would have turned water into wine at His friend's wedding, if that was the case. I think that the issue was that people were habitually spending money and time doing things that did not profit the Kingdom of God. I believe that Jesus still takes issue with those who continually feed their own ego without a thought of helping those less fortunate.

It is a sobering thought that we could live a totally godless life on earth. But many people chase after frivolous things with no thought of tomorrow. Yes, they may be happily enjoying life, but one day end up in eternal flames just like the rich man in Chapter 33.

I have trouble with this subject. I have read Mary K Baxter's "A Divine Revelation of Hell." If it is true that Hell is really burning now, just like Jesus said in that parable—if it is true that it is so hot that just a drip of water will relieve you—then, that is not a place you want your friends to go to. That is not a place you want to end up going to. It should not be a place that you would want anyone to go to.

Having to buy every new gizmo that comes onto the market to keep up with the latest craze is ridiculous: it will be outdated before you even work out its full potential! By indulging oneself with continual extravagant living means that those who need money to minister the Gospel here or in other countries will almost certainly be denied. Also, by being stingy on earth, eternal rewards are in serious doubt. We need to realize that people are heading for a lost eternity and suffering terribly not only because *of wrong choices they make, but often because of the selfish choices that God's own people make!*

I am not here to bring condemnation and shame to my readers, but I need to give a wake-up call that people are suffering needlessly, when by sharing our resources, we could make such a difference to the outreach of the Gospel message. But, only God's compassion flowing in a person will cause them to release their money to others.

If you have compassion, your attitude towards money and giving to the Lord is wide open. If you do not have compassion, mercy and the love of God flowing in you, you will be very tight fisted with your money. That is really what verse 21 says: "He, who lays up treasure for himself, will not be rich toward God."

So treasure is not just about stocks and bonds. I have been told that most Americans could not survive two or three weeks without an income or bank savings money. Treasure, in the West includes buying a house and having a brand new car plus other luxuries purchased on credit. For them, that is all the kind of treasure they chase after.

We, in the West, live in a "throw away" and an "instant" society. People have a "try-before-you-buy" mentality. Couples live together before committing to marriage. Even Christian couples don't seem to see this as "fornication." Or they marry, but if their spouse does not make them "happy" they simply move on and try someone else. Commitment is an old fashioned idea these days. Happiness is the twenty-first century word! Even products we buy today are not designed to last because the manufacturer wants them to have a short life expectancy so you will buy their updated version.

In our parent's day people were happy to have a modest two-three bedroom cottage and saved for each piece of furniture. Today however, many youngsters expect to live in lavish four bedroom homes, 2 bathrooms, an office and sundeck. Then they go and buy a whole house full of furniture on credit. We are money mad and credit is our accepted resource. There is so much danger in this mentality. But even if you do have a healthy bank balance, this will not guarantee happiness.

When we are spiritually rich, we will have an abundance of the good things in life, including material possessions. Part of living an abundant life is having enough for your own needs, plus having enough to help someone less fortunate. That is God's heart! He doesn't want His own kids to be scrimping and saving to make ends meet. Jesus wants us to have an abundant life. (John 10:10)

God loves to bless His children! It is a myth that is perpetuated by the world, that Christians should be in poverty, lest people should think that they are selfish or not giving enough to the poor. A lot of aspersion is cast upon Pastors if they have a new car, or live in a nice home. But Jesus never said that Christians should be in lack. What He is saying in this parable is that we need to watch our attitude towards money and the things of this world. Matthew 6:21warns: *"Where your treasure is, there your heart will be also."*

If we allow money and the material things of life to dominate our thoughts and be our focus, we end up idolizing those things, and our heart will be geared towards the pursuit of them. The well known saying: *"The love of money is a root of all kinds of evil"* comes from Scripture - Timothy 6:10. Note that it is the *love of money* that is the problem, not the money itself. It is clearly our attitude towards it that can become a problem.

Instead, we need to regard our finances as a tool to equip us to be good stewards for God. Rather than becoming possessive about our money and allowing the world to dictate what we spend it on, let us instead allow God to move us in how we spend our money, which is ultimately His anyway because He gave it to us. People say "what I do with my money is my business!" Just remember, it is God who gave you the intellect and the physical capacity to do things, and the mental drive to reach your goal, which enabled you to get a job in the first place. Many people don't have these things: they were born with disabilities or have had no positive input into their life.

There is a real joy in giving and in knowing that people are blessed. I pray that this parable has put money and the worlds "treasure" into perspective and that as you put heavenly treasures first in your life, you will know what it is to live in abundance, for this is God's promise to us in Matthew 6:33 which says: *"Seek first the Kingdom of God and all these other things will be added to you."* God does not want you to miss out on the good things in life!

When God's priority, becomes our priority, we will not be able to contain all the blessings He will shower upon us. God is an extravagant God in everything He does! You only have to look around at nature to know that! The word "stingy" is a worldly attitude; it doesn't ever relate to our God who promised in Ephesians 3:20 that *"He is able to bless us exceedingly abundantly above all that we ask or think."*

What is your imagination like? Do you dream great dreams? God can do all that and far more!

CHAPTER 35

THE PARABLE OF THE SALT WITHOUT TASTE (MATTHEW 5:13)

Matthew 5:13 reads:

"You are the salt of the earth; but if the salt loses its flavor, how shall it be seasoned? It is then good for nothing but to be thrown out and trampled underfoot by men."

Jesus here was talking about salt being no longer salty. Has anyone told you that you are good for nothing? Or did your teacher ever tell you that you would never amount to anything? Have you been told by your parents that you are useless? It's not a good feeling: it makes you feel humiliated and even rejected.

Before we begin our parable, I just want to let you know that when people place negative words on your life, they are actually cursing you. On the cross, Jesus not only took the world's sin and sicknesses upon Himself but He also took every curse in the whole world upon Himself. He relinquished all curses on our behalf by becoming a "curse" for us! (It is interesting that the devil causes unbelievers to curse the name of Jesus all the time!)

Proverbs 18:21-22 says: *"Death and life are in the power of the tongue and those who love it will eat its fruit."* Our words can have a positive or a negative impact both on ourselves and on others. We are to personally claim the power of the blood of Jesus over every curse that has been placed on us and in His name, break its power in our lives!

In the Old Testament people focused on the external matters of the Law, but Jesus was focused on the internal matters of our heart. Hence Jesus wants us to be salt to others by living responsibly and by bringing the flavor of God into the world's corruptive nature. Did you know that salt is used in fertilizers, but if it is used in excess, it will make the soil sterile: nothing will grow! In the same way, when we season our food, we are to just sprinkle: we are not to overload it with seasoning.

Jesus was certainly not saying that you are good for nothing if you are a Christian and you are not having an impact on the world. When Jesus walked on earth, He preached law and grace. *He is the grace of God* and He preached the message of love. Jesus shared the practical ways of how to express love to others. Yes, Jesus was all about love, but He was deliberately setting God's standards so high, that His hearers would realize that they could never measure up in their own strength. When we come to that knowledge we are in a good position to seek personal salvation. Until then we will remain lost.

Jesus expounded the Law in such a way that it just made it impossible to be free from sin. For instance, He shared that to look at a woman with lust was to commit adultery in your heart. That statement alone would convict most men if they are honest.

The inference that Jesus made about "un-salty" salt being good for nothing, but to be thrown out and trampled underfoot by men – can be most offensive! Many Christians are trampled underfoot by others in life. Many believers are condemned and judged unfairly because of their Christian life, but suffering and persecution for righteousness' sake is a good thing and something to be treasured. Jesus is talking about something more here.

How can anyone *become salt?* I have heard it said and preached many times that salt not only enhances the flavor of food but that it is also a natural preservative. Salt helps to stop bacteria from growing. Therefore, salt in Christians can prevent the growth of sin in their life and in the lives of others. There are many ways we can become salt in the world. For example, in your workplace when people are swearing and gossiping, you can set a passive standard by noticeably refusing to take part, or you can even take a more positive stand by verbally correcting them. It depends on your temperament and your allegiance to your faith.

I have spent hundreds of hours watching videos of Andrew Wommack. That is why I keep mentioning him in this book. He told a story about his experience in basic training in the Army. He was in a room with about fifty men, waiting to be paid. Standing with him was a foul-mouthed and angry man who was blaspheming God. In every sentence, he was dragging Jesus into his anger issue. He was constantly blaspheming and swearing. Andrew, who could not stand it anymore, said to him, "Stop it man! Just stop it!"

The astonished man threw a punch at Andrew, but then Andrew said something which stopped the man in his tracks and he did not hit Andrew anymore. He asked the man what the name of his girlfriend was and then said to him: "How would you react if every time someone was angry, they yelled out her name, and used her name as a cuss word?"

The man didn'tanswer. In fact every person in the room just stood in silence for about thirty minutes, as they waited to be paid. After that episode, none of the fifty men in basic training would speak to Andrew. Each lunch time he would sit by himself and he was ostracized, but he stood up for righteousness' sake.

Well, that is being salt. That was a reminder to the men that there were standards they had crossed. Being salt is standing up and correcting something when it is not right.

This past week I found out something that was not right. When I found out about it I went and told someone to do something about it and make it right. The situation was resolved.

Being salt is refusing to sit by and ignore an injustice, an untruth, or a wrong attitude or action. There is a famous cliché that says, 'evil seems to triumph when good men do nothing.' I am not big on quoting clichés in anything. In fact, I think that is the first time in this series of parables that I have used a cliché, but it is so true. We are supposed to make a difference in this world. We are supposed to stand out.

The moral decline of America and other places in the world can be directly associated with the lack of integrity, personal holiness and devotion to God by the Christians living there. The opposite of being salty is to be passive. When we are passive we open the door to the devil to win in a situation without even having to fight.

People don't really listen to what you say until they have watched you do what you do. It is shameful to know that I am talking to someone on Facebook or online for half an hour, and then when I ask him when do they have to go to bed or when are they going to go, they would answer, "No, it is okay. I am at work." I find it appalling that a Christian would spend his work time talking to me! If I had known it within the first five minutes, I would have broken off the conversation. Because of it, I am now more aware of American time zones!

But non-Christians see this happen! Not many non-Christians read the Bible because without the help of the Holy Spirit, it is too hard to understand. The only "Bible" that they see is you and me. That is essentially what being salt is. We are called to *show* Christ to them. The word Christian means "little Christ." Jesus Christ would not spend any time on Facebook talking, while He is supposed to be working for a boss. Jesus does not condone that kind of behavior.

Life can be very interesting when you can hear the Holy Spirit and be directed by Him. God knows how to make you shine and how to bring His righteousness to any situation. The Holy Spirit knows which people are going to be saved and come to the Lord one day and He can use you to be a bridge to those people. Just being different to people can have a drastic effect on their salvation. In this dark world, it does not take much to stand out and be more than the average person. That is what being salt and light is all about!

The Christian life is a matter of swimming upstream, Andrew Wommack says even a dead fish can float downstream. It does not take much to float downstream, but the Christian life is a swim upstream. Righteousness means right standing with God. It can never be earned, but it is given as a free gift to us by Christ at salvation. The Bible says that we have the mind of Christ, therefore let His mind show out in your life.

I hope that you have been blessed by what I have shared.

CHAPTER 36

THE PARABLE OF THE SERVANT'S DUTY
(LUKE 17:7-10)

The Parable of the Servant's Duty, found in Luke 17:7-10 reads:

"Which of you, having a servant plowing or tending sheep, will say to him when he has come in from the field, 'Come at once and sit down to eat'? But will he not rather say to him, 'Prepare something for my supper, and gird yourself and serve me till I have eaten and drunk, and afterward you will eat and drink'? Does he thank that servant because he did the things that were commanded him? I think not. So likewise you, when you have done all those things which you are commanded, say, 'We are unprofitable servants. We have done what was our duty to do.'"

Notice the word "unprofitable." This same word is found in Roman 3:10-12. *"There is none righteous, no, not one; there is none who understands; there is none who seeks after God. They have all turned aside; they have together become unprofitable."*

I have to say that out of all the parables, I personally struggled more with this one. I told myself it was low self esteem! It is quite understandable to feel inadequate when we first become a Christian but over time we are to learn to see ourselves as God sees us - that we are covered with the righteousness of Christ. Nevertheless, I still struggled in my soul area because there were obviously still remnants of hurt and pain in my life that needed to be placed under the blood of Jesus. I would like to be free to share about that.

When I was near the end of my twenty year addiction, I was taught what true repentance was and saw the difference between being truly repentant and just being mournful or sorry for my sin. I had that described to me in a one-hour sermon, and someone took me aside afterwards and counseled me for half an hour about true repentance.

He said to me, "Matthew, until you are sorry for raping the girls that you are sleeping with—until you are sorry for being someone like a perverted father, taking and abusing these girls (even though you are paying them)—you are abusing them for having sex with someone who is not your wife. Until you are desperately sorry for what you are doing to them and for abusing your own flesh; until you are sorry for wasting your own money and trying to find love in the wrong places; until you are sorry for abusing God; until you have given some deep and personal thought about your abusive addiction; and until you are truly mournful and sorry in those areas, you will never find repentance. The bottom line is that until you stop doing these things you are NOT repentant!"

I thought about that. It only took a week to agree with what I had been told. Then one Sunday at church, where we could call out prayers in the middle of the worship service, I was going to repent of my sins publicly. Then I heard Jesus say: *"When you do it, I want you to admit, that all 'your righteousness' is like filthy rags."*

But you see I also had a huge big problem with saying that my good deeds were filthy rags. I felt that I was essentially a good person. (Somehow, in those days I could separate in my mind my addiction, from my "good works" for God.)

Whilst I would never say that I hated the Scriptures that talked about being "unprofitable," I wanted to believe that they were simply wrong! I had a problem with Jeremiah 17:9 too, saying that: *"The heart of man is desperately wicked. Who can know it?"* That day in church, I inwardly struggled for some time, but finally, I accepted its truth. Yes, I was convinced that even *"my good deeds"* are filthy rags in God's sight. So, when I prayed my prayer, I really meant it. I said out loud, "My righteousness is filthy rags." Immediately God set me free from that addiction because the spirit of lust left me.

On Tuesday, when I was paid and I was tempted, the degree of temptation was reduced to something I could handle so I was able to resist it. I truly praised God that day.

The reason I am sharing this illustration is that I personally had an issue with going to Jesus and saying, "I am an unprofitable servant. I only did what was my duty to do." It was a pride issue with me! I felt that I was doing a good job for Jesus and I was well pleasing in His sight. He has shown that He really loves me and told me He does, but essentially, when it really comes down to it, without Jesus I would be going to Hell. Without His cross and His salvation, I would be lost eternally.

As His follower, I am really His servant. John 15:14 says, *"You are My friends if you do whatever I command you."* Although I am His friend, I am first His servant. With all the money in the world, even if I could write bestselling books and make millions of dollars for the Kingdom of God, it could never repay Jesus for taking the rap for my sin. I could never repay Him if I lived a thousand years or more!

So, when I look at it that way, I know that I truly am an unprofitable servant. The Bible says that Christians are part of the worldwide "Bride" of Christ; they are priests of God; they are peculiar people to the world; they are a brand new creation; I also know that I have the DNA of Jesus Christ because His Holy Spirit indwells every Christian. It was not beneath Jesus Christ to come and serve lost humanity. It is not beneath Jesus Christ to serve us and intercede for us now in Heaven. So, it should not be beneath me to say that I am an unprofitable servant, and all the good things that I do, are only what He has commanded me to do.

We say we have a low self-esteem but really we have the very opposite! If you too have a problem with this, one way to deal with it, is to consider what a high price Jesus paid for us. Without Him, we would not even have life. He is both our Creator and the giver of eternal life. There is no way we could enjoy His peace or look forward to an eternity in heaven without His work for us on the cross. If you considered the great price that Jesus paid and how there is nothing we could do to earn our salvation, like me, you will come to a point where you will be able to accept that yes, we in ourselves are "unprofitable."

I originally recorded this on video and didn't have it typed up. I disagreed with this parable of Jesus. I thought it was not relevant anymore, but God has convicted me, because everything Jesus said *is relevant*. I couldn't do a parable series and say one of the parables is not relevant today and successfully pull it off—and have people believe it. It would be like a rotten apple in a bunch of fresh ones.

The fact that the parable uses the word "unprofitable" is the reason why it strikes so close to the bone in my life. It forces me to confess that there is nothing essentially good in me. It is God's Holy Spirit and the blood of Jesus covering me that is good. I can do wonderful things with Christ's help like writing this book in the power of the Holy Spirit. But without His intervention this book would be un-salty rubbish! The friendship of Jesus has taught me, that left to my own devices, I would be totally helpless. I am a lost cause without God.

There will be many readers who will disagree with what I have said. But both the Old Testament and the New Testament agree on the truth that without the intervention of God in our life, all humanity is stained with sin. If this were not so, the Father would not have had to send His Son to die on a brutal cross to redeem us from Satan. To argue otherwise is to argue with the Creator! The Bible says: *"Let God be true but every man a liar."* (Romans 3:4) Pride is so entrenched in our soul, that it seems inconceivable that there is nothing good in us without God.

It always comes back to the same issue: we compare our goodness with other people and forget that God is the only One who is good. We were born with a sin bias: that is why it will take us a lifetime to come into line with God's ways. I guess some people just struggle with it more than others.

Before the Gospel is liberating, it is offensive! If you are finding it offensive it means the Holy Spirit is working in you. Until we come to the knowledge that even our very best works are filthy compared to the holiness of God, then we are not open to be saved from sin. Take heart dear reader, Jesus said *"I did not come to call the righteous, but sinners, to repentance."* (Matthew 9:13)

If this message has offended you, know that I know how you feel. I pray that God's truth will be revealed to you personally. Then like me, you can rejoice that you are a sinner because confessed and repentant sinners are the only people who will go to Heaven. If you remain self-righteous, there is no other provision God has for you!

CHAPTER 37

THE PARABLE OF THE SHEEP AND THE GOATS (MATTHEW 25:31-46)

I am not one who has seriously studied Eschatology, which is the study of "End Times" events in their chronological order. However, I will attempt to give you a brief summary of what I believe the future has in store for us. I shared in Chapter One about an event that is called the "Rapture" of the church. This "snatching away," of Christians into the air to meet Jesus, will happen in a blink of an eye and will not be noticed by unbelievers until after the event, when millions of people go missing all around the globe. No more than seven years after this supernatural event, Jesus will physically set foot on earth. All the saints from the time of Adam will be in the clouds witnessing this momentous scene played out on earth. The following parable will then be fulfilled. In verses 31-33, we read *"When the Son of Man comes in His glory, and all the holy angels with Him, then He will sit on the throne of His glory. The nations will be gathered before Him, He will separate them one from another, as a shepherd divides his sheep from the goats. And He will set His sheep on His right hand but the goats on the left"*

Therefore, we are told that Jesus will sort people into two groups. At His right, will be believers, both Jews and Gentiles. They would have surrendered their lives to Jesus since the Rapture of the Church. Many of these would have mysteriously lost loved ones at that time, and would have remembered that these Christians used to talk about such an event happening. Too late, they will realize that the Bible was true and they had been left behind. They would also realize that a great time of tribulation was coming to the earth and they would be hated and even murdered by the establishment of the day. These people would be longing for the day when Jesus would physically return, so that they would be safe. Many Jewish believers present would have come to faith because they had received special revelation during the tribulation period that the Lord Jesus Christ was indeed their long awaited Messiah. Both Jews and Gentiles in this group are referred to as the "sheep" in the parable and will be wonderfully rescued by Jesus at this stage.

Also, many other believers, both Jew and Gentile, will have been already martyred for their faith and will be among those who are witnessing events on earth from the clouds.

139

The second much larger group of people referred to as "goats" by King Jesus will be those who have hated the believers and would have surrendered their lives to the leadership of the Antichrist and his accomplice: the False Prophet. They would have willingly agreed to have the mark of the beast implanted on their forehead or wrist and would have openly worshiped the "antichrist" in the temple in Jerusalem.

The Book of Revelation says that the holy angels are going to come and reap the harvest. There is therefore, the harvest of the righteous and the harvest of the wicked. So those two harvests go up before Jesus, on Judgment Day, He separates the people just as the parable says into sheep and goats The Antichrist and the False Prophet will be cast alive into the lake of fire and the goats will be killed by the sword. Revelation 19:21.

The practical portion of the parable that means so much to me personally comes from verses 34-36: *"Then the King will say to those on his right hand, 'Come you blessed of my Father, inherit the Kingdom prepared for you from the foundation of the world: for I was hungry and you gave Me food; I was thirsty and you gave Me drink; I was a stranger and you took Me in; I was naked and you clothed Me; I was sick and you visited Me; I was in prison and you came to Me.'"*

We must remember that God had made his first Covenant in the Old Testament with the Jewish people and until the Cross these were the ones that the Father sent Jesus basically to minister to. That is why Jesus spoke as He did to the Gentile women mentioned in Matthew 15:21-28. Jesus had said to her in verse 26 *"I was not sent except to the lost sheep of the house of Israel!"* However because of her great faith He healed her daughter.

When Jesus was put on the cross for the sin of all humanity, the grace of God extended to the whole earth not just to the Jews. But in the seven year period of worldwide tribulation that is soon coming, God's attention will then be re-focused on His original people. The non-believing Jews and unbelievers from the other nations of the world will be severely judged by what their attitude towards God's people was during the tribulation period.

The words *"I was a stranger"* is translated in another Bible as: *"I was homeless."* I want my series on the parables of Jesus to be written in modern language so that is can be applied today. It says, "For I was hungry and you gave me food" I direct my question to you my reader who sit in church each week; Do you know that desperate people come to churches all the time seeking food. Does your church have a food pantry so that the Pastors can help them? You could make that at a priority at your weekly shopping.

There may be people even sitting in your church who are struggling feeding their loved ones. You could invite them to your place occasionally at least. Some people in churches have addicted spouses who spend the grocery money on gambling or beer. If you give them clothes or food parcels, their spouse cannot sell these items for their addiction.

Do you know that many people thirst for spiritual water and look in the wrong places for it? Christians have the true spiritual water. It is the Holy Spirit of God in our lives that brings true refreshment to our soul and spirit. People need to know that nothing else will satisfy their thirst. A Samaritan lady spoke to Jesus at the well in John 4:4-26. She found out about spiritual water that forever quenches thirst and she wanted some of it.

You could give these thirsty people some Christian DVD's or books, a Bible, or other recourses, so that they will come to the knowledge of biblical truth. Jesus said to the crowds gathered at a Jewish feast in John 7:38 – *"He who believes in Me, as the Scripture has said, out of his heart will flow rivers of living water."*

When the Holy Spirit begins to work in a person's life they become hungry and thirsty for the things of God but may not be able to afford even a Bible. They may come to church early and stay late in the hope of fellowship. Don't disappoint them.

People resist giving money to homeless people in case it is abused but you can always buy food or clothes for people especially their children. You could even perhaps volunteer some of your time in a soup kitchen. Then you will come to know those who need help and you could find ways to personally befriend them.

You could take a needy person to and an Op-shop. Also you don't have to be in jail to be imprisoned emotionally, mentally or physically. Many people are confined to their homes. Taking them a nice cake and making a friend of them will boost their day. In time, they may even feel comfortable in visiting you. Also, there are actual "Prison" ministries where friendly Christian workers would be always welcome.

Even in hospitals or in Aged Care Homes there are people who would love to be visited. These places can be sterile and lonely for many people. They would welcome the chance to reminisce or to tell you all their stories. You could perhaps share your story or read to them. Then there are people who deliberately isolate themselves because of past hurt, but even these people you could pray for at least.

There are heaps of people who are desperately lonely even in your church. Visiting with people who tend to isolate themselves, or the ones that live by themselves would make their day. Some people have become suspicious of others, but even this wall can be broken down by love. Right up to life's end, we need to be like Jesus to people.

Some people are difficult to love. But when we show His love to these people, it is a way to show our love to Jesus. For instance, He says that when we feed or give drink to the hungry, we are actually ministering to Him, when we visit someone in prison or in hospital it is like we are visiting Him and giving Him our love and time.

The Sheep and the Goats Parable is a parable that sparks compassion for others. Don't be like the man who looks at his reflection in a mirror and then forgets what he saw. The brother of Jesus said that we are to be doers of the word and not just hearers. (James 1:22) I have given you a practical application of this parable in today's world. Go and multiply. Go and do the good works of the Savior. You will not regret it I can assure you.

CHAPTER 38

THE PARABLE OF THE SIGN OF JONAH (MATTHEW 12:38-42)

In Matthew 12:38-42, we read about the parable of "The Sign of Jonah."

"Then some of the scribes and Pharisees answered, saying, 'Teacher, we want to see a sign from You.'

"But He answered and said to them, 'An evil and adulterous generation seeks after a sign, and no sign will be given to it except the sign of the prophet Jonah. For as Jonah was three days and three nights in the belly of the great fish, so will the Son of Man be three days and three nights in the heart of the earth. The men of Nineveh will rise up in the judgment with this generation and condemn it, because they repented at the preaching of Jonah; and indeed a greater than Jonah is here. The queen of the South will rise up in the judgment with this generation and condemn it, for she came from the ends of the earth to hear the wisdom of Solomon; and indeed a greater than Solomon is here.'"

First of all, let me quote the end of verse 40. It says, *"...so will the Son of Man be three days and three nights in the heart of the earth."*

If you have ever wondered where Hell is located, it is in the heart of the earth. We know this because other Scriptures infer that Jesus descended into the bowels of the earth to declare His final victory over sin and death to the devil and his prisoners. He then physically rose from the tomb on the third day. The stone was not rolled away to let Jesus out of the tomb, but it was rolled away for our sake: that we may know that death could not hold Him down. Jesus is alive! Scientists agree that the core of the earth is molten lava. It is very hot down there. That certainly suits the environment of Hell, with the burning sulfur and molten lava. So if someone ever questions you: "Where is Hell?" It is where Jesus briefly visited before He rose from the dead. Hell is in the heart of the earth.

During the pre-resurrection time, there used to be "Paradise" down there too, a place that was separated from Hell by a big chasm. In Chapter 33 I taught on this subject. The righteous people were in Paradise and the unrighteous people were in Sheol. In the

Parable of the Rich Man and Lazarus, the rich man was in agony while Lazarus was in the bosom of Abraham. Since the resurrection of Jesus, Paradise was emptied out and is now located in God's dwelling place in Heaven.

As I said in Chapter 33, I do not believe that Jesus was merely telling a parable here. Lazarus was obviously a real person or Jesus would have referred to him as a "certain beggar" and not by a personal name. If Lazarus actually existed then we know that the whole account in Luke Chapter 16 was an actual event.

It is a comforting thought to know that Abraham—someone who the Jewish people looked up to as their father—had Lazarus in his bosom, holding him and comforting him. It is also good to know that in Heaven, we have a memory. If we have suffered on earth it would be good to know that we are being comforted and the tears would stop flowing even when we remember the hard times on earth. This makes the joy, peace and serenity of Heaven so much more compared to our hard earthly life.

Jesus says in verse 39, *"An evil and adulterous generation seeks after a sign."* We live in a generation which is like that. There are certain factions within the church who believe that miracles still happen just as they did in Bible days and then there are others who condemn signs and wonders and think that anyone who is operating in the gift of healing and miracles is a false prophet and not from God. They have a right to their opinions, the same as I have a right to my opinion. There are many accusations about the Pentecostal church that do hold weight. People can make accusations and find some sort of substance in what they are saying about the excesses of the Pentecostal church in some ways.

But then I have been amongst some Pentecostals who experience the joy and bliss of the Holy Spirit. These people are free; they are not bound by religion. They are most often prosperous. They are most often joyful and extremely fulfilled. Their lifestyle and presence manifests the wisdom and peace of God. Some people would say that bursting out in laughter is not a good thing. Anyone can say that until they are in a middle of a depression and they burst out in laughter and it fills their whole being with joy and peace.

So, part of the church condemns signs and wonders, and it is probably from verses like these that generate such opinions. Also, teachers who do not believe in the miracles of this generation help perpetuate such opinions, but remember that Jesus says a sign might be given to a generation that is adulterous. The Holy Spirit, in James 4:4, said that anyone who seeks after his own, to spend things on his own pleasures is an adulterer. I will just turn to the scripture and read it for you in context.

James 4:2-4 starts:

"You lust and do not have. You murder and covet and cannot obtain. You fight and war. Yet you do not have because you do not ask. You ask and do not receive, because you ask amiss, that you may spend it on your pleasures. Adulterers and adulteresses! Do you not know that friendship with the world is enmity with God? Whoever therefore wants to be a friend of the world makes himself an enemy of God."

This is the type of adulterer that Jesus is talking about—a generation that is serving the lusts of the flesh—a generation that is devoured by consumerism, consumed by a lust for wanting more and more—a generation that only pays lip service to Jesus Christ, but their real god is their bellies—their real god is the things that they can buy and consume, and the things that bring temporal joy and happiness.

An adulterer is a person who is married, but flirts and has sex with another person. As Christians we are called to be the bride of Christ, we are called to love God with all our heart, mind and soul, and so when we focus all our attention, time and money to other things or we lust after other things, we are really committing adultery against Jesus Christ. This is the sort of adulterous generation that we live in, the same as the generation in which Jesus lived.

"...and no sign will be given to it except the sign of the prophet Jonah" (v.39b)

So, what is the sign of the prophet Jonah in this generation? Well, you will find in Revelation 11:3 that the two witnesses are the last prophet Elijah and, I believe, Enoch. Some people think these prophets are Moses and Elijah, who represent the Law and the Prophets who were transfigured before Jesus, John and Peter in Matthew 17:2. Other Bible scholars say they represent the two olive trees or the two lamp-stands which are symbols of the witnessing church. Many things in Scripture are not clearly set forth and these two witnesses are purposely unidentified. .

It says in Revelation 11:7-12: *"When they finish their testimony, the beast that ascends out of the bottomless pit will make war against them, overcome them, and kill them. And their dead bodies will lie in the street of the great city which spiritually is called Sodom and Egypt, where also our Lord was crucified. Then those from the peoples, tribes, tongues, and nations will see their dead bodies three-and-a-half days, and not allow their dead bodies to be put into graves. And those who dwell on the earth will rejoice over them, make merry, and send gifts to one another, because these two prophets tormented those who dwell on the earth.*

"Now after the three-and-a-half days the breath of life from God entered them, and they stood on their feet, and great fear fell on those who saw them, and they heard a loud voice from Heaven saying to them, 'Come up here.' And they ascended to Heaven in a cloud, and their enemies saw them."

So, in this last day—in this adulterous generation—we need a sign like Jonah. Jonah was three days in the belly of the whale. Jesus disappeared off the face of the earth for three days and came back. These two witnesses—our current sign of Jonah—will be killed and lie on the streets dead for three and a half days. I assume that their spirits will be in Heaven for that time, and then they will come back.

Our title text in Matthew 12:42 referred to a certain Queen. This was the Queen of Sheba who had heard all about the extremely wise King Solomon of Israel. She was anxious to meet personally with him and brought with her a hundred and twenty talents of gold. (This would be forty ton of gold.) At that time, the annual revenue of gold in Solomon's Kingdom was 666 talents—normally a bad number. Six hundred and sixty-six talents of gold were brought to Solomon's Kingdom every single year, which is now billions and billions of dollars' worth of gold. This one Queen brought a tremendous offering of gold to Solomon to measure her respect of him.

In this same text, Jesus spoke of three people: Jonah, the Queen of Sheba and Solomon. Jesus was saying "that someone better than these was in their midst." However, Jesus did not get recognition! The Scribes and Pharisees had still been asking Jesus for a miraculous sign.

The mere fact that the Scribes and Pharisees were still in unbelief as to the real identity of Jesus was amazing: it totally verified their utter spiritual blindness! It is the same today, people want a sign of the truth of the Gospel and when they see a miraculous healing, they still refuse to believe. The truth is: It is not that a person cannot believe but instead people choose not to believe. Evidence is not the issue it is our personal will that is the issue and *people do not want to believe so they simply choose not to!*

Jesus said in verse 41 that the men of Nineveh will rise up in judgment against this generation. Some preachers say that even some of the Gentiles of Nineveh who had no biblical history were going to be saved. They are going to come back in a righteous way and judge the generation in which Jesus spoke of.

What is the application for this? One of the main points is that we have to treasure Jesus above all else. We can live in a generation that is adulterous and which is seeking after a sign, but we should not be lusting after the things of the world. We do not have to be adulterous. We can live in an adulterous world, but we can be not of this world. We can make Jesus the true focus of our devotion—the true focus of our time.

Reading a book like this is a good thing—a good practice for you to do, but even better than reading a book is to put its teachings into practice. A good way to put this book into practice is to minister to other people—buy yourself multiple copies and give them to your non-Christian friends!

Even though Jesus is rejected as God by many people, He is recognized as a famous and influential scholar in the world's history books! Therefore His unique teaching, by the use of parables, has been spoken about ever since He walked on earth.

CHAPTER 39

THE PARABLE OF THE TARES IN THE FIELD (MATTHEW 13:24-30 AND 13:36-43)

The actual parable that will be considered in this chapter's teaching is found in Matthew 13:2430.

"The kingdom of Heaven is like a man who sowed good seed in his field; but while men slept, his enemy came and sowed tares among the wheat and went his way, but when the grain had sprouted and produced a crop, then the tares also appeared. So the servants of the owner came and said to him, 'Sir, did you not sow good seed in your field? How then does it have tares?' He said to them, 'An enemy has done this.' The servants said to him, 'Do you want us then to go and gather them up?' But he said, 'No, lest while you gather up the tares you also uproot the wheat with them. Let both grow together until the harvest and at the time of harvest I will say to the reapers: First gather together the tares and bind them in bundles to burn them, but gather the wheat into my barn.'"

For years, this parable eluded me. I did not fully understand this story about the "tares." It says that the wheat and the tares are growing in the same place. It says that the enemy sowed the tares. Well, we know that the enemy of the wheat field is Satan. If the wheat and the tares are growing in one place, well then it could also be that they are growing in the church. Once the wheat is sown, Satan comes and sows his tares in the church.

The following explanation of the above parable is given by Jesus in Matthew 13:37-43. *"He answered and said to them: "He who sows the good seed is the Son of Man. The field is the world, the good seeds are the sons of the Kingdom, but the tares are the sons of the wicked one. The enemy who sowed them is the Devil, the harvest is the end of the age, and the reapers are the angels. Therefore, as the tares are gathered and burned in the fire, so it will be at the end of this age. The Son of Man will send out His angels, and they will gather out of His kingdom all things that offend, and those who practice lawlessness, and will cast them into the furnace of fire. There will be wailing and gnashing of teeth. Then the righteous will shine forth as the sun in the Kingdom of their Father. He who has ears to hear, let him hear!"*

146

The "tares" were quite common in that particular area and they looked like wheat growing. It was not until the grain appeared near harvest time that they proved to be counterfeit wheat. Jesus is comparing nature's tares to the counterfeit Christians that the devil plants into God's church. Jesus warns us to watch out for these false brethren. In Matthew 7:20 Jesus said "by their fruits you will know them." In other words: talk is cheap but genuine believes will produce good lasting fruit.

Also, certain people in the church have open minds and hearts for the things of God, but they have not come to a level where the Spirit has ministered to them to the point of salvation. For example, I have a good friend who now comes to my church. She loves singing the songs and the choruses. She is very open to "church," but she hasn't yet opened her heart to "Jesus." Therefore, it's a good thing to have non-Christians in church. It's better than them being at the beach or in the clubs. Christians often judge non-Christians, but Jesus loves all people! You'd be surprised that many of them are open to the Gospel. This gives us hope that our time spent with them may have eternal benefit.

But the "tares," the counterfeit Christians are not just in the churches! Jesus said that the field is the world and He meant the whole world: these "tares" are everywhere we go.

Verse 38 says *"The seeds are the sons of the kingdom, but the tares are the sons of the wicked one,"* Every person belongs to the wicked one right up until the time they are saved. At the moment of salvation, Jesus bursts His light upon their heart. Consequently, once they believe and confess that the Lord Jesus Christ has risen from the dead and has saved them from their sin, they become a child of righteousness. (Romans 10:9-10)

And we have the promise of Jesus that those who are given to Him, He will never lose. Many people (including myself up until eight weeks ago) believed that a Christian can lose their salvation—that one can be saved, then fall away and lose their salvation through sin. I do not believe that anymore. I believe the Holy Spirit is good enough to turn anyone around, because God looks upon the heart of His children.

Anyone who trusts their own works of righteousness or their own personal holiness to enter the Kingdom of Heaven will put little thought or faith in the perfect work that was achieved on the cross of Jesus Christ for them. The righteous are righteous from the time of salvation. Jesus Christ imputed His righteousness onto them even if they don't appear to be very righteous. In God's eyes, they are righteous because He sees His Son's blood covering them and He sees the Holy Spirit in their human spirit. *"For God took the sinless Christ and poured into Him our sins. Then in exchange, He poured God's goodness into us"* 2 Corinthians 5:21 Living New Testament translation.

Now to Matthew 13:39a - *"And the enemy who sowed the tares is the devil."*

The earth is run by minions of the Devil. What is so powerful about the devil in the life of a non-Christian is that the unbeliever is not even aware that a good proportion of his thoughts, motivations and temptations come from the evil one. Some Christians have been in the faith for some time, yet they are not aware of how often Satan drops his poisonous thoughts into their mind. We can't blame the devil all the time because old patterns and mindsets from our "old sin nature" lead us astray. It takes work and time to establish the *"new patterns and mindsets that are sown by the Holy Spirit"* into our soul area. But gradually these changes will be evidenced by others in a positive way.

Whenever you are tempted to speak out against someone or gossip to someone—the times you cheat your boss in any way—the times that you deliberately ignore your own conscience —all the sins that you commit are temptations of the evil one, or are the result of fleshy habits that need to be replaced by Godly ones.

Up until salvation our soul is the boss in our life! However, when the Holy Spirit brings God's life to the human spirit, the soul must learn to take orders from a new boss! This new authority is called the "renewed born-again spirit." The process of the human soul being renewed is a difficult life-time process! The more you surrender day to day decisions to the spirit, the more you will be able to surrender harder decisions to God. The soul is made up of three very strong compartments: the mind or your ability to process information, the emotions or your ability to show positive or negative feelings and lastly the most deadly – your will: the ability to make wise or unwise decisions.

Ingrained in every human being is self-centeredness which has at its root, human pride. If Christians are being tempted, so much more is a person who is not saved. Whilst we are all part of God's creation, only those who have received Christ are the children of God. All unbelievers are still under the rule and authority of the devil: they by nature resist the things of God and are not aware that it is Satan that they serve.

Ephesians 2:1-3 says: *Once you were under God's curse, doomed forever for your sins. You went along with the crowd and were just like all the others, full of sin, obeying Satan, the mighty prince of the power of the air, who is at work right now in the hearts of those who are against the Lord. All of us used to be just as they are, our lives expressing the evil within us, doing every wicked thing that our passions or our evil thoughts might lead us into. We started out bad, being born with evil natures, and were under God's anger just like everyone else.* (Living New Testament translation.)

The enemy has a big campaign to keep people in darkness. For many, many years, I was in darkness about the true righteousness and the finished work of Jesus on the cross. I was born-again and had God's Holy Spirit residing in my human spirit but my soul was not conformed to the truth of God's word. If I had died I would have gone to heaven but I was allowing Satan to drop his deadly thoughts into my mind. Therefore, I lived a defeated life and was actually a hindrance to the kingdom of God. There are many Christians that fall in this category.

For many years, I had a spirit of religion and legalism, and I believed that my own good works were a vital factor of maintaining my salvation. I believed that if I did not behave—if I did not read the Bible, do good works, go to church and do a whole lot of ministry for the Lord—there was a good chance I was going to go to Hell. I had to balance the scales as it were, because I thought certain sins in which I did, were taking me to Hell. I was bound up and I was a very unhappy Christian.

Since the Lord has resurrected me and opened my eyes, I have become a new man. A gigantic weight has been lifted off my shoulders. This book is something that the Lord has inspired me to write: it's not me trying to earn brownie points with God!

Let's go back to the parable, verse 40 says: *"Therefore as the tares are gathered and burned in the fire, so it will be at the end of this age."* As mentioned in my previous chapter, the book of Revelation speaks of two harvests. Jesus says in verse 41: *"The Son of Man will send out His angels, and they will gather out of His Kingdom all things that offend and those who practice lawlessness."*

Some disgruntled people complained to Jesus: *"Lord, Lord, have we not prophesied in Your name, cast out demons in Your name, and done many wonders in Your name?"* Jesus replied, *"Depart from me, you who practice lawlessness"* (Matthew 7:21-23).

You see, you can only go to Heaven through the finished work of Jesus Christ. If you try to appeal to God by trying to earn your way to Heaven through your own works or the works of the Law, you fail automatically.

Lawlessness is sin. *"Whoever commits sin also commits lawlessness, and sin is lawlessness." 1 John 3:4.* Practicing lawlessness is doing things contrary to the will or word of God. The main point here is that the people who offend Jesus are going to be cast into the fire according to verse 42 of our second title text: *"and will cast them into the furnace of fire."* These are non-Christians: they are not saved because their sin of unbelief prevents salvation to take place.

Jesus loves everyone. His blood that was shed on the cross was for every single person. Jesus wants everyone to be saved. 2 Peter 3:9 says: *"The Lord is not "slack, concerning His promise, as some count slackness, but is longsuffering toward us, not willing that any should perish but that all should come to repentance."*

God, the Father has so much compassion, love, grace and mercy flowing from His throne towards wicked men. However, He gave man a free will to choose to love Him or not. God will not violate His own word. If He ever did, the whole world would fall apart. The people who do not know God have right up until their death to change. However, if they are still alive at harvest time at the end of the age, when the angels of God reap the world, it will be too late for them to turn to God. That is why it says in 2 Corinthians 6:2b – *"Behold, now is the accepted time; behold, now is the day of salvation."*

None of us know when death will come! Jesus is the only way to be saved. *"There is one God and one Mediator between God and men, the man Christ Jesus who gave Himself a ransom for all." 1Timothy 2:5-6.* Jesus Himself proclaimed that He was the only way to God and that no one could come to the Father except through Him. (John 14:6)

An unbeliever will not readily read the Bible. But you could give this book to a non-Christian friend to show them that there is a loving God who has done everything He can do to woo them to Himself. God takes no pleasure in punishing those who reject Him but to deny the only way to salvation, gives Him no other option. Sin or sinners can never enter God's Heaven for it would no longer be heaven for anyone! This and other parables show that non-Christians will weep in remorse for allowing pride and unbelief to rule their brief life on earth.

Verse 43b says: *"Then the righteous will shine forth as the sun in the Kingdom of their Father. He who has ears to hear, let him hear!"* These are the ones clothed in Christ's righteousness – they will shine like the sun! Jesus quoted a prophecy which had been written in the late sixth century by God's prophet Daniel – *"Those who are wise shall shine like the brightness of the firmament. And those who turn many to righteousness like the stars forever and ever."*

Christians are the ones referred to here as the "wise" who "shall shine like the brightness of the firmament." The word "firmament" simply means "the vault or expanse of the sky; the heavens". The verse continues on by saying, *"And those who turn many to righteousness like the stars forever and ever."*

Not all of us have the gift of evangelism. Not everyone has the ability to share the Gospel. This book will be available one day on the internet for free. At the back of the book, there will be an internet address where you can send the book to hundreds of your friends for free. So, this is a way you could spread the Gospel and perhaps bring your friends and family to a saving knowledge of Christ.

Also, if you invest money in foreign missionaries, like Heidi Baker of Iris Ministries, or many other ministries in the East, your money can be used to save many souls. Supporting Christian television satellite stations is also a wonderful way for you to share in the spreading of the Gospel. You can become one who turns many to righteousness through your investment and you will shine like a star forever and ever.

So, I hope that you have learned many things from this parable and my comments arising from it.

CHAPTER 40

THE PARABLE OF THE TEN MINAS
(LUKE 19:11-27)

We pick it up at Luke 19:11

"Now as they heard these things, He spoke another parable, because He was near Jerusalem and because they thought the Kingdom of God would appear immediately.

Jesus is saying: "There is going to be a delay. There is going to be some time between now and when the end comes."

The Scripture continues on: *Therefore He said: "A certain nobleman went into a far country to receive for himself a kingdom and to return. So he called ten of his servants, delivered to them ten minas, and said to them, 'Do business till I come.' But his citizens hated him, and sent a delegation after him, saying, 'We will not have this man to reign over us.'*

The parable here and the parable in the next chapter differ in some ways, but they are both about the stewardship of God's blessings to us. This parable is concerned about stewarding money wisely, while the second one is about being a wise steward of our talents. Every good thing we possess comes from God – we are to be His wise caretakers!

The chemicals in my brain do not function properly, but God still uses me, for He has compensated my lack, in giving me other special blessings that others may lack. Because of this, I don't consider myself worse off than anyone else. In fact I seem to have greater awareness of the spiritual world than those who function normally! God has His reasons and one day I know that I will receive His total healing. When we finally accept, that all we have is not ours to do with what we want, but does in fact belong to God: then our attitude entirely changes. We are called to be good stewards of God's blessings whatever they might be!

So he called ten of his servants, delivered to them ten minas, and said to them, "Do business till I come." (In my Bible notes, it says that a mina was a weight of money equal to fifty shekels. In those days it was worth about three month's salary.)

151

You would not give this amount of money to a person who has no aptitude for business. To invest like that would be foolish. For instance, if all you have ever known is living on welfare and you have never worked a day in your life, it would be foolish for someone to have you run their organization, requiring you to work sixty hours or more a week. I'm not condemning a person who doesn't work for there are many reasons why people do not work. I am using this as an illustration to say that when this nobleman gave these people the ten minas and said, "Do business until I come," in verse 13, it means that he trusted them and believed that they *could* make wise business decisions.

"And so it was that when he returned, having received the kingdom, he then commanded these servants, to whom he had given the money, to be called to him, that he might know how much every man had gained by trading." (v. 15)

The Master expected to find good results from astute trading. Today, we could assume that it was like the stock market, but at that time, it was probably like buying and trading produce and making a business with the capital. Recently, I have heard of charities and Christian foundations that give micro-finance loans, small loans of ten to a hundred dollars to people in poor countries. This would allow the poor to start a small business for themselves. They would be able to buy chickens, pigs or any produce to sell in the market, or for ladies to sew marketable clothes. Within a year, if they do well, they would be able to pay back their loan with interest, but instead they only need to repay the original money they borrowed. When each loan was repaid, it would then be re-loaned to another similar worthy cause. In this way, people are not only being brought out of poverty, but they receive tremendous satisfaction of a job well done. The people in our story have been given a similar opportunity to prove themselves.

Then came the first, saying, "Master, your mina has earned ten minas." And he said to him, "Well done, good servant; because you were faithful in a very little, have authority over ten cities." And the second came, saying, "Master, your mina has earned five minas." Likewise he said to him, "You also be over five cities." (Verses 16-17)

Parables are parables; each given to explain a simple point. I understand that this story is not absolutely literal. For instance, if every Christian in the world was given authority over ten cities, there wouldn't be enough cities for Christians to rule. The point is that in this parable each person was given the same opportunity.

Here is the Master, (Jesus) who has gone off to a far country. He is saying: "If you are faithful with what I give you, I am going to give you more!"

We are caretakers of everything God gives us. We have zero control over the world's economy, but we do have control over our economy – and when we know that it all belongs to God and He has entrusted us to use it for Him, He will make sure that we receive more resources for His work and also more for our own pleasure.

Jesus rewards those who work faithfully for Him. There is a system with Jesus: work and reward. We cannot work our way to salvation and nothing we can do can make Jesus love us more, but Jesus is a smart and astute Master. He knows how to reward the hard workers and the people with a heart after Him. You do not have to be God to understand that if you are going to put someone in control of something important then he should be someone competent. A person must have a good track record in order to be given certain positions. No one fresh out of school is placed as CEO of a major corporation. Even the multi-millionaire owner of the business will not promote his son to such an illustrious position in his company until he has proved himself with certificates and actual experience.

The second servant made a smaller profit and was rewarded but in verses 20-27 we read:

"Then another came, saying, 'Master, here is your mina, which I have kept put away in a handkerchief. "I feared you, because you are an austere man. You collect what you did not deposit, and reap what you did not sow.' And he said to him, 'Out of your own mouth I will judge you, you wicked servant. You knew that I was an austere man, collecting what I did not deposit and reaping what I did not sow. Why then did you not put my money in the bank, that at my coming I might have collected it with interest?'

"And he said to those who stood by, 'Take the mina from him, and give it to him who has ten minas.' (But they said to him, 'Master, he has ten minas.') 'For I say to you, that to everyone who has will be given; and from him who does not have, even what he has will be taken away from him, but bring here those enemies of mine, who did not want me to reign over them, and slay them before me.'"

I certainly do not believe that a born-again Christian can go to Hell. If we misuse God's money, gifts, or talents it will mean that we will have an unfruitful life here on earth and even much regret after death, but I don't believe you would go to Hell! But you will most definitely lose rewards meant for you in Heaven when *"each one's work will become clear; for the Day will declare it, because it will be revealed by fire; and the fire will test each one's work, of what sort it is. If anyone's work which he has built on it endures, he will receive a reward. If anyone's work is burned, he will suffer loss; but he himself will be saved, yet so as through fire."* (1 Corinthians 3:13-15.)

This one servant had his mina taken from him. I believe that this person had never actually come into God's kingdom in the first place, or if he was a Christian he would experience great remorse in heaven for his actions on earth.

Another point I want to make: If a Christian becomes so angry at God, to the extent that he has told Him to get out of their life, not just once in an anger-spit but over a long period of time, God will oblige. He will never over-ride our free will choices. So there may be people who do lose their salvation. But God hasn't taken the initiative, the person themselves has wanted it that way! (Jesus promised in John 6:37 that He would never cast out any of His children.) If a Christian was cast out they would certainly know about it! Therefore if you are worried that you have overstepped yourself in God's grace, be at peace. The mere fact that you worry about such things, means that the Holy Spirit is still in you. You must understand this otherwise the devil will play havoc in your mind.

People in the West know of Jesus Christ but God says in Romans 1:19-20 that He has put knowledge of Himself into every person on earth. *"For the truth about God is known to them instinctively; God has put this knowledge in their hearts,* (Their conscience.) *Since earliest times men have seen the earth and the sky and all God made, and have known of His existence and great eternal power. So they will have no excuse* [when they stand before Him on Judgment Day]

Creation reveals the fact that there is a Creator! Even remote tribes ignorant of the Gospel know there is a god of some sort and have their own form of religion. These people just need to have a personal encounter with the God of the Bible! It's not up to us to judge unbelievers, but it's up to us to be a light to them. A Christian is always trading on the stock market of God. They should be trading "life" and bringing glory to God's name.

Now back to the parable. We are to be good stewards of God's resources – this includes His money! God's economy works totally opposite to the world's economy and it's just so much better! God has made our financial budgeting very simple and fair. Whatever He has allowed us to receive, we are to give back to him ten percent. We tithe because we are secure in the fact that God alone is our provider – therefore God is pleased. . *"Without faith it is impossible to please Him, for he who comes to God must believe that He is, and that He rewards those who diligently seek Him." Hebrews 11:6*

This is not going back to the covenant Law. No! It's exercising faith! God has always rewarded faith. How was Abraham saved? Was it by his works or by his faith? Why was he blessed – He *believed* God! Nothing has changed, when we truly believe God, we know that all His principles will work to our good. If we tithe out of a sense of duty, we are left to ourselves to budget the remaining ninety percent! (We have given the rest away in vain!) Whereas, if we tithe *by faith*, God works out the rest so that we even have some left to give to the poor. God is so fair and wise: He doesn't name a particular figure to give Him, just a particular percentage, so even a small child can be taught the principle of tithing. God's ways are so much higher than ours.

He wants us to use money wisely so that some of it is invested into His kingdom purposes and then He will elevate us and give us even more opportunities and authority. So if we receive a wage, a salary, or benefits from the Government – see these things as a blessing from God. Even our ability to be *able to work* comes from God! He gave us the intelligence, the physical ability and the opportunity to work. If we refuse to give back to God His small portion, it proves to Him that we don't trust Him as our Provider.

We can be really poor and still benefit abundantly. It's such a fair system God has put in place for us. This is a message to inspire us! The tithing principle revolutionizes lives! In verse 17, He says: *"Well done, good servant; because you were faithful in a very little, have authority over ten cities."* It is a comforting thought here – you only have to be faithful "over little."

If there is anything that you can take from this teaching— know that all the little work that you do is going to be highly rewarded by God and He desires to bless you abundantly, even more than you can imagine. Conduct your business His way and I will guarantee you will never regret it!

CHAPTER 41

THE PARABLE OF THE TALENTS
(MATTHEW 25:14-30)

The Parable of the Talents found in Matthew 25 is again about wise stewardship of what God gives us. It tells another story about a man who traveled to a far country and left his servants to invest wisely while he was away. This time instead of giving his servants equal amounts to do business for him, as in the previous chapter, here he gives different amounts of opportunity to just three people. First, He gave one servant five talents, then another servant two talents and a third servant just one talent. In those days, a talent was considered a fortune because it represented six thousand denarius. To help put this in context, just one denarius's was a normal day's work for a laborer, so you can see that the master had exercised great faith in these particular servants.

As the story goes, when he returned from his journey, the one to whom he had given five talents had made another five. So this servant gave his Master ten talents back. The second servant also had doubled his investment – his two talents had been increased to four. But, the one who had been trusted with only one talent had not been faithful in discharging his responsibility to his master for he just buried his allotment.

His pitiful excuse was: *'Lord, I knew you to be a hard man, reaping where you have not sown, and gathering where you have not scattered seed, and I was afraid, and went and hid your talent in the ground. Look, there you have what is yours.'*

"But his lord answered and said to him, 'You wicked and lazy servant, you knew that I reap where I have not sown, and gather where I have not scattered seed. So you ought to have deposited my money with the bankers, and at my coming I would have received back my own with interest. Therefore take the talent from him, and give it to him who has ten talents.

'For to everyone who has, more will be given, and he will have abundance; but from him who does not have, even what he has will be taken away, and cast the unprofitable servant into the outer darkness. There'll be weeping and gnashing of teeth'" (Verses 24-30.)

Now, this parable speaks about a man who went to a far country, just as Jesus has gone away to a far place. (Our Master went back to Heaven, but He has promised to return soon.) Before going away the Master in the parable gave the talents to each servant, each according to their ability.

Let's look at this word "ability." There are some people who are just born clever. Some may even have parents who can give them the very best education possible. These people have a great start in life and are considered highly privileged people. They would have no financial problems: no intellectual problems because they have done well at the best universities; they have received the best encouragement and mentoring available; they also have been loved by family members and highly esteemed by others. I believe that these are the type of people who were given five talents.

Not many people who come from poor families end up ruling a state or a country. People from more privileged backgrounds seem to make their way into politics and leadership. When the Lord was distributing the talents, He was giving them—the five, the two and the one—each according to the recipient's ability.

Therefore, take comfort in knowing that the Lord knows your ability. He is not going to ask for something that is too hard for you to do. He does however require that you use your ability in a faithful manner. The master was not impressed with the lazy servant who squandered his God given ability. This type of behavior rarely happens by mistake: it is most often made by a personal and deliberate choice by the person themselves.

At birth, we are all given natural talents and abilities and God wants us to use these for His Kingdom. There are many people who may not be consciously aware of their abilities are but others who love them can point them out. Generally, talents are found in what we can do well or the positive things that we love doing more than anything else. E.g. some people are hopeless at drawing things, yet others find themselves drawing at every opportunity. Others may be naturally musical and find peace in playing an instrument. A talent includes things that you desire to pursue because you are confident that you will be able to perfect it in life.

Spiritual gifts are different to natural talents. Don't be confused between the two. Regardless of natural talents, a person can have many spiritual gifts and vice versa. No Christian needs to be restricted by the things they have inherited at birth, such as low IQ. Neither should a Christian boast of things God gave them that are different to their parent's abilities. We should all be thankful for whatever talents or gifts we have.

However "spiritual" gifts are reserved for those who are filled with the Holy Spirit. They are quite separate than our other natural gifts or talents. These spiritual gifts must first be known by us and then acted upon. You can find a simple test on "Google" that will help you discover them. Some Spirit filled Christians automatically use a spiritual gift and are not even conscious that the ability has come from the Holy Spirit. We all need teaching on this subject so that we can more effectively use God's gifts.

When you combine your natural talents and your spiritual gifts, life becomes really exciting. There are three people who presently stand out in my mind who have done this: Benny Hinn, Kenneth Copeland and Joyce Meyer. Joyce particularly, is an outstanding speaker who constantly applies truth in practical ways by using everyday terminology and experiences. However, I believe that all three people have been promoted by the Lord together with many others. They have been given much authority in God's Kingdom to do great works because they fully use their talents and their gifts to the best of their abilities.

Someone who has been given two talents and is using their spiritual gifts may be one who is a Pastor of a church or speaking at conferences or going from church to church as a guest speaker whilst shepherding and preaching in their own church.

Most of us would easily relate to those who have been given just one talent. I have a simple camera—a cheap five hundred dollar camera—and I sit down and make "YouTube" videos. I have an inexpensive computer and write articles and put them on the Internet. Thousands of people watch these videos and read these articles each month. Doing that is just using my one little talent and my spiritual gifting. The technology of the internet brings amazing and instant multiplication. It is certainly a tool both God and the devil use in to-days world!

I do not like to think that any servant of God can be found squandering their talent to the extent that this last servant did. Scripture teaches that salvation is a free gift and Jesus has promised to never cast out a believer, (John 6:37) so the passage is not talking about loss of salvation. Perhaps the hard words said by Jesus in verse 30 may refer to the loss of a person's reward at the Judgment Seat of believers.

You can read all about this Judgment by looking up 1 Corinthians 3:11-15. Verse 15 says: *"If anyone's work is burned, he will suffer loss; but he himself will be saved, yet so as through fire."*

I spoke on the Judgment Seat of Christ in the previous chapter but will continue now. This particular judgment will not be against sins we have committed, because Jesus has already been judged for them and God is legally bound not ever to judge sin *twice*. In our courts of law this is called "Double Jeopardy" and God is not into doing that! In fact, God has chosen to forget our sin and wipe them from His memory forever. This judgment will take place in Heaven and is only for Christians - there will be no unbelievers present in Heaven! This "Day" will determine the eternal rewards we will receive by the Lord Jesus or the loss of rewards for our works of service while on earth. This reward system is based only on how we have lived our life *since becoming a Christian because everything before that time has been wiped clean and is not even remembered by God anymore!* This particular servant in our parable would forfeit the blessing and joy of reward by his unfaithfulness in stewardship.

We are responsible to God for what we do with the resources he has entrusted us with. This includes our finances, our opportunities, our talents and our gifting He has given to us. The "weeping and gnashing of teeth" mentioned in this parable would reflect the servant's remorse for lost opportunity. This is because the individual judgment made on that Day will come into play for that person for all eternity. There will no other future assessments or judgments by the Lord Jesus. Now on earth, we are to plan for the future!

We are to take seriously the things God has entrusted us with. One future day we will be so pleased that we have not wasted our privileges. Also, commit yourself to do a Spiritual Gifts test. Discover your personal gifts and begin to work in them. As I have said, there is nothing more exciting than walking in your spiritual gifts.

I believe that I have the gift of teaching, the gift of encouragement, the gift of prophecy and the gift of evangelism. These gifts I am very aware of and I use them as the opportunity arises. Occasionally God has graciously given me a word of knowledge or a word of wisdom and this has been exciting, but scary. (What if I get it wrong?)

Everyone has a particular purpose that God planned long before their conception! To get a handle on this read the whole of Psalm 139 – it will blow you away! Most often your purpose can be found in what you want to do, your dreams, your desires and your biggest ambitions. These things often reflect God's destiny for you, so you need to make small steps and work towards them.

For many years, I have wanted to preach. I had a friend who bought a camera and we both started to preach a little bit and then he sold the camera to a Pawn Broker because he needed money. We could not preach anymore and that upset me, but it had planted a seed and a desire in me.

A couple of years later, the Australian government gave people on a disability pension some money, supposedly to help boost the economic downturn. I used this money to buy myself a camera and soon I started to make videos on YouTube. If you search YouTube under my full name, I have a few hundred videos. I believe I am walking in my destiny. I hope in the future not only to be preaching to people on the Internet, but I hope to be preaching to audiences and in churches, but we have to take things step by step. In the meantime, God has been working on my theology, building line upon line, precept upon precept. That is His way of growing us. We can move slowly into our destiny or quite fast. It all depends on the Lord and His wisdom in knowing where we currently are or how much we can absorb.

You can be taking steps to equip yourself to become more proficient at individual parts of your destiny before you move into the whole thing. So I encourage you to work out your natural abilities and most importantly, your spiritual gifts. Dream big and tell God how much you appreciate the work He has started in you. Always remember that what God starts in any one of us, He always finishes! We have His word on this: *"Being confident of this very thing; that He who has began a good work in you will complete it until the day of Jesus Christ." Philippians 1:6.* In fact, the Holy Spirit has seen fit to repeat His message in different words! See 1 Corinthians 1:8 and 2 Timothy 4:18. God reinforces our confidence in His ability so that the devil will not be able to convince us that it is all up to our ability.

Don't be hard on yourself! God is committed to the task of perfecting you. God Bless.

CHAPTER 42

The Parable of The Ten Virgins
Matthew 25:1-13

If you are reading all of the parables in this book, you will probably be happy with what has been done. If you are not, well maybe this is just the parable for you.

Ten virgins went out to wait for the bridegroom. Five took spare oil for their lamps and the others didn't! This first five had wisely prepared for a long wait while the others had not. The bridegroom was very late in coming and all ten virgins eventually fell asleep. When the bridegroom finally came, the five wise virgins used their spare oil to light their lamps and the other five virgins begged to have some oil. *"But the wise answered, saying, No, lest there should not be enough for us and you; but go rather to those who sell, and buy for yourselves."* (25:9.) The five wise virgins then went with the Bridegroom to the party. When the foolish ones returned with more oil, they were too late and missed out on all the festivities. This is a very brief summary of the story Jesus told.

The sermons I have heard on this parable have had little practical application. We need to dig deep! The fact that all ten virgins had oil in their lamps means that they were all Christians because in the Bible oil signifies the Holy Spirit. Therefore they were all saved. Salvation can be likened to being pregnant. No woman can be a little bit pregnant – she is, or she is not! In the same way no one can be a little bit saved – you are, or you are not!

The Holy Spirit is not a commodity that one can dissect! He is a Divine Person, being the third member of the Holy Trinity of God. He is equal to the Father and to Jesus Christ in every way. Some say: the Father is the Divine Executive, the Son is the Divine Architect and the Holy Spirit is the Divine Contractor. We are told that Holy men of God wrote the Bible under the direct inspiration of the Holy Spirit. (2 Peter 1:20-21) The Holy Spirit is a person not just a "force or power" that the Jehovah Witnesses will tell you. If the Holy Spirit is living in your life, know that He is the Father's gift to every born-again believer! He is the seal that we belong to God. 2 Corinthians 1:21-22 says: *"Now He who establishes us with you in Christ and has anointed us is God, who also has sealed us and given us the Spirit in our hearts as a guarantee."*

159

The difference between a traditional church and a Pentecostal church is that a traditional church says that once you have the indwelling presence of the Holy Spirit then you are fully equipped to live a victorious Christian life. However, a Pentecostal church teaches that whilst you receive the "presence" of the Holy Spirit at salvation, there is such a thing as a second anointing of the Holy Spirit, called the Baptism of the Holy Spirit.

Two things occur at this Baptism. The first and most obvious to the believer will be to receive a new prayer language from God. In time, others will notice the increased love the believer has towards both God and man. Helpful information about this Baptism is given in the back section of this book. Like a toddler starting to talk, the prayer language may be quite basic at first, but it will develop and mature with practice. Later on, the Lord may bless a believer with multiple prayer languages.

Not all people have the faith to immediately receive this anointing. It is not something that we are to stress over but we should continue to actively seek it. Jesus said: *"If you then, being evil, know how to give good gifts to your children, how much more will your heavenly Father give the Holy Spirit to those who ask Him!" Luke 11:13.* I do not believe that this Scripture refers to salvation. How many unbelievers ask for the Holy Spirit? Just recall when you were saved. You were convicted of sin and you just wanted to surrender your life to Jesus so you called out to Him to save you and to forgive you. It was not until later that you found out that the Holy Spirit had taken up residence in your life.

The second result of this Baptism is that the Holy Spirit will give the believer one or more of His nine gifts mentioned in 1 Corinthians Chapter Twelve. This gifting will be in line with the particular kingdom work God has pre-ordained each Christian to do. You will see that in this listing are the gift of tongues and the gift of interpretation of tongues used to assist a prophecy that has been declared to the church. Please be sure not to confuse the prayer language above with these two "gifts" of tongues I have spoken of here.

Note that there is a distinction here: *all the "nine gifts" of the Holy Spirit are given to edify others, but our heavenly prayer language is given to edify us personally!*

We can then go deeper with God and our prayers will not come from our mind but directly from God. I must add that some Christians have the wrong belief that God gives us our own personal "prayer language" without our co-operation. Yes, *He gives us the words to say* but we must voluntarily offer our vocal chords, our tongue and our mouth to Jesus, before He can baptize us with His Holy Spirit. Both the receiving and the use of this anointing will always remain our choice. God will never take away our free-will!

We cannot only have "part" of the Holy Spirit living in us, but often He has only part of us! Our allegiance to Him may be divided: in the flesh, we can actually choose to allow our old nature to be boss! Therefore, our joy and our preparedness for the Lord's return will vary. That, I believe is the difference between these two groups of virgins: the wise virgins were fully committed to wait as long as it took, while the others were not!

The universal church encompasses all denominations worldwide. It is the Bride of Christ.

People from every background can be part of His Bride! The common denominator is the Holy Spirit at work in their hearts. Therefore, there are no first or second class Christians. Every Christian is who he is because God's Holy Spirit lives in them. You either have Christ, or He is still waiting at the door hoping to be invited in. However, there are various degrees of "commitment" and "maturity" within the universal church of God

At times in the past, the preaching of this parable didn't ring true to me. I not only like to hear Scripture taught, but I also need to find a practical application to God's word. The Scriptures should give us meaning, purpose and direction in our day to day life. Therefore, if it's possible to be a foolish Christian virgin, I want to be constantly alert for the bridegroom. It has been two thousand years now since Jesus physically ascended up into the clouds. When He comes back for His bride, he will return in like manner.

While the disciples watched: *"He* Jesus) *was taken up, and a cloud received Him out of their sight. And while they looked steadfastly toward heaven as He went up, behold, two men stood by them in white apparel, who also said, "Men of Galilee, why do you stand gazing up into heaven? This same Jesus, who was taken up from you into heaven, will so come in like manner as you saw Him go into heaven." Acts 1:9b-11*

Jesus had just told His disciples not to depart from Jerusalem, but to wait for His Holy Spirit. He said in Acts 1:8 *"You shall receive power when the Holy Spirit has come upon you; and you shall be witnesses to Me in Jerusalem, and in all Judea and Samaria, and to the ends of the earth."*

Earlier, in John 20:21-22 we read: *"Jesus said to them, 'Peace to you! As the Father has sent Me, I also send you.' And when He had said this, He breathed on them, and said to them, 'Receive the Holy Spirit.'"* This event happened after the resurrection of Christ and *before* He ascended into the clouds. The disciples received the "presence" of the Holy Spirit, but a short time later, in the Book of Acts Chapter Two, these same disciples received the "power" of the Holy Spirit. This new anointing enabled them to be no longer cowards, but to boldly proclaim the risen Christ to the Jews. This miraculous anointing caused three thousand souls to be converted to Christianity in just one day!

Christians are first to be witnesses in their own home and family, then, they are to be witnesses in their everyday area of contact. Lastly they are to be a witnessing tool to the ends of the earth. This is our mandate from God. This is our assignment on earth.

Jesus has delayed His return! In Chapter One I explained how He was going to return in the clouds and snatch up to Himself every world-wide born-again believer. He will come like a thief in the night or at an hour we do not expect. We are to be on constant alert!

"Behold, I tell you a mystery; we shall not all sleep, but we shall all be changed – in a moment, in the twinkling of an eye, at the last trumpet. For the trumpet will sound, and the dead will be raised incorruptible, and we shall be changed." 1 Corinthians

15:51-52.

To the world, "dead" means dead! But God says when a Christian dies, they are asleep! Remember the twelve year old girl who had died and Jesus told the mourners that she was not dead, that she was asleep. He said the same thing about His close friend, Lazarus, when He was told that he had died a few days earlier. That is why when a Christian departs from this life, we know that death has lost its sting! Physical death becomes a triumphant door that allows our loved one to enjoy a glorious new life in heaven.

Many of the parables share a common theme. Our responsibility until the Master returns is to be about God's Kingdom business. So that when He finally comes back for us He will say "Well done, good and faithful servant. Enter my Father's kingdom which has been prepared for you since the foundation of the earth."

Another common theme in the parables is that some people were given things they didn't use. The man with the one talent did not invest it! The religious leaders ignored the injured Samaritan although they could have helped him! We today have many opportunities to bless others but it is easier to turn a blind eye. Jesus would not judge us if we did not have the means to help others. So, could it be that the foolish virgins are people who are saved, but have no abundance, mercy or grace to give to others.

Could it be that missing the party, actually means missing out on the fullness of the abundant anointing of Jesus Christ? Could it be that some Christians are happy and satisfied, walking around in the presence of the Lord, full of joy just like a true bride is with her groom, while other Christians are walking around depressed and sad, not living a life of joy and blessings that God has for them?

I read in a book about an atheist who said he did not want to become a Christian because most Christians seem to him, to be like people who have a headache that they can't shake off! Perhaps these people stifle the Holy Spirit from bubbling up with joy and peace. They therefore appear to have no relationship with Jesus Christ. Could it be that the foolish virgins are people who are not experiencing the fullness of Jesus Christ? Someone in that situation is not the best answer for a person who is unsaved. They would not illuminate light, which is what we are called to be and do in this world.

The perfect Christian life is to have enough joy, security, peace and love overflowing us that we can share it with a brother who is not doing too well. It is good for the Holy Spirit to have access to *all our life* so that we can be a source of encouragement to others. A wise believer would be so filled with the Spirit of God that His presence, vitality and power bubbled out to all who were open to receive. God's kind of love is meant to be contagious! I believe that this parable and the parable of the Sheep and the Goats will encourage you to share your overflowing oil with others less fortunate.

My mental illness has caused me to be wrongly judged by others. Still, it gives me great fulfillment to do what I am called to do - to walk in the gifts that God has given me, and it supplies me with enough joy to overflow into other people's lives and encourage them.

Jesus was filled with the Holy Spirit, that He healed all those who came to Him. We are to share His ways with others. He went away, but has promised to return. Jesus gave His disciples an incredible mandate in Matthew 10:8 and in Matthew 28:19-20. He has given us His authority and His grace. Every Christian has Christ, but does He have all of us?

Some of my teaching on the Holy Spirit may be new to you so I trust that I have not confused you. God bless you.

CHAPTER 43

THE PARABLE OF THE SOWER
(MATTHEW 13:3-9 AND 18-23)

I hope that in reading this parable, you will receive some new insight. I received some of this information from an apostle who came to my church, but I never considered that the slant he gave to this parable would affect me. I have never been the same since.

Matthew 13:3-9: *Then He spoke many things to them in parables, saying: "Behold, a sower went out to sow. And as he sowed, some seed fell by the wayside; and the birds came and devoured them. Some fell on stony places, where they did not have much earth; and they immediately sprang up because they had no depth of earth. But when the sun was up they were scorched, and because they had no root they withered away. And some fell among thorns, and the thorns sprang up and choked them. But others fell on good ground and yielded a crop: some a hundredfold, some sixty, some thirty. He who has ears to hear, let him hear!"*

Then in verses 10-17, Jesus explained the reason why He spoke in parables. He wanted the people to see, hear and understand. That is what the parables are for; to give understanding, but they make the seeker search truth out. For many years, I have been trying to search the deeper meanings of the parables. This book has been the result of much study and meditation, and I hope that you will be blessed by what I have to say.

He says in verses 18-19: *"Therefore hear the parable of the sower: When anyone hears the word of the kingdom, and does not understand it, then the wicked one comes and snatches away what was sown in his heart. This is he who received seed by the wayside.*

Now, let me establish what it says here in verse 19 about hearing the word of the Kingdom, but not understanding it. There are a couple of reasons why people might not understand the Scriptures.

Number one is that the preacher may not have explained a passage well enough, and so the listeners do not understand. But the major reason why people do not understand new teaching is that they hold onto old teaching. The flesh will try to resist change!

164

I am not rubbishing Christ's church here; I grew up in a mainline denominational church and was saved at the age of eight in such a church. Well meaning friends of mine have told me that apostles, prophets and the nine gifts of the Holy Spirit were given to the church by God, in order to firmly establish it. They believe that once all the Scriptures were faithfully recorded, there was no further use for these other things. The complete word of God is all that we now need to become a mature Christian. Therefore, when a Pastor teaches like this, their congregation believes it to be true. After all, the Pastor has a "Theological" degree and his audience is not professionally trained. Bear in mind that the Apostle Paul encouraged us to find out for ourselves what Scripture says!

The Holy Spirit has given me the gift of prophecy. At times He has given me a word of knowledge or wisdom to validate a prophecy. I would estimate that during the course of my life I have given about four thousand prophecies to people. Three quarters of these prophecies have been given to total strangers on the streets. I would also say that each one had a powerful effect on its receiver about things in their life that only God would know. I am very grateful for these gifts because they have helped so many people over the years. Prophecy is a message from God and the gift of knowledge and the gift of wisdom give a particular directional word of God.

I have no problem knowing that the spiritual gifts exist and have a powerful effect. Apostle Paul said, "The best gift is the gift of prophecy," and I know that this tremendous gift is amazing. However, if you attend a church that denies the gifts of the Holy Spirit and then hear me talking about prophecy, immediately you think: "No, that does not exist. That teaching is of the devil." No man can open a closed mind! You need a revelation from the Holy Spirit direct to your spirit for you to change your doctrine.

You my reader may be one who believes that 1 Corinthians 13:8-13 refers to the "*unfinished Scriptures*" of Paul's day and that now that we have the completed Scriptures, supernatural gifts are no longer necessary! I believe otherwise. I believe that a time will come when prophecies, tongues and knowledge will cease. But they will pass away only when the Lord Jesus Christ returns for His Bride and not a moment before.

You see, *Our Lord Jesus Christ is that which is perfect!* When we see Him face to face at the Rapture, there will no longer be any need for supernatural gifts. In the meantime, the church needs these gifts to come against the attacks of the enemy and to manifest the glory of God to all mankind. We are told that *"Jesus Christ is the same yesterday, today, and forever." Hebrews 13:8.* Therefore, the Holy Spirit is the same yesterday, today, and forever. God does not change. The Holy Spirit gave His gifts to His church two thousand years ago and He still gives gifts to His church today!

Yes, the Holy Spirit operated differently in the Old Testament because the people were under the Old Covenant. The prophets of God told the people that a new time was coming. The New Covenant of God has opened a new way based on what God's Son has accomplished. Praise God, we can now be "filled permanently" with God's Holy Spirit!

The book of James 1:17 says: "Good gifts come down from the Father," but as soon as I start talking about the gifts of the Holy Spirit, a reader who does not believe in the Pentecostal gifts may immediately switch off. There are many teachings that are true, but some never take root in a person's life. This is because the person listening switches off and says to himself that the teaching that he is hearing is wrong! There is so much that God might want a person to hear, but that person switches off, because what is being taught does not agree with what he has been taught beforehand. This is the seed that is sown on the wayside. Does that make sense to you? In order to learn in this world, we need to have open ears. We need to listen to things with an open mind and let the speaker explain what he is saying by the Word of God. If we switch off straight away when something contrary is said, we miss out on many blessings!

"But he who received the seed on stony places, this is he who hears the word and immediately receives it with joy; yet he has no root in himself, but endures only for a while. For when tribulation or persecution arises because of the word, immediately he stumbles." Matthew 13:20-21.

Some teachers say that people may hear the salvation message, but when tribulation arises, they fall away because they have no root in themselves. Some think that it's not a person's fault if someone offends them at church or something drastic happens. Satan is there to attack people as soon as they have given their life to Christ, and so they may fall away. But a more appropriate meaning is this: every time the Word of God is preached, it takes time to settle into a person or for a person to come into alignment with it and start to obey what was taught.

For instance, this book of parables has various insights. It teaches readers many things in order for them to work out their own salvation and things to practice in their daily lives. Now, people could begin to put into practice one of the things that I have taught. They may decide to help a homeless person as I shared in the parable of the Sheep and the Goats. Suddenly some homeless man starts acting violent towards them so they give up this idea because persecution or tribulation had come to them.

Therefore, it is necessary that when the Word of God convicts you to move out in a new way, you must stay on track of your conviction. Then you will begin moving closer to Christ in a more efficient way, and in Christ, there is new freedom and liberty. Satan is aware that you have moved in that new direction. You are becoming more effective for the Kingdom of God, so he rises up in opposition against you. Tribulation and persecution will come against you, directly associated with your new obedience. Now, if you are shaken by Satan's attacks, well then, you will stumble and possibly fall away, and that is what the parable is talking about in regard to the stony places.

"Now he who received seed among the thorns is he who hears the word and the cares of this world and the deceitfulness of riches choke the word, and he becomes unfruitful" Matthew 13:22.

This verse is warning that the cares of this world and the deceitfulness of wealth choke the Word and it becomes unfruitful. The Kingdom of God has to be expanded. It costs a huge amount of money to broadcast Christian teachings on TV. It costs large amounts of money to take the Gospel to foreign countries. So often, people who are in those ministries could do so much more if they had more finances. Anything I earn from the sale of this book will go back into God's work. Therefore I am not promoting my book for personal gain. I truly believe that it is an excellent tool for my readers to pass on to others or to buy multiple copies for people they have been praying for: people who need to know Jesus and also people who are open to learn more about the Scriptures. You could direct people to the website version of this book or advertise the link on Facebook.

The thing that stands in the way of most Western Christians is the deceitfulness of riches and the cares for the things of the world. If I am talking about making a two hundred dollars investment in copies or printing of this book, most often people will not go forth and spread this word to their friends, because of that money. Most often, the god of this world, Satan, uses money to prevent the will of God being accomplished. So many things come back to money and Jesus would not have shared this parable and said that the cares of this world and the deceitfulness of riches stop people, if it did not. People also care about their reputation, that is why they do not share the Gospel or practice much of what is taught in the Bible, because they are worried about what other people would think.

Verse 23 says, *"But he who received seed on the good ground is he who hears the word and understands it, who indeed bears fruit and produces: some a hundredfold, some sixty, some thirty."*

When you hear, understand and practice the Word of God and tribulation arises, continue to press on and do not let the distraction deter you. It might even start costing you money. It may start costing you your reputation, but I encourage you to endure. If you persist through the cares of the world and the deceitfulness of riches, the Word of God is being planted deeper and deeper in your heart. It will bear fruit and it will have a big return. You might find that difficult to believe, but the Scripture says that it will.

I pray that everything you learn from this book will compel you to live a richer Christian life. You do not have to do all the things I suggest straight away. Just do one of them and watch it multiply. Be aware that persecution and tribulation may follow, because Jesus warned us that it might. But know that *"He who is in you is greater than he who is in the world."* 1 John 4:4.

Go and bear much fruit for Jesus. Ask God to totally fill you with His Holy Spirit and to cause you to exercise His supernatural gifts. I hope that I have given you some insight into this parable.

CHAPTER 44

THE PARABLE OF THE TWO DEBTORS
(LUKE 7:41-50)

The passage in Luke 7:41-50 reads:

"There was a certain creditor who had two debtors. One owed five hundred denarii's, and the other fifty, and when they had nothing with which to repay, he freely forgave them both. Tell Me, therefore, which of them will love him more?"

Simon answered and said, "I suppose the one whom he forgave more."

And He said to him, "You have rightly judged." Then He turned to the woman and said to Simon, "Do you see this woman? I entered your house; you gave Me no water for My feet, but she has washed My feet with her tears and wiped them with the hair of her head. You gave Me no kiss, but this woman has not ceased to kiss My feet since the time I came in. You did not anoint My head with oil, but this woman has anointed My feet with fragrant oil. Therefore I say to you, her sins, which are many, are forgiven, for she loved much, but to whom little is forgiven, the same loves little."

Then He said to her, "Your sins are forgiven."

And those who sat at the table with Him began to say to themselves, "Who is this who even forgives sins?"

Then He said to the woman, "Your faith has saved you. Go in peace."

This Parable of the Two Debtors is found within the context of the woman who anointed Jesus' feet with expensive and fragrant oil. This is a well known story in the Gospels, and we are going to draw out some points.

At this time, Jesus was residing at the house of a Pharisee. This leader liked Jesus to come to his place for it gave the man prestige! Being leaders in the Jewish faith, they were very important people in society and were mostly very devout. They spent their whole life trying to make sure that God's will was being done.

Let me indulge myself here. Imagine if I was an international speaker who had two hundred and fifty speaking engagements a year and at night, you could watch me on

Christian Satellite stations. Let us say, I had twenty bestselling books. In other words, I was one of the most well known and loved speakers in the world. What if I was that person and I came to your house to share some time with you, discussing anything that you chose to bring up and answering any of your questions? Wouldn't you feel honored to have my company? I believe that was exactly how Simon, the Pharisee, felt when Jesus was his guest.

Jesus was very humble. Today, many Christians condemn the Pharisees, but they really thought they were doing the best they could and were far more devout with their own faith than many Christians are today. At that time, Jesus was at Simon's house. Then, the most well known sinner in town burst into the house and started washing Jesus' feet.

Let us look at the parable, from verse 37-38: *And behold, a woman in the city who was a sinner, when she knew that Jesus sat at the table in the Pharisee's house, brought an alabaster flask of fragrant oil, and stood at His feet behind Him weeping; and she began to wash His feet with her tears, and wiped them with the hair of her head; and she kissed His feet and anointed them with the fragrant oil.*

Many people say that she was a prostitute, because of what the Pharisees said in verse 39, *Now when the Pharisee who had invited Him saw this, he spoke to himself, saying, "This Man, if He were a prophet, would know who and what manner of woman this is who is touching Him, for she is a sinner."*

Simon believed that this woman was making Jesus unclean: she should not be touching Him. Under the Jewish law, Jesus should have rebuked her! The Pharisees thought, "If this Rabbi is really who He says he is, He should stop this nonsense! It is disgusting and He is asking for trouble. If He is really a prophet He would know who she is and He would have nothing to do with her, but would tell her to stop making Him unclean."

Actually, I gave you a few more words than were recorded in the Bible. I just expanded on the thoughts of Simon, and this is where the parable kicks in, verse 40, *"And Jesus answered and said to him..."*

You, like I did, might wonder, what did Jesus answer? Simon had not even spoken. He had merely thought these things to himself, but here we see that Jesus answered his critical thinking! This is very interesting for it reminds me of something that I do. People sometimes ask me saying, "How do you speak to Jesus in visions?" And I answer them and say, "I speak in thoughts."

Here, Jesus did not answer the thought directly, He instead told a parable. "Simon I have something to say to you," and so Simon said "Teacher, say it."

Simon called Jesus "Teacher" as a sign of respect, because even though Simon had negative thoughts about Jesus at this time, he knew that anyone who is learned in the things of God is very open to someone who is more learned.

A teacher of the Word of God is someone you want to listen to even if you disagree with some points that they say. So, showing respect that Jesus was His very special guest and that he wanted to hear anything He had to say, he said "Teacher, say it."

Jesus said in verses 41-43: *"There was a certain creditor who had two debtors. One owed five hundred denarius, and the other fifty, and when they had nothing with which to repay, he freely forgave them both. Tell Me, therefore, which of them will love him more?"*

Simon answered and said, "I suppose the one whom he forgave more."

And He said to him, "You have rightly judged."

In the Parable of the Vineyard, it was mentioned that a denarius is equivalent to a day's wages. This means that one debtor owed five hundred days wages and the other one owed fifty days wages. A good wage in Australia for a pretty good job is two hundred dollars a day. Five hundred days wages is therefore one hundred thousand dollars; and fifty days wages is ten thousand dollars.

The point that Jesus is making is that if we feel that we have a giant size debt to pay and someone pays it for us then we will be far more grateful than a person who thinks they only have a small debt owing. Our gratitude is therefore linked to the size of our debt.

Imagine a situation. Someone loaned you a hundred thousand dollars to buy a house. Later, you lost your job and consequently, you were about to lose your house. Then you appealed to the person to give you more time to pay the debt and he says, "Don't worry about it. Just keep the money, friend. It's fine, keep your house."

There is nothing you would not do for that friend who forgave your debt! You would baby sit their children, you would work for them in their company for free. You would do anything for them and you would be in tears because you would not be able to repay.

And so, in verses 44-50, *then He turned to the woman and said to Simon, "Do you see this woman? I entered your house; you gave Me no water for My feet, but she has washed My feet with her tears and wiped them with the hair of her head. You gave Me no kiss, but this woman has not ceased to kiss My feet since the time I came in. You did not anoint My head with oil, but this woman has anointed My feet with fragrant oil. Therefore I say to you, her sins, which are many, are forgiven, for she loved much, but to whom little is forgiven, the same loves little."*

Then He said to her, "Your sins are forgiven."

And those who sat at the table with Him began to say to themselves, "Who is this who even forgives sins?"

Then He said to the woman, "Your faith has saved you. Go in peace."

We sometimes hear of a drug dealer or a gang leader or a former high priestess witch who has become a Christian and their testimonies are so compelling. What makes these people's stories so compelling is that they are stories from deep dark depravity to the saving light of Jesus.

The good news of this parable is that everyone can be forgiven by Jesus Christ and every person that comes to Him receives salvation. *"For whoever calls on the name of the Lord shall be saved." Romans 10:13*

Yet, the point of this parable is similar to the parable of the prodigal son. The dirtier you lived your life, the more it seems the celebration is in Heaven when you find Jesus.

In this book, I have shared with you my many years of addiction to the sex industry and I had often wondered why my love for Jesus was just so much more devoted than many Christians I knew. The Holy Spirit has pointed to the words of Jesus in this parable. The fact that I have been forgiven for so many sins makes my love for Jesus deeper than perhaps others who have not lived such a degrading lifestyle.

My debt is such a large debt and yet I know that He has fully forgiven me.

Many people look at sex addicts, the heroin dealers, the drug lords and even the poor homeless people and think that these people are so hard to bring to Jesus, but the opposite is true. The more depraved that you are, the more tender and broken your life is and the more you will respond to the love of the Savior.

I personally believe that this woman who wept at the feet of Jesus was His devoted friend Mary Magdalene. Later on she became Jesus' follower and may have even financed His ministry out of the money that she had. Who knows? Perhaps when I meet her in Heaven one day, I will ask her.

This parable is deeply personal for me to share and one of my all time favorites.

I have met people with a passion and love for Jesus similar to mine who have sinned very little in their life compared to me, so please do not get disheartened thinking that you need to be a terrible sinner to love Jesus a lot. We are all in different stages of sin and God has no favorites in His Kingdom.

This was not the only time Jesus said "Your sins are forgiven," Once Jesus said these words to a paralyzed man and again he said it to a woman who had been caught in the act of adultery. Here, at Simon's house, the guests commented among themselves, but the host did not push the fact that Jesus was actually declaring Himself to be God.

Do you, my reader freely acknowledge that Jesus is God? You need to.

CHAPTER 45

THE PARABLE OF THE TWO SONS
(MATTHEW 21:28-32)

This is the Parable of the Two Sons. I pray that what you gain from this teaching will minister to your spirit. The passage is found in Matthew 21:28-32.

"But what do you think? A man had two sons, and he came to the first and said, 'Son, go, work today in my vineyard.' He answered and said, 'I will not,' but afterward he regretted it and went. Then he came to the second and said likewise, and he answered and said, 'I go, sir,' but he did not go. Which of the two did the will of his father?"

They said to Him, "The first."

Jesus said to them, "Assuredly, I say to you that tax collectors and harlots enter the kingdom of God before you. For John came to you in the way of righteousness, and you did not believe him; but tax collectors and harlots believed him; and when you saw it, you did not afterward relent and believe him."

Jesus might have appeared to be harsh with the Pharisees here. He was giving them a rebuke. It's a loving thing to grow up in a family and have a father rebuke and discipline you in love. Regardless of His rebuke, Jesus was a very loving Person.

Heidi Baker of Iris Ministries, a well known missionary who operates a healing ministry, wrote a book called *Compelled by Love* on the beatitudes, which is part of the Sermon on the Mount found in the Gospel of Matthew. In the foreword, her husband Rolland Baker wrote that wherever he went, people he asked about the Sermon on the Mount would say they were not sure it was possible or practical to live what Jesus preached.

It is indeed impossible to live a life that way without the empowerment of the Holy Spirit, but Heidi believed that it was not only possible, but that it is the way we should live our life. A Christian cannot just love Jesus and obey the commandments given in the Sermon on the Mount by his own strength or will-power. Let us be filled with the mind of Christ and live a supernatural life in a supernatural dimension. When you follow the promptings and thoughts that come to you from the Holy Spirit, then you are living a life that Jesus said is possible in the beatitudes.

The Sermon on the Mount is still part of the Law. Legalists say that if you don't obey it, you are not going to be worthy. The Law is meant to bring you to your knees and say, "Jesus, Jesus, please help me." It's only when you come in submission, that the power of the Holy Spirit is released. As a Christian, when you come to the end of yourself, and say, "I just cannot stop sinning. Lord, please help me," that is when the Lord steps in and operates supernaturally through your life.

The Pharisees were so strict in obeying the Law that sometimes Jesus had to rebuke them because they had a mindset that was stuck in obedience to the Law even above love and compassion. Their heart attitude toward their fellow man was uncaring and pathetic!

Jesus told this parable regarding the two sons, and he said someone came to the first man, "Son, go and work today in my vineyard." The son said, "No, I am not going to work in your vineyard." And then later he changed his mind and worked in the vineyard. He said to the second man, "Work in my vineyard." And he said, "Yes." But then he didn't do it.

Jesus was saying that the Pharisees profess to follow the Law: they profess to want to please God and to obey Him. On the one hand, they were saying that they want to obey everything that God commanded, but when John the Baptist came to preach repentance, they resisted. So it was like they were saying "Yes" to God, but then in the end didn't follow through. However, the prostitutes, tax collectors and sinners, whose lifestyles indicated a rejection of God, changed their minds when they realized that they fell short and needed to draw close to God. They are like the son who initially said "No", but then changed his mind and came to work in the vineyard after all.

See, it's a lot easier for someone who has sinned greatly to come to Jesus, because they know only too well, their many faults. They are lost and have no answers for the questions in life. It's amazing when someone who doesn't know God comes: falls on his knees and gives his life to Jesus, but it is a terrible thing for a prideful person, who is puffed up with self righteousness, to think that he is obeying the whole Law.

It is really hard to teach a person like that. It's almost impossible to correct a person who thinks they do everything right! The Bible calls these people scoffers: they are un-teachable. Scoffers were around in the days of old and will still be around in future days.

"A wise son heeds his father's instruction, but a scoffer does not listen to rebuke; A scoffer seeks wisdom and does not find it, but knowledge is easy to him who understands; The devising of foolishness is sin, and the scoffer is an abomination to men; Scoffers set a city aflame, but wise men turn away wrath; Scoffers will come in the last days, walking according to their own lusts."(Proverbs 13:1, 14:6, 24:9, 29:8, and 2 Peter 3:3)

The Pharisees were very good at interpreting the Law, justifying themselves and saying that they were perfect by the Law's standards. That was the reason why Jesus shared this parable. Essentially, Jesus used a parable to say to the Pharisees, "You want to please the Father, to be righteous and to do everything the Father says, but here I am, a prophet, telling you a new and better way, but you will not receive it. Nor will you receive the baptism of John. You will not receive Me! I have a new yoke for I am a Rabbi with a new form of teaching. There is a new way of doing things now. You need to turn around and follow My way, but you will not do it. You are obstinate, stubborn and extremely proud: you are full of self-righteousness."

"The sinners and the tax collectors are entering into the Kingdom before you. They are like the son who said, 'I would never come.' They were people steeped in sin. They were so far from God and then they relented and said, 'No, God is the answer: I will obey Him! I will put away my life of sin and I will start to walk in a righteous and holy way.'"

This parable still rings true today. To the sinner, there is hope! To the person who has rejected Jesus all their life, they can still change their mind; God will be only too pleased to welcome them into His Kingdom.

You might be a person who thinks that you are good enough and do not need God. You might be a sweet and kind person who does more good things than bad things. You might be very spiritual and have your own private ideas about God, but you cannot believe that Jesus is the only way to the Father. You might be like these Pharisees of old who thought they were justified by all the good things they did, but they rejected the words of Jesus Christ.

The judgment against sin towards all people has been paid for by Jesus. Happy is the person who acknowledges this fact and responds to Jesus. The pride of scoffers, on the other hand makes them look after themselves. They believe that they have all the right answers! These people refuse to acknowledge that they even sin and if they ever did sin, then they themselves will make retribution for it! God sees their folly but will never take away their free will to choose death instead of life.

Which son are you? Are you going to work in the vineyard for God?

CHAPTER 46

THE PARABLE OF THE UNJUST JUDGE
(LUKE 18:1-8)

We read this parable of the unjust judge in Luke 18:1-8, starting with the first verse:

Then He spoke a parable to them, that men always ought to pray and not lose heart.

We are to pray and not lose heart. I will give you an example of this. For years and years, my mother knew that I had an addiction to prostitutes and for years, she prayed that I would find release. She loved me as a son, but she knew that I was in sin. I also had no end of trouble with mental illness. Also, my sin had given Satan an inroad to my life.

It came to a point where frustration made me extremely angry. I had much bitterness and pain towards God and un-forgiveness towards my natural father. At the same time, I was going through a spiritual transition and Satan hated it. He was using my mental illness, and negative attitudes to hurt both myself and others. I struck out against my mum and just crossed her off. With furious, white hot anger, I banished her by saying, "Do not ring me anymore." I did the opposite of respecting and honoring my parents. I totally abused her; I swore my head off and told her I wanted nothing to do with her.

I told my pastor and she was very concerned. Meanwhile, my mother just continued to pray me. Not so much to see me, or to get me back, but she just prayed that I would be okay. She hoped in her heart that one day her relationship with me would be restored.

I know I really broke my mother's heart. I had not spoken to her for fifteen months. Then, in March 2010 my brother told me that my grandmother had died. God convicted me to contact her, so I decided to shop for a nice card and wrote on it that I was open to hearing from her. Immediately our relationship was restored. My mother had not lost heart.

Let us continue with the passage: *"There was in a certain city a judge who did not fear God nor regard man. Now there was a widow in that city; and she came to him, saying, 'Get justice for me from my adversary.' And he would not for a while; but afterward he*

175

said within himself, 'Though I do not fear God nor regard man, yet because this widow troubles me I will avenge her, lest by her continual coming she weary me'" (Vs 2-5).

A woman kept coming back to court: she continually pestered the judge. We can't do that in the Australian court system but we can go to one level of court and if we do not get justice, we can appeal to a higher court. There are three levels of court in this country and if we lose in them, we will not get justice. It seems that this woman was able to come back again and again to this judge. Finally, for selfish motives the judge said: "I am going to give in to this woman; otherwise she is going to wear me down."

Jesus continued: *"Hear what the unjust judge said. And shall God not avenge His own elect who cry out day and night to Him, though He bears long with them? I tell you that He will avenge them speedily. Nevertheless, when the Son of Man comes, will He really find faith on the earth?" verses 6-8.*

If we have a wrong conception of God, we will struggle with faith. Many people believe that God is the source of all diseases, suffering and calamities in the world. They assume that because God is the Superior Being, He has full control over everything on earth: therefore, justice should reign and bad things should not happen!

But let's think about that. We have people in government who are responsible to run our country in a fair and just manner. We have a police force that is trained to handle crime and to protect us. These people have legal control over us, but does that mean that everybody comes under their control? No, of course not! Why? Because we all have a free will to choose what our actions will be. In theory, they should be in control but in practice, they are certainly not!

God is the Supreme Being, but He refuses to over-ride man's free will. Hence we have a world totally out of control. The Bible says that Satan is the god of this world and that is true. He has legal authority *over all unbelievers*. God gave Adam and Eve control over earth and they by their disobedience abdicated their control to Satan. It is for this reason that the world is in such a mess!

Many people see God as an unjust judge: they are actually bitter and secretly or openly hostile towards Him. Life can be hard and we struggle in many ways and we assume that if God loves us, He should remove all the struggles from our life. So much of our lives are dependent on what we know and believe. The truth that we know will set us free: truth is found in the Bible and in the Person of Jesus Christ who said: *"I am the truth."* (John 14:6). Again in John 1:17 – *"For the law was given through Moses, but grace and truth came through Jesus Christ."*

A good preacher can refute error by speaking truth into our life. I only recently discovered that suffering is not from God, but is the result of Adam's sin and the effect that Satan has in this world. Truth brings healing to our life. There are so many factors involved in being set free. We start to become free when we know the truth about God—(1) Who He is: what He is responsible for and what He can do. Then (2), we have to know who we are in Christ and what we can do in God's name. We need to pray in faith based on what we know about these two things. An important point *is to know what we are responsible for and what we are not responsible for!*

Many non-Christians have bitterness and anger in their hearts towards God for things that have happened in their life that they believe God could have prevented. Evil things, such as suffering happens every day, not because God doesn't care, but because we live in a world full of sin and sinners. We live in a fallen world where Satan has much authority.

In Chapter 30, the parable of the Pearl of Great Price, I spoke about living simultaneously in two kingdoms: the visible and the invisible. The invisible kingdom has two opposing camps: one belongs to God and the other belongs to Satan. Until we are born-again, we belong to Satan's kingdom. He is the legal authority over our lives! Suffering comes from two sources only: Satan and his demons or by the wrong choices made by us humans.

Even Christians who have been transferred from Satan's kingdom, to God's kingdom by the work of Jesus on the cross: can become prey to the devil's hate, if they do not cling to God and resist the enemy. A great Bible verse to put into practice is James 4:7-8a - *"Submit to God. Resist the devil and he will flee from you. Draw near to God and He will draw near to you."*

The opposite of resisting something, is to be passive towards it. A passive Christian will become prey to all the enemy's attacks: we need to use spiritual weapons against Satan. These weapons include praise and thanksgiving to God, prayer, and also *verbally resisting Satan* by using the word of God against his deception and assaults. We are told in 1 Timothy 6:12 to fight the good fight of faith! God has given us special armor to fight a very real spiritual war! (You may need to re-read Chapter 19 on the King's War Plans.)

To know the word of God is absolutely essential for our survival against sin and the devil. Also, we need to draw on the power of the Holy Spirit before we even begin to fight the devil. We are told to first submit to God. That means to recognize his awesome power, victory and authority in our life. Second, we are to openly and verbally out loud resist the attacks of the devil. Remind him that he is a defeated foe and has no authority to rule in our life because we are covered by the blood of Jesus. Use God's words against him. When we follow this principle, the devil will flee!

Read the story of when Jesus was led by the Holy Spirit into the wilderness for forty days to be tempted by Satan. Note how he would not succumb to the enemy's taunts, but used the word of God against every suggestion that Satan made. In the end, Satan left Him alone. If Jesus needed to fight Satan, we certainly have to.

The record of this temptation is found in Mathew 4:1-11. It has been recorded for our benefit so that we can learn how to combat the devil and win. The Holy Spirit led Jesus to this testing time before He began His short three year ministry on earth. The line had to be drawn: Satan had to be put in His place right from the beginning. The same thing happens when we begin to minister: Satan will do his best to thwart our plans and we have to hold our ground just like Jesus did in the power of the Holy Spirit.

Sometimes bad things happen because of foolish choices we ourselves have made or foolish choices made by others that have affected our life. For example: Christians can be involved in an accident caused by a drunken driver! Innocent children can be sexually abused by a pervert who has lust from the devil in his heart. We can innocently go into a bad marriage with the mistaken idea that our love will cause our spouse to overcome their gambling addiction or whatever.

But this parable is saying that God hears our prayers like that unjust judge. The parable says that God will avenge—He will answer our prayers. He will make sure things are done right. Jesus emphasized that we should pray like that and not to give up. Know that God doesn't work in the same time-frame as us. This can be frustrating, but it builds perseverance in us. If, in the meantime, we decide to take matters into our own hands and execute our own revenge, we in fact prevent God from working on our behalf. God says "Okay my child, I will just step aside!"

Instead, ask God to exercise His justice on our behalf. The Bible says in Hebrews 10:31 *"It is a fearful thing to fall into the hands of the living God."* Personally, I would prefer the anger of another human to be foisted on me than God's anger to be released onto me! If we react to negative situations God's way, we will discover that it's the best way!

To explain this parable fully would take an entire book. There is so much to cover and the best I can do is advise you to watch Andrew Wommack at the address I give at the end of this book.

CHAPTER 47

THE PARABLE OF THE UNJUST STEWARD
(LUKE 16:1-13)

The parable in Luke 16:1-13 says:

He also said to His disciples: "There was a certain rich man who had a steward, and an accusation was brought to him that this man was wasting his goods. So he called him and said to him, 'What is this I hear about you? Give an account of your stewardship, for you can no longer be steward.'

"Then the steward said within himself, 'What shall I do? For my master is taking the stewardship away from me. I cannot dig; I am ashamed to beg. I have resolved what to do, that when I am put out of the stewardship, they may receive me into their houses.' "So he called every one of his master's debtors to him, and said to the first, 'How much do you owe my master?' And he said, 'A hundred measures of oil.' So he said to him, 'Take your bill, and sit down quickly and write fifty.' Then he said to another, 'And how much do you owe?' So he said, 'A hundred measures of wheat.' And he said to him, 'Take your bill, and write eighty.' So the master commended the unjust steward because he had dealt shrewdly. For the sons of this world are more shrewd in their generation than the sons of light.

"And I say to you, make friends for yourselves by unrighteous mammon, that when you fail, they may receive you into an everlasting home. He who is faithful in what is least is faithful also in much; and he who is unjust in what is least is unjust also in much. Therefore if you have not been faithful in the unrighteous mammon, who will commit to your trust the true riches? And if you have not been faithful in what is another man's, who will give you what is your own?

"No servant can serve two masters; for either he will hate the one and love the other, or else he will be loyal to the one and despise the other. You cannot serve God and mammon."

We see here that this steward was petrified when his master found out that he was not doing his job well. He was lazy and not very good at managing his master's accounts.

He didn't care about collecting bills for the master and he was losing money hand over fist for him, but when he was about to lose his job, he said to himself, "I can't go and dig roads. I can't do manual labor. Hard labor will kill me and I am too ashamed to beg."

Someone who is jobless doesn't have a sense of security. In those days, if you couldn't do the hard manual labor required on farms, things were tough for you. This steward may have been overweight and unfit. If that was the case, then he would find manual labor difficult and he would have to beg, and begging takes great humility. Therefore, this steward devised another option: he put a plan in action to secure his future!

We read his plan in verses 4 to 8. He basically went to his master's debtors and gave them big discounts on their accounts and then collected all of the money. He knew he was ripping his master off and eventually he would be fired, so he had set himself up to look good in the eyes of the debtors. He figured that those whom he had given discounts to, would give him work when he lost his present job. He was thinking that when he became poor and had no food, he would need a job. He figured that those, to whom he gave hefty discounts to, would be merciful to him by giving him food and lodging.

This man was both lazy and shrewd. He had been living off his master's income and had been dishonest in administering his master's funds. Like some of the government workers who waste the people's money, this manager was just a waste of space. He was self focused and lacked integrity: he didn't care about his master's business at all, but was out to just save himself from calamity.

When he realized that he couldn't bring himself to dig ditches or to beg, because he lacked the humility to appear desperate, he knew he was in a bad situation. Therefore, he became cunning and worldly "wise" with money. When he gave huge discounts to the people who owed his master money, they willingly paid the balance. Who wouldn't?

But remember, at that time he was still employed by the master, so his statement of account that the bills had been settled was legal tender. The master couldn't come back and say: "My steward was unfaithful. Pay me the rest." It was legal because the manager was still exercising authority on behalf of his master. The manager wanted to build up friendship with the debtors in the hope that one of them had an easy job for him in the future. He was building up future protection for himself at the master's expense.

Verse 9, *"And I say to you, make friends for yourselves by unrighteous mammon, that when you fail, they may receive you into an everlasting home."*

These are difficult words. We cannot buy our way to heaven, but our stewardship to God is definitely a good indicator of our relationship to Him. Therefore, money can be used for an eternal home. Jesus was taking the example of this unjust steward to be applied to His Kingdom. He hinted at using the money of the unrighteous mammon on earth to build up a foundation and a security in the Kingdom of Heaven.

Paul talks to Timothy about a similar thing in 1 Timothy 6:17-19 *"Command those who are rich in this present age not to be haughty, nor to trust in uncertain riches, but in the living God, who gives us richly all things to enjoy. Let them do good, that they be rich in good works, ready to give, willing to share, storing up for themselves a good foundation for the time to come, that they may lay hold on eternal life."*

This was the Apostle Paul speaking to Timothy under the influence of the Holy Spirit. This is a message for us! Paul was referring to rich people. If you are in the West, even if you are on a social security pension, you are richer than ninety percent of the people in the world. Paul was saying, "Do not be proud. Do not be haughty nor trust in your wealth or in your job, but trust in God and share your money."

The above passage says that we should be ready to give and be willing to share our resources all the time. By doing so, we will store up for ourselves a good foundation for the time to come. The Kingdom of God has certain principles - Christians should be willing to share and to do good works. Also, it's helpful to know that *"the wealth of the sinner is stored up for the righteous."* (Proverbs 13:22b)

Back to our parable: Luke 16:10 - *"He who is faithful in what is least is faithful also in much; and he who is unjust in what is least is unjust also in much."*

Jesus believes money is the least thing in the world. There are a lot harder things to do in the Christian faith than tithing and giving money to deserving causes. Compared to tithing, it's much harder to deal with persecution, or to bear with someone who is being extremely difficult to deal with, or to forgive someone who has maligned your name or attacked you. We must allow God to change any tight-fisted attitudes and bring us in line with His purposes because He wants us to use money wisely and give to others.

In Luke 16:11, God does not want us self-deluded! He is simply saying: "I cannot trust people with my other treasures, if they cannot be trusted with the money I give them."

Verses 12 and 13 continue: *And if you have not been faithful in what is another man's, who will give you what is your own? No servant can serve two masters; for either he will hate the one and love the other, or else he will be loyal to the one and despise the other. You cannot serve God and mammon."*

This man used his master's money to serve himself and build up riches for his own benefit. If we use all our money on ourselves with no thought of others or God, we have the potential to become just like this unjust steward. We need to see ourselves in this parable. Jesus wants us to realize money is important in this world and it has been given to us for a good reason. We should administer our money correctly and our Master, Jesus, should definitely receive His share.

To sum this up, God is saying that you have to choose who you serve. Money is the least. You need to get over the love of money and start giving your money to God and trust Him. God gives us tests, not for Him to see what we are made up of, but for us to see what we are made up of. Bear in mind: if you are not trusting God in the least of things, how can He bless you in the most blessed things that will count for all eternity.

I don't mean to be on your case, but this is what God is saying here: money should be the least of your concerns. If you are generous with your wealth and give with open arms to the Lord, then the Lord is your Master. If you are not generous in sharing material things then money could be your master. This parable is as simple as that to understand.

What people don't realize is that when you see all your money as belonging to God: He knows this and financially honors us. He is then free to multiply our resources, just like He did with the feeding of the huge crowd with a small boy's lunch. Similarly, we don't understand how a small seed grows but God does. God delights to be able to create! When our money belongs to Him, He does far more with it than any budget we can devise. I know this from personal experience and millions of other Christians would be able to confirm this truth. It's amazing! God's book-keeping skills are supernatural.

It is not my intention to fill you with condemnation and guilt. The opposite is true: I want to build your faith in God. It takes great soul searching and faith to start giving, especially when you have a small income like mine, but the joy of doing it far outweighs the pain, I can assure you. As you discover God's faithfulness to you in financial matters, it increases your faith that He will also come through for you in other far more important matters, such as saving your loved ones.

CHAPTER 48

THE PARABLE OF THE UNMERCIFUL SERVANT (MATTHEW 18:21-35)

This is a well known parable. It is about a man who owed a massive debt to his master, but was forgiven that debt. The master had compassion on him. However, when this same man, found a fellow servant who owed him a small debt, he threw that person into jail for not paying his debt. When the master heard of this, he was outraged and said: "I forgave you a huge debt, yet you refused to show mercy on your fellow servant and forgive his debt. Because of your hard-heartedness, I no longer forgive you of your debt and I demand that it be repaid. You will be thrown into jail until then."

Let me see what insight the Holy Spirit will give me for this parable.

Matthew 18:21-22 says: *Then Peter came to Him and said, "Lord, how often shall my brother sin against me, and I forgive him? Up to seven times?" Jesus said to him, "I do not say to you, up to seven times, but up to seventy times seven."*

Does that mean we are to forgive someone four hundred and ninety times and then we can stop forgiving them? No! Jesus was using two very important numbers: seven and ten. Seven times seven is forty nine but ten times that is four hundred and ninety. Both these numbers are highly significant in the Bible: nothing happens by chance with God! What Jesus was saying is that we are to forgive a person *ad infinitum*. We are to forgive a person into eternity.

The following points come from a book by Robert D. Johnston called "Numbers in the Bible." Apparently, the number seven is the symbol of *"spiritual perfection."* In the first book of the Bible we read an account of the first six days of God's activity on earth - He then rested on the seventh day! Enoch who never died, but was taken by God, was the seventh generation from Adam. Moses was the seventh generation from Abraham. In the last book of the Bible we read about: seven churches, seven candlesticks, seven stars, seven lamps, seven angels, seven spirits, seven seals, seven trumpets, seven bowls made up of seven plaques and so on. The Apostle Paul wrote to seven different churches and three other individuals – ten altogether.

Ten too is another important number to God: even in this book, there are ten virgins, ten talents, ten minas and ten coins. Our whole numbering system is structured around the number ten. Ten denotes: *"Man's responsibility to God - ten speaks of judgment!"* There were Ten Commandments written by the finger of God. A "tithe," one tenth of our income belongs to God. In Genesis Chapter One: the words "God said" occur ten times. Noah and his family were saved from God's judgment of flood in the tenth generation. Pharaoh's heart was hardened ten times: there were ten plagues. There were ten lepers. The antichrist's world power will be made up of ten kingdoms, symbolized by ten toes and ten horns.

However, to balance this: every child of God has been given a tenfold security promise. Let's look at Romans 8:38-39. "I am persuaded that neither *death*, nor *life*, nor *angels*, nor *principalities,* nor *powers*, nor *things present*, nor *things to come*, nor *height*, nor *depth*, nor *any other creature*, shall be able to separate us from the love of God which is in Christ Jesus our Lord." Our future is very secure in Christ – our judgment for sin was taken upon the physical body of our Lord Jesus Christ. The only type of future judgment will relate to our "rewards" or "loss of rewards" determined by our faithful stewardship on earth as a Christian.

Actually, both the numbers seven and ten were used by Jesus in this parable. *"Therefore the Kingdom of Heaven is like a certain king who wanted to settle accounts with his servants, and when he had begun to settle accounts, one was brought to him who owed him 'ten' thousand talents."* (Matthew 18:23-24).

Ten thousand talents was a tremendous amount of money. Wikipedia says that one talent could pay a man for six thousand days of work. Therefore, ten thousand talents is a gigantic debt—so huge that the master commanded that the man's wife and children be sold as payment.

In a former parable, I shared that in Roman times, a father could sell his child as a slave up to three times. Once he had money, he would redeem the child back and then sell him again. In this parable, the master commanded that the servant sell his wife, children and all that he has. So a portion of the payment of the ten thousand talents would be re-paid.

Verse 26 says that the servant therefore fell down before him saying, *"Master have patience with me, I will pay you all." Then the master of that servant was moved with compassion, released him and forgave him all his debt.*

Both the servant and the master knew the debt was un-payable, so the master exercised grace and forgave the huge debt. In this parable, Jesus shared something that is a deeper truth. So let us be very clear about this: the fact that salvation is readily available is the grace of God. It is His "undeserved" favor towards us: it's a debt that we could never repay. Nothing that we could ever do, could possibly even begin to repay that debt!

If I won a million dollars I couldn't even repay Heidi Baker or Andrew Wommack for what they have done for me. Let alone what Jesus has done for me! To be accepted by Him as His own child and to be able to spend eternity in heaven is far beyond all the riches of earth! A trillion million dollars wouldn't even come close to meeting that debt. I would have no hesitation in giving a million dollar win away to further the message of the Gospel because the salvation of "lost souls" means everything to God. This is why we have the "master" in this parable forgiving such a gigantic debt.

You will notice in this parable that the servant said, "Have patience with me, I will repay you." The truth is: the Bible says we were separated from God for all eternity. No amount of money could save us from going to hell. Then God, our Creator came to earth in the form of a human and with His own blood, He paid the ransom price for our forgiveness and restoration to wholeness. The sin debt was fully paid for and we were totally forgiven forever. This man, who had been forgiven in the parable, should have been so grateful for the grace shown by the master that he should have said to his debtor: "Man, don't even worry about repaying me. I have just received a windfall – your debt to me is waived!"

The Parable continues: *"But that servant went out and found one of his fellow servants who owed him a hundred denarii; and he laid hands on him and took him by the throat, saying, 'Pay me what you owe!' So his fellow servant fell down at his feet and begged him, saying, 'Have patience with me, and I will pay you all.' And he would not, but went and threw him into prison till he should pay the debt. So when his fellow servants saw what had been done, they were very grieved, and came and told their master all that had been done. Then his master, after he had called him, said to him, 'You wicked servant! I forgave you all that debt because you begged me. Should you not also have had compassion on your fellow servant, just as I had pity on you?' And his master was angry, and delivered him to the torturers until he should pay all that was due to him.*

"So My Heavenly Father also will do to you if each of you, from his heart, does not forgive his brother his trespasses" (Matthew 18:28-35).

What is the message? Jesus was saying that we need to forgive all the people that wrong us. We have been forgiven and we will continue to be forgiven by God for thousands of wrongs that we have done.

Yesterday, I went on a Christian chat site and the people sort of ganged up on me and attacked me because of something that I said. It made me very angry and part of me wished I could jump through the computer and hit people on the other side of the Internet. I told my roommate Stephen about it and he laughed. Still today, I am upset about it and had a thought a while ago about going online and having another argument. This is the sort of debt we need to forgive. I may come across as the nicest guy ever when all is said and edited, but despite that, my human pride still gets the better of me!

There are so many illnesses, sicknesses and demonic oppressions that come from not forgiving others. We suffer when we refuse to forgive. There exists a sort of emotional and spiritual torture that we put ourselves through when we hold bitterness and un-forgiveness in our hearts. I feel that this anguish is what Jesus is referring to with the torturers. Sometimes we feel that we have a right to punish people and make them pay for hurting us. Jesus is telling us that we have been forgiven for so much more than anything anyone else can do to us, and it is our duty, as a believer in Him, to forgive.

People do not realize but when they refuse to forgive, the person who offended them goes on enjoying life! But we put ourselves in bondage while they are free! How stupid is that!

But far worse than that: when we refuse to forgive we give the devil an open door to do with us whatever he wants. We can't claim protection from God because we have deliberately put ourselves out of His umbrella of protection. We need to repent and to ask God to enable us to forgive. If He knows that we genuinely want to forgive, then He will supply the power to finish the work. *If we refuse to be even willing to forgive*, His hands are tied! Jesus said to call out to Him all who are weak and heavily laden and He will give you rest for your soul. In our own strength it's difficult to forgive, but all things are possible with God. If it were not so, Jesus would not have shared this parable with us.

Let the one who hurt you off the hook, because the bitterness hook has two barbs: the hate you have for others comes back to hook you. Let God deal with the offender and ask God to heal you in your heart by His amazing grace. God bless you.

CHAPTER 49

THE PARABLE OF THE UNPREPARED BUILDER (LUKE 14:28-30)

The theme in this parable is covered in an earlier parable, but it is good to be reminded about this regularly. Let's read this parable in its context, beginning from Luke 14:26-27.

"If anyone comes to Me and does not hate his father and mother, wife and children, brothers and sisters, yes, and his own life also, he cannot be My disciple, and whoever does not bear his cross and come after Me cannot be My disciple."

When I first saw this, I thought well Jesus doesn't mean to literally hate our family, He must mean to love them less than we are to love Him. But I discovered that in the context of this statement that Jesus really did mean to hate. When you study the Greek text we find that certain crowds of people had been consistently following Jesus wherever He went. He knew that their motives were prompted by self-centeredness and not for God's glory. They were following for self gain: food, prestige, the miraculous, whatever!

Jesus deliberately used shock tactics regarding commitment to Him. Many people would have been offended and walked away in disgust. Shock can have a cleansing effect! In this case it sorted out the takers from those who were genuinely searching for truth.

Our spouse, our children and our parents are the closest relationships we have. They will stick by you even if other people desert you or give up on you. We can rely on those who really love us to stand up for us no matter what. Yet, Jesus was saying that unless we love Him far more than our immediate family, we cannot be His disciple.

There is a big difference between a convert or follower and a disciple. Jesus didn't tell us to make converts, He said to make disciples. We read this in the great commission He gave the church in Matthew 28:18-19a. He said: *"All authority has been given to Me in heaven and on earth. Go, therefore and make disciples of all the nations."* A disciple is committed long term! To survive, we have to love Him more than anything or anyone else. If not, Satan will see to it that we won't hold the line for long. Jesus must be preeminent in our love scale.

The word "hate" here is a metaphor: it's a word of comparison. Jesus is saying: "My relationship with you is to be above every relationship you have." Do you know there is one person you love more than any other person in the whole world? This person is you! Let me illustrate: in a group photo, who do you focus on? You of course! If it's a good photo of you - then you say it's a great group photo. Mostly, you don't even bother to check out the faces of the others, you just look at your own face!

We must daily surrender our own selfish life to Him: it's an ongoing process. As mentioned in other parables, we are in a spiritual war. The act of dying to ourselves will need to continue to our physical death or to the Rapture, whichever comes first.

Galatians 5:16-17 says: *"I say then; Walk in the Spirit, and you shall not fulfill the lust of the flesh. For the flesh lusts against the Spirit, and the Spirit against the flesh; and these are contrary to one another, so that you do not do the things that you wish."*

This fixation about our own importance is why many marriages fail. One spouse will love themselves more than they want to honor their commitment vow to God. If our spouse doesn't fulfill our needs, we want a divorce so we can find someone who will fulfill us.

If we love even our self more than Jesus, we are not worthy of Him. His grace however, will bring us to that point. Some religious sects have majored on this verse because the devil wants to destroy families. Young people have been convinced to leave home and the security if offers, to go join some weird group who are out to control their lives.

Jesus set a very high standard here. The apostle Paul said: *"I can do all things through Christ who strengthens me."* (Philippians 4:13). We cannot love God in our strength, but with the Holy Spirit's help, we can love Jesus more than our loved ones and even our own life. To be honest, until Jesus is in that place, life simply isn't as rich as it could be. You see, the trouble is when you become a Christian and you start to act in godly ways, sometimes your family will start to act differently towards you. If you are the only Christian in your family, there probably will be persecutions and tribulations.

Back to our parable, Luke 14:27- *"And whoever does not bear his cross and come after Me cannot be My disciple."* Here, Jesus is reinforcing the high cost of commitment. Salvation is free, but it costs you everything you have! It is one thing to sing about loving Jesus but it's another thing to be a disciple. A disciple is someone who practices the things that Jesus taught.

Jesus continues: *"For which of you, intending to build a tower, does not sit down first and count the cost, whether he has enough to finish it— lest, after he has laid the foundation, and is not able to finish, all who see it begin to mock him, saying, 'This man began to build and was not able to finish'?*

Living the Kingdom way is hard. When people around you find out you are a Christian, they are going to be watching you, just like the builder of this tower. It is not going to be easy "leaving" your old lifestyle for the things of God.

Let's say, you are going to build a block of apartments, rent them out and make a lot of money. It has been your dream and you begin the project in faith. You have a good job and you are confident that you could arrange the finances for the construction. What if in the middle of the project, you suddenly lost your job and you couldn't pay the loan back?

Or, say you had money and you projected a cost, but you made a wrong calculation. It's wise, before you start something like this, to first sit down with good accountants and make a cost analysis for the projection. Because, if you start putting up half a block of apartments and then you stop building due to lack of money, everyone in the area is going to laugh at you.

Jesus was essentially saying that the Christian life is like that. If you decide to become a Christian, people are going to watch you and they will be the first to ridicule you if you decide that it's too difficult and you no longer have the enthusiasm to continue. We should know at the outset that the journey in being a disciple will be hard.

Through this book, I encourage you to make the decision to give your life to Him. Pray out loud the prayer written in the appendix of this book and experience the changes that the Holy Spirit will bring about in your life.

For some Christians, things may not continually go as well as they thought it would. Maybe you feel stuck in a rut, depressed, hurt or broken; maybe you lack vision or purpose: or maybe you feel over-looked or unfulfilled. Satan loves to bring problems. Well, that is not the life God has planned for you. God has a life for you where you live in total abandonment to Jesus Christ and you are fully surrendered to Him.

A sailing ship without the sails up, just coasts along: it takes effort to put those sails up and once they are up, the boat meets the resistance of the wind and it sails. The boat will not only sail with the wind, but can go against the wind in a tack. Now, if you don't have your sails up to catch the Spirit of the Living God; if the wind cannot move your sails; if you have not given your life to God and said, "I surrender Lord" but you are still trying to run your own life, then you are like a ship with no sail up! You are going nowhere.

If you are hundreds of miles out to sea: you could starve. You will be at the mercy of the seas, which will break all over you if your sails are not up. You have to learn how to move in the Holy Spirit. In this parable Jesus has pre-warned us that Christianity comes with a cost. Therefore, if you have made a decision for Christ, take comfort that Jesus also lived on earth: He knows first- hand how difficult things are here.

You can experience true love, success, joy and peace. You can have purpose in life. Your sin-muddied life can become a life of holiness and righteousness. You can be transformed by God, but it comes at a cost. Be prepared to pray to the Lord and surrender your life fully to him. Ask Him to take control: truly you will never look back!

CHAPTER 50

THE PARABLE OF THE VINE AND BRANCHES (JOHN 15:1-17)

"I am the true vine, and My Father is the vinedresser." John 15:1. Here, we see that Jesus is the vine and the Father is the one in charge, because He is the vinedresser.

"Every branch in Me that does not bear fruit, He takes away: and every branch that bears fruit He prunes, that it may bear more fruit." John 15:2

Once you start bearing fruit by doing Kingdom business, Jesus makes you stronger and causes things to happen which bring spiritual growth. Some growth comes through trials and afflictions, and those things may appear to come against you. However, things such as disease and destruction do not come from God, because He is a good God! Know that God may put us through our paces like a coach puts an athlete through race after race, practice after practice, to push and coach him. Jesus says here that God will coach us: He will prune us. He will cut us back and make us perform better.

"You are already clean because of the word which I have spoken to you." John 15:3. Jesus is saying: "You are righteous; you are clean; you are washed. Everything is fine when you place your faith in Me."

"Abide in Me, and I in you. As the branch cannot bear fruit of itself, unless it abides in the vine, neither can you, unless you abide in Me." John 15:4

Abiding in Jesus is more than going to church, praying and reading the Bible. It is about allowing Him to run your life by having the Holy Spirit give you directions. Every Christian has the capacity to hear from the Holy Spirit: all it takes is prayer and practice. Abiding in Jesus is like having His sap run out from the vine through the branch to bear fruit. So, if we are connected to Jesus and are allowing the sap to flow, we are abiding in Him. It is essentially doing and living as the Holy Spirit says. If you are making all the decisions yourself, you are not abiding. Life is fun and easier when you allow the Holy Spirit to give you directions each day.

Jesus said He wanted me to do a video series on the parables. I have now finished all the videos. Then, He wanted me to have them transcribed into a book. I planned to pay the transcribers and editors from my pension each fortnight but Jesus told me to get a loan for one thousand dollars so that I could pay it all at once and finish the book quickly.

To abide is to follow step by step instructions from the Holy Spirit. I found the list of parables on Google, but I am totally amazed by the way Jesus is helping me. Abiding in the Vine is working hand and hand with the Holy Spirit, which is the Spirit of Jesus living in me. The parable of the vine and branches is one of my favorite passages and teaching this parable a few chapters from the end is just amazing.

"I am the vine, you are the branches. He who abides in Me, and I in him, bears much fruit; for without Me you can do nothing" John 15:5

Originally, with one week's work, I hope to bear a tremendous amount of fruit and that is truly amazing. You see I spoke the book, I didn't manually type it. Because of that, it needed a great amount of editing. If you have the resources, buy the book or you can look at the free website version that you can post on Facebook. When you abide in Jesus—when you are doing what He tells you to do by tuning into the Holy Spirit quietly communicating with your human spirit, you will bear much fruit.

In our own strength, we are helpless; without God we can do nothing. I am helpless on my own, but as a Christian, I am never alone! God is always with me. He goes everywhere I go. That is why we should be mindful of not taking Him to places He would not enjoy. The issue that most Christians have is they are not "depending" on Jesus. They are not listening to Him: their lives are so busy that they can't hear the Holy Spirit. If we read the Bible and get connected with Christ, we will know how to hear His Holy Spirit.

"If anyone does not abide in Me, he is cast out as a branch and is withered; and they gather them and throw them into the fire and they are burned" John 15:6

We see here that if we do not bear fruit—for instance, although we go to church, pray and do godly things, if we have never surrendered our lives to Jesus—we will wither. One thing is for sure: Jesus once again mentioned that there is going to be a fire for people who do not accept Him and walk with Him in this life. There are so many people who are "outwardly religious" but their heart is far away from God: they have no personal relationship with Jesus because even if they once said a prayer of invitation to Him, it may have been empty words coming from a hard heart and prompted by wrong motives.

"If you abide in Me, and My words abide in you, you will ask what you desire, and it shall be done for you" John 15:7. I'm not strong on asking for things, but I do know that sometimes, when I pray for other people's desires, my prayers for them are answered.

I know my mother's one desire, was that her mother would be saved. For almost thirty eight years she hung onto this promise and also one in Psalm 138:8 which says: *"The Lord will perfect that which concerns me."* She kept on claiming these verses for her mother's salvation. In 1978, she had received a prophecy that when her mother was old and was in some kind of home and was alone, then she would be able to lead her to Jesus. And that is exactly what happened. God had spoken to my mum on two occasions a year before grandma's death, and told her that He was going to save her. My mother was so excited and shared that with all her friends. She was so excited even at her death-bed, because she knew Jesus was there! Her joy was overwhelming! It was the greatest testimony of the peace of God that she has ever experienced. Death had lost its sting!

James 4:3- *"You ask and do not receive, because you ask amiss, that you may spend it on your pleasures."* There is a type of asking that God will not answer; that is when you want things for selfish motives. If your motives are wrong and He knows that the things you are asking for are not good for you, you can ask God for them and they will not be given to you. However, if you have the Holy Spirit in you, you will know what to pray for, and when you are abiding in Christ, you will ask only for the will of God.

"By this My Father is glorified, that you bear much fruit; so you will be My disciples" John 15:8. Do you know that the way to find fresh oranges is to go and find an orange tree? It should be the same way with Christians. When you bump into a person who is so full of love, compassion, joy and peace, you will know that you have met a real follower of Jesus Christ. You may watch some interviews of Heidi Baker on YouTube, and you will see God's love pouring out of her. You will see that she is a blessed "little Christ."

If you have ever met my Pastor, you will know that Christ is alive! Every Christian has within them, the nine fruit of the Holy Spirit, but not all believers walk in that fruit. My Pastor is the only person I have had the privilege to know, who consistently shows forth the love of God toward all people. Jesus wants us all to bear His fruit so that people will be attracted to the Savior. People ask me, "Why do you do what you do? Why do I do it? It is because Jesus loves me and it is His will for me to do it.

"As the Father loved Me, I also have loved you; abide in My love" John 15:9

Many people are afraid of the love of Jesus. They have been rejected and hurt so many times; they will not accept Jesus' love. Jesus says, "Let my Holy Spirit show you that I love you. Abide in Me. Start to accept My love. Start to listen to Me. Commune with Me; start to fellowship with Me and everything will be fantastic."

"If you keep My commandments, you will abide in My love, just as I have kept My Father's commandments and abide in His love" John 15:10

Jesus came down from Heaven and did everything the Father told Him to do. In the same way, Jesus wants us to do what He tells us to do. This is not to come from a sense of obligation, that we are destined for Hell if we do not obey Him, but out of love for Him. It's the most practical way to live our life. Life is just so good when we do it God's way!

"These things I have spoken to you, that My joy may remain in you and that your joy may be full" John 15:11

I have been so full of joy since July 2010, when I was transformed by the doctrine of grace. Since then, the load of self righteousness, guilt, shame and condemnation has been lifted off my back. My whole life has been full of joy; I am energized. I almost feel that I am on some drug induced "high" at times. The verse in John 15:11 is true in my life.

"This is My commandment, that you love one another as I have loved you" John 15:12

Some people think that Jesus doesn't love them much. They can't visibly walk and talk with Him or see Him in the flesh like the early disciples did. To other people, Jesus is an historic figure and that's all. That is why it's hard for them to love others; and that is understandable. You need to mix with people who are full of Jesus and let them love you, so you will have an example of His special love for everyone. My pastor and her daughter are the expression of Jesus' love for me. By their example, I am able to love like them. Above all, Jesus has loved me so much: I have a tremendous relationship with Him and have spoken to Him many, many times and so I genuinely love a lot of people.

"Greater love has no one that this than to lay down ones life for his friends" John 15:13

Jesus did this for all of us. Likewise, we can all lay down our lifestyle for another person. We can spend less on our own desires and give money to people who are not as well off. The day to day laying down of our lives for others is what Jesus wants from us.

"You are My friends if you do whatever I command you" John 15:14

In another parable, Jesus said that we are wise when we build our lives on His commands. Living the way that Jesus commands us, means that He will become more than just God's Son to us, but He will become our closest friend.

"No longer do I call you servants, for a servant does not know what his master is doing; but I have called you friends, for all things that I heard from My Father I have made known to you. You did not choose Me, but I chose you and appointed you that you should go and bear fruit, and that your fruit should remain, that whatever you ask the Father in My name He may give you" John 15:15-16

We think that we are the ones who choose Jesus, but that is not so: He chooses us! That's why no one can come to Him unless His Holy Spirit has already started a work in them. Perhaps God has been working in your life for years and you have been sub-consciously resisting Him. It's great to know that it is God who initiates the relationship because then we have confidence that it will remain: He will not divorce you! What He starts, He finishes and He says that He hates divorce!

So, when you are abiding in Jesus, you will do what the Holy Spirit puts in your heart; you will prove that you love Him and you will bear much fruit. If your life is directionless and purposeless, you need to listen to the Holy Spirit.

"These things I command you, that you love one another." John 15:17 This is a commandment, not a request! In verse 12, Jesus said that we are to love others as much as He loves us. Earlier in John 13:34, He had said the same thing. That is such a high calling! It is impossible to do in our own strength! The only way we can fulfill this calling is to draw close to Him so that His love can flow out to others through us.

The successful Christian life is to allow Jesus to give you constant directions and you will not only find purpose in life, but you will bear fruit that remains. God bless.

CHAPTER 51

THE PARABLE OF THE WATCHING SERVANTS
(LUKE 12:35-40)

The main emphasis in this parable is on "watchfulness." We are to be in a state of continual readiness for the Lord to call us to Himself at the Rapture. The parable then goes on to speak about the Wedding Supper of the Lamb. Let's begin at verse 35 through to the beginning of verse 37. "*Let your waist be girded and your lamps burning; and you yourselves be like men who wait for their master when he will return from the wedding, that when he comes and knocks they may open to him immediately. Blessed are those servants whom the master, when he comes, will find watching.*"

The owner of the house has gone out to a wedding and knows that he will be very late coming home. He doesn't want his servants to go to bed in his absence. Instead, he wants the light of his home to be burning and his servants keeping a diligent watch over his possessions in case thieves try to break in and take what belongs to him.

Verse 37b says: "*Assuredly, I say to you that he will gird himself and have them sit down to eat, and will come and serve them.*" Upon his return, the master would reward their watchfulness and their faithfulness in obedience, for he himself would gird up his wedding garments and would prepare a supper for them.

Verses 38-40 continues: "*And if he should come in the second watch, or come in the third watch, and find them so, blessed are those servants, but know this, that if the master of the house had known what hour the thief would come, he would have watched and not allowed his house to be broken into. Therefore you also be ready, for the Son of Man is coming at an hour you do not expect.*"

I have to ask you: Do you know the Lord Jesus? You need to – don't put it off! Be aware, there is a thief who infiltrates our minds to divert us from the things of God. He will use every form of deception he can to stop us from knowing and obeying God's word. His name is Satan and he sends his demons to rob, kill and destroy those that Jesus died for.

Do you know when Jesus is coming back? No one knows the day or the hour only the Father in heaven. Jesus did however give us many signs to look for before His coming and these signs are all coming together in our time today.

Are you girded and ready for warfare in doing God's work? Men, in Bible times would tuck the skirts of their long robes into their belt so that they would be ready for serious action and not be impeded by their clothing.

Are you prepared? If Jesus was to come at any moment, would you be involved in God's kingdom business? Is your life focused on doing things that would please Him?

Are you just sitting, watching and waiting for the return of the Lord? We need to keep ourselves actively informed of what is going on in the world to-day, especially events concerning the nation of Israel. Iran's president has openly said that Israel must be wiped off the face of the earth. Iran's nuclear arsenal is ready and could impact the world as never before imagined! This is just one example of what is happening in our life time.

Satan knows his time is short. He is stirring up opposition in the world to *everything that is precious to God*. By being aware of current events and prophecies in the Bible, we will develop a sense of "urgency" about the lateness of the hour. Then, we will be focused on God's priorities and things of a temporal nature will not distract us!

People want to know what they need to be doing in order to prepare for Jesus' return. They begin to study the Book of Revelation, but this is a very difficult book and it does not really tell us what we need to be doing *now!*

Jesus has already told us what we need to be doing! We are to be actively involved in God's Kingdom business! In some of the parables we have covered so far, He wants us to care for the poor, the hungry, the homeless and the depressed. I suppose I have gone on and on about the homeless in this book, because the homeless are extremely needy and damaged. I have a special empathy for them because I went through what they are going through. I had parents who loved me but I was far too ashamed of my addictive lifestyle that I couldn't bring myself to go home. I hope that one person who buys this book might actually go, make a friend of the homeless, feed and clothe them and make them feel special.

To understand the Bible it's important to know a few things. Whilst our day starts at midnight and ends at midnight, *the first hour* of the Jewish day starts in the morning: our time 6.00am.

The evening and night was divided into watch periods. The first watch was called the "Evening watch" - it went from 6.00pm – 9.00pm (Our time)

The second watch was called the "Midnight watch" - it went from 9.00pm to midnight.

The third watch was called the "Cockcrow watch" - between midnight to 3.00am.

The forth watch was the "Morning watch" - 3.00am –6.00am – *the start of a new day!*

"Watch therefore, for you do not know when the master of the house is coming—in the evening, at midnight, at the crowing of the rooster, or in the morning." Mark 13:35. Does this mean Jesus won't come during the day hours? Who knows? Just be ready!

If your master was away at a wedding and he was coming home to get ready for bed, he would want to know that his house was being looked after and that no one could break in. He would want to be sure that everything was in order. The return of Jesus has been likened to a thief coming in the night. Meaning – thieves come when we least expect it?

Through the course of these parables, we have come to realize that there is a lot that we can do. We can minister in the gifts that God has given us. We can fully utilize our money, time and resources to further the Kingdom of God. We are not to be stagnant or be standing in one place. We are not to be on the wide path leading to destruction like all the unbelievers.

Instead, we are to be on the narrow path going *against the ways of the world.* (See Matthew 7:13-14) We can be shining our light in our community: we can be a house on a hill and a bright shining light to everyone we meet. It's time for the introverts to swallow their pride and to be bold for Jesus! You can have confidence in the transforming power of the Holy Spirit. It says in 1 Corinthians 2:16 that we have the mind of Christ. We can therefore put on the mind of Christ and break free of any barriers or apathy that keeps us silent.

Watching is essentially doing the will of the Father. Many people are interested in the last days and listen to teaching on the Book of Revelation to know future events. All I know, is that Jesus said to *live and preach the Gospel!* Even in the book of Revelation, it says the angel sounded the trumpet and the Gospel of the Lord went out to all the nations. At that time the angels of God will be very active on earth.

From the time of Abraham to the time of the death of Christ, God's priority had been towards the salvation of the Jewish people. They were the ones that He originally covenanted with to be His people and He would be their God. Jesus knew a new era was to begin. At the Last Supper before His death, He said a New Covenant would be in force by His blood. A covenant of Grace would begin where "everybody" would be called to be part of God's Kingdom, not just the Jewish people!

Two thousand years have passed since then and it is only been since May 1948 when the Nation of Israel came into being that many Jews have begun to recognize the new age of grace. The Jewish people not saved before the Rapture, will have a major role to play on earth, because great numbers of them will come to salvation during a terrible time of tribulation. They will be among the many, many people who will be martyred for their faith because they will refuse to follow the Antichrist.

A friend of mine, Yianni, had a vision. He saw a couple of very long tables in Heaven. The tables went off into eternity for miles and miles. He said everyone was seated at these tables and each person had on their hands some kind of gold rope. Fruit and other food ran continuously down the centre sections of the tables. Jesus came along the table and was personally and lovingly serving each person at the table.

Months before my grandma came to the Lord; my mother had a dream about seeing a white folded "place card" standing up with her mother's name boldly written in a beautiful font – like perfect handwriting. She woke up and made a card just like she had seen. A few weeks later, she spoke to a prophet friend at a wedding and he said "It looks like Jesus has got your mother's place card all ready for the Wedding Supper of the Lamb." She was so excited because in her heart she had made the same conclusion.

At this extra special feast, the Master, our Lord Jesus Christ, will be waiting on His bride, who will be clothed in beautiful white wedding garments personally selected by the Groom. This holy bride is made up of tens of millions of men, women, boys and girls, aborted babies, people with intellectual handicaps, the innocent ones, people of every race, color and culture from the time of Adam! Can you imagine the scene? Just as well it is Jesus who is hosting this spectacular event. Otherwise, it would take years to be served.

This event will occur in heaven, sometime after the Rapture of the church. The Lord Jesus Christ is serving food to those He loves. This parable speaks prophetically about that event. Will you be seated at that special table? When Jesus brings home the people that were busy doing His will, He is going to wait tables on them!

Do you know if you are going to be at that wedding reception? Have you made your decision for Christ yet? If you have surrendered your life to Him, I will see you there!

Don't look for an overweight person as seen on my videos! I will have my new slim body then - because at the Rapture everyone will receive a glorified "perfect" body which is able to live in the atmosphere of heaven and be able to pass through things at will and travel in the blink of an eye. We will still be able to recognize our loved ones but they will look the best they have ever looked. (No one will need Jenny Craig or Botox in heaven!) I think it's wonderful that we will still enjoy eating great food! What a great day that will be!

CHAPTER 52

THE PARABLE OF THE WISE BUILDER
(MATTHEW 7:24-27)

The wise builder parable can be found at the end of the Sermon on the Mount. We will begin with Matthew 7:24-25.

"Therefore whoever hears these sayings of Mine, and does them, I will liken him to a wise man who built his house on the rock: and the rain descended, the floods came, and the winds blew and beat on that house; and it did not fall, for it was founded on the rock.

Jesus does not waste His words. Therefore, we can be sure that every word He has spoken in the Bible has meaning and relevance in our society and especially to the Christian life. We should not disregard any word that Jesus has said merely because we do not understand what it means. Instead, we should put His words to prayer and we could ask mature Christians to share with us their interpretation.

Here, Jesus is telling a parable about a wise man who is building his house upon the rock. According to verse 24, this "rock" is the perfect and safe foundation on which to build a successful and obedient life on.

For us to understand what Jesus was saying, it would be helpful to read all the commands He gave in the Sermon on the Mount. In that famous sermon, Jesus taught many principles as to how the Christian is to conduct his life. Essentially, we can assume that everything Jesus taught in the Gospels is the proper way to live a God pleasing life. Then our life would be a testimony of God's saving power. However, always bear in mind that our Savior's earthly teaching was before the Cross, before the new Covenant of Grace began. This is very important when you are trying to understand about law and grace.

Not long after the death and resurrection of Christ Jesus, the official Church was formed. God then raised up special people to teach on the Covenant of Grace. God had a certain Jewish man in mind: his name was Saul. This man had been highly educated and was steeped in the Laws of the Old Testament. He was an extremely devout and articulate scholar who as a zealous religious leader ruthlessly defended his Jewish faith.

Because God had in mind an amazing work for Saul, the "risen" Christ personally confronted him in a dramatic life-changing encounter. (See Acts 9:1-18) Saul's faith did a total back-flip! Suddenly all his former legalism was revolutionized by God's grace. God changed his name to Paul. This amazing man, under the inspiration of the Holy Spirit wrote a huge portion of the New Testament. The study and application of his writings helps us to understand God's full purposes in our life.

We read in the book of James that we are a fool if we listen to something and fail to apply it. Instead we are to *"be doers of the word, and not hearers only, deceiving yourselves" James 1:22*. A person can be filled with deception, if he only listens to the Word and doesn't apply it in his own life.

You do not find many multi-millionaires in the world not "driven" in regard to business matters. All their waking hours are consumed with ways of gaining greater outcomes with their time, money, resources and employees. You do not find any athletes in the world competing at the Olympics and receiving a gold medal who has not endured tens of thousands of hour's working at his sport. You do not find a gold medalist in a specialized sport that has not studied and applied the best and latest techniques of that particular sport. If he does not apply the latest techniques, he might find that at the next Olympics, someone else wins the gold and he is no longer the world record title holder.

If the people who succeed in the world know how to follow techniques and best practices, we too as Christians, need to follow the advice of our Master, Jesus Christ. It is especially relevant that as followers of Jesus, that we obey His commands. He warns us in His parables of the cost of following Him. For example: we are to love our mothers, sisters, wives and children less than we love Him. Also, we would need to deny our own selfish desires so as to fulfill His. Yes, genuine Christian living comes with great personal cost.

The amazing thing, that unbelievers do not realize, is that when the Holy Spirit enters our life, *He actually changes our desires*, so it doesn't seem anywhere near as difficult to walk God's way because we will want to go that way. I love the way God has made it!

I want to inspire people and not fill them with guilt. Yet, it's self-deception to call ourselves Christians and not do what Jesus said. It simply makes sense that you don't go out into the pouring rain in the middle of winter without an umbrella—without clothing that will protect you from the rain. No one in his right mind goes for a couple of hours walk in the pouring rain in the middle of winter, if they value their health.

So too, Jesus is saying here, anyone who listens to His words must apply them, because that is the way to live like a rock upon "The Rock." There *are* going to be storms in life! In the Parable of the Sower, we were told that as soon as we hear and apply the word of God, tribulations and persecutions will come. That is why it is vitally important that we are founded on God's Rock in the principles and teachings of Jesus Christ.

Jesus came to give us an abundant life. Therefore, He is not someone who wants to steal your joy or wreck your life. Jesus is the wisest Person we could have as our role model: if He says to do something, things will go great in our life! It is no use saying that Jesus is your Savior, without Him being your Lord. It is useless saying that Jesus was the master teacher, if you do not apply His teaching.

Hearing the information is only half of it. If you read this book and you think: "That was a great book, I really enjoyed reading it," but you do not apply the parables to your life, then your time has really been wasted. But if anyone reads this book and applies the principles associated with it, then he is building his house upon the right Rock.

Jesus went on to say, "But everyone who hears these sayings of Mine, and does not do them, will be like a foolish man who built his house on the sand: and the rain descended, the floods came, and the winds blew and beat on that house; and it fell, and great was its fall" (Matthew 7:26-27).

Jesus and His teaching is the foundation of the Christian life. If you don't build on this foundation, your life dreams may crumble. There is nothing scarier than trying to live the Christian life without a solid foundation. If you are a Christian in name only, you are self-deceived and you will experience bitterness, hurt and resentment against God.

If you are living the principles of the Word of God, you have this promise from the Master Himself that your house will stand, even though circumstances may appear to be threatening all around you. If your life is centered on the Lord Jesus Christ and His words of wisdom, your house will stand.

The wonderful thing about the Gospel is that we are constantly urged not to do things in our own strength: these are called self-righteous works of the flesh! The only way we can possibly please God is to do things in the power of God's Holy Spirit. By doing things in His strength, He gets the glory and not us! In return though, we receive all His wonderful blessings!

May you know and enjoy every one of His blessings as you draw closer to Him.

CHAPTER 53

THE PARABLE OF THE WISE AND FAITHFUL SERVANT
MATTHEW 24:45-51

Here too, Jesus is sharing about His second coming. Matthew 24:44 says: *"Therefore you also be ready for the son of man. He is coming at an hour that you do not expect."*

And the parable: Matthew 24:45-51 reads: *"Who then is a faithful and wise servant, whom his master made ruler over his household to give them food in due season? Blessed is that servant whom his master, when he comes, will find so doing. Assuredly, I say to you he will make him ruler over all his goods, but if that evil servant says in his heart, 'My master is delaying his coming,' and begins to beat his fellow servants, and to eat and drink with the drunkards, the master of that servant will come on a day when he is not looking for him and at an hour that he is not aware of, and will cut him in two and appoint him his portion with the hypocrites. There shall be weeping and gnashing of teeth."*

This sound horrific! Will Jesus really cut someone in two? I believe there are people who genuinely think that they will be accepted by God. When they find themselves left behind all their dreams will be cut into two: they will emotionally be cut into pieces. Jesus is going to send the angels to reap the earth. He said in Matthew 24:37-41 - it would be just like in Noah's time when the people were partying and the flood came suddenly. So it will be with the coming of the Son of Man: two men will be in the field, and one will be taken. Two women will be at a mill and one will be taken! Watch therefore, for you do not know what hour your Lord is coming. If we knew when a thief was planning to enter our house we would be on guard. In the same way we are to be ready for Jesus!

After Jesus finished the parable of the wise and faithful servant, He taught on the ten virgins, where half of them missed out on what Jesus wanted to give them because of inadequate preparation. Our Lord then went on to teach about two people who doubled their talents as compared to the one servant who did nothing with what was entrusted to him. Jesus also proceeded to teach about the sheep and the goats, the people who fed the hungry, poor, and homeless; looked after the sick, and visited those in prison and the people who failed to do any of these things.

Jesus had an amazing way of going from parable to parable. He had a way of saying something—then further saying it, then further saying it, then further saying it. Andrew Wommack also explains a point in four or five different ways until you get it. If you catch his point the first time around, he just reinforces the truth four different times in different ways with different illustrations. Jesus Christ is the same. Personally, I need that type of repetition for my pre-set mind to eventually get the drift!

Jesus is again talking about going away, leaving the earth and then coming again with His angels to harvest, and now He is speaking about servant-hood again. Every Christian is to be a wise and faithful servant who is left in charge while the Master is away. We are to administer the gifts and the talents that God gives us. Jesus goes further into the talents parable and says that you are not a faithful servant if you were given talents, but don't apply them. He says that you are a goat if you have gifts, talents, abilities and resources, yet you do not share with the broken hearted. You are not faithful, if you don't share; you are not faithful if you don't apply your talent and you are not faithful if you don't live the Christian life in such a way that you have your oil or lamp continually burning.

On the other hand, the unwise or evil servant is the one who is entrusted with the goods of the Kingdom, but actually "abuses" that honor.

Now how could they be abusive? What is the practical application of this evil servant? What differentiates the wise and faithful servant from the evil one? Well, it says here that the evil servant begins to beat his fellow servants and eat and drink with the drunkards. He is a hypocrite, he might sit in church each week and do his religious thing, but in his free time, he acts like all his unsaved friends.

During the time of Noah, people were eating and drinking and giving in marriage when the judgment of God came upon the whole earth. In fact, Jesus mentioned Noah in the previous discourse.

We have continual choices every day! We are given the precious resources of time, money, talents and opportunity. If we are squandering all of God's blessings, then we are not measuring up. If for instance, we go to work to earn our money and yet we squander all our time in front of the television watching useless programs, or spend all our resources on things not really profitable for us or anybody else, then we have just wasted our resources.

Opportunities come and go, make sure you use your opportunities to create eternal value. This world is passing away and only the things done for eternity have any substance. We cannot recall time and live it different. God's top priority has always been in developing relationships: vertical and horizontal! He is more concerned about our character than our personal comfort. When we desire His character, every project we undertake will make a positive difference to the lives of others. Self gratification is an unwise use of resources.

Many people will look at this and say, "Well I don't hurt other people, like the evil servant in the parable." This is true, you may not be abusing other people, but you could be neglecting those who are being abused. You know, this wise servant was in charge of his master's household: he had people answering to him. You might say to yourself, "Well I don't have people answering to me. I'm not in charge. I'm not abusing anyone."

Well you may be surprised that our chocolate, coffee and many other goods we consume, come from farms overseas. Many of these workers are slaves. Men come from African villages where young children are told a lie. They are told that they are being hired to have a good job, an opportunity to earn an income for their families, but they are then taken to another part of Africa. They then have their passport stolen and they are forced by violence to work for no wages from sun up to sun down every day of the week.

Many of our goods are bought from the third world countries where people are working for pitiful amounts of money. We are living off other people's hurt. Many of us are buying things cheap in this world not knowing that we are living off the backs of people who are being abused.

There is a thing called Fair Trade. There is a way that you can buy things fair trade, which means the people that make the goods *have not been abused in any way* and they have been paid a fair wage for their work. That is one way you could be a wise servant.

In the parable of the sheep and the goats, Jesus shows how we can give out food to the hungry, drink to the thirsty and clothes to the naked or homeless. If we fail to help our neighbor and just live a lavish Western lifestyle—we must think twice. I may live on a pension, but I enjoy a good lifestyle compared to someone in the third world. Two-thirds of the world lives on less than two dollars a day. So, even people on a pension earn a lot more money and have a better lifestyle than most people overseas.

People may respond that they are not sitting down and drinking with drunkards and therefore are not the wicked servants. But what do drunks do? They drink for pleasure and to forget about the hard life that they have had. We can be similar in the way that we buy things in the West. We are constantly spending our money on things that bring us pleasure. We are happy for a time with our new toy, but then the pleasure of the new purchase fades and we are off shopping again to get another fix. Just like a drunk, we are drunk with buying things of no profit to God or His Kingdom.

God loves us and He sent Jesus to teach us these things. Jesus is in Heaven, but He is watching. We are meant to be servants of His household: we are to be an example. We are meant to benefit others, as well as to enjoy life.

If you want to be faithful, then be faithful with the time that you have. Share your time doing things that are profitable and share your resources with the poor. This is being a wise and faithful servant.

CHAPTER 54

THE PARABLE OF THE WISE STEWARD
(LUKE 12:42-48)

The Lord said, "Who then is that faithful and wise steward, whom his master will make ruler over his household, to give them their portion of food in due season? Blessed is that servant whom his master will find so doing when he comes. Truly, I say to you that he will make him ruler over all that he has" Luke 12:42-44.

Many parables of Jesus speak about honor and reward. Jesus is a rewarder of people who do good work for Him. Some people would say that we are all equal in the Kingdom and that God does not favor any one person over another. This is true. We are all saved by the grace of God. We are all saved through the blood of Jesus Christ shed at Calvary, but it seems that the Lord was saying here that those who have been faithful on earth— those who have been wise—those who have used what was entrusted to them on earth wisely—are going to be rewarded and made ruler over many other people and things.

Let us take Sydney, Australia. We need one ruler over the whole city, but it is made up of many suburbs and each of the suburbs could do with a Mayor. Then, there are different functions in each of the suburbs. There are people in charge of the water, people in charge of electricity and people in charge of education. There are different positions within the suburb so there are many levels of responsibility in the society that we live in.

It is true that when Jesus Christ returns He will physically rule from Jerusalem for a thousand years and then after that time, this earth will be burnt up and He will create a new Heaven and a new earth. During the future one thousand year reign, called the Millennium, there will be many positions of leadership in the new Kingdom on earth. Jesus is going to have people who are faithful to Him in these leadership roles. If He promotes someone to be head over all the suburbs of the city of Sydney, they will need to have had excellent administrative experience.

Often, people look at their life on earth and wonder whether their credentials or achievements will be used in Heaven. People work in jobs that they love and cannot imagine themselves doing any other type of job. Perhaps this could be true. When you work on earth, you may do a similar job in Heaven. Jesus was hinting at this. He said that He will make you ruler over many things if you are faithful in what you do now.

There will be many positions up for grabs and opportunities available for the average person. Not everyone will fully apply themselves in the Millennium. Even now on earth, not everyone will live to the potential that God has set for His people.

Jesus is not a hard taskmaster: He is an encouraging Savior. He allows you to develop your gifts naturally and then gives you more practical experience until you become proficient. Jesus promotes people through levels of authority. Not only will there be promotion in the Kingdom to come when Jesus reigns on earth, but there is promotion in the Kingdom for those on earth today, who prove themselves worthy.

Some people prove that they are wise stewards of God's money, resources, time and talents on earth. This is not just something for the future. If you look at people like Joyce Meyer, Benny Hinn, Joseph Prince and other preachers, you will find that they have been promoted to television ministries, book writing ministries, tapes and CD ministries and big convention ministries. They have big and powerful ministries on earth today. They have been promoted and given much glory and power in today's world.

These parables do not have to be in the future tense. Jesus preached the parables for a few reasons—as a promise of what is going to happen in the future, but also for a practical day by day experience. I hope that you are catching the practical application of this parable today.

"But if that servant says in his heart, 'My master is delaying his coming,' and begins to beat the male and female servants, and begins to eat and drink and be drunk, the master of that servant will come on a day when he is not looking for him, and at an hour when he is not aware, and will cut him in two and appoint him his portion with the unbelievers. And that servant who knew his master's will, and did not prepare himself or do according to his will, shall be beaten with many stripes. But he who did not know, yet committed things deserving of stripes, shall be beaten with few. For everyone to whom much is given, from him much will be required; and to whom much has been committed, of him they will ask the more" Luke 12:45-48.

You will note that in the previous chapter, I have spoken of an identical passage recorded in the Gospel of Matthew. Here, I have to say in conclusion, this being the last parable that all the "stripes" mentioned here are avoidable. While growing up, you knew as a young child that you would be punished if you broke your curfew or you stole money from your father's wallet. You were given definite boundaries, so that when you ignored the rules and found yourself in trouble, you knew that your disobedience would incur punishment from those in authority. You did not *have* to suffer bad consequences: you did not *have* to receive punishment but you decided to take the risk of being found out - you could have easily avoided the situation by being obedient in the first place.

So, too, with this parable: I believe that a Christian doesn't need to receive correction from Jesus Christ, because the Holy Spirit will bring them to a place of repentance. If we are sensitive to the promptings of the Holy Spirit, punishment would not be an issue.

However, the Bible is adamant that there is punishment for people who are opposed to God's will in their life. There are certain people who are using and abusing others to acquire wealth. There are people who are drunk and violent and people who are totally self-centered with no thought of others in their life. At the moment of death, these same people will know what lies before them!

But everyone has the opportunity to come to know Jesus and do things the right way. I'm not saying that Christians always do things right! The difference between a Christian and a non-Christian is that they see sin for what it is and call out to God for His mercy. His forgiveness cleanses them and the matter is forgotten. They have the assurance that though they constantly fail, they will never be cut off from the family of God. Because they are not clothed with their own righteousness, but have Christ's righteousness imputed to them, they know that their future is in safe hands.

Our Heavenly Father, just like our earthly parents, will chastise His own children in order for them to learn an important lesson. However, just like in the natural world, our obedience to God means that His godly "stripes" are unnecessary. Bear in mind, that this passage warns us that those who have been given much opportunity much will be expected from them and to those who have been given little opportunity much less will be expected from them.

Our earthly legal system too, has its consequences. Some devious people however, manage to beat the legal system by not ending up with the full punishment they deserve. But God is bigger than any earthly judge! His judgments cannot be interfered with by man! No one will be able to cheat God's system! We can deceive others and even ourselves, but God sees not only what we outwardly do but He knows what we inwardly think. He knows the true condition of our heart.

"There is no creature hidden from His sight, but all things are naked and open to the eyes of Him to whom we must give account." Hebrews 4:13.

There is only one sin that excludes a person from heaven: that sin is the rejection of the Lord Jesus Christ. To live your life independent of God will mean that you will spend eternity, independent of Him. To live a life independent to the God of the Bible means that Christ died for that person in vain; unless of course they do respond to the Gospel.

Jesus said: *"For He whom God has sent speaks the words of God, for God does not give the spirit by measure. The Father loves the Son, and has given all things into His hand. He who believes in the Son has everlasting life; and he who does not believe the Son shall not see life, but the wrath of God abides on him." John 3:34-36.*

These are very hard words for an unbeliever. However, I pray that you will begin to read the Bible and find out for yourself how very much God loves you and how wonderful it is to come into an intimate relationship with the Creator God. There is no better life!

God bless you. I pray that you will write to me, post me a comment or ask me a question. God bless you. Bye.

CONCLUSION/APPENDIX

I hope that you've enjoyed the reading of The Parables of Jesus made simple. I trust that it's been both informative and interesting and you've learned much from it. I've had a number of reviewers read the book so far and I've been very pleased that it has intrigued them, inspired them, and encouraged them.

This book has been written for various readers: long term Christians, new believers and for people who have not yet come to salvation. Specifically, I want to talk to people who have read this book and who are not of the Christian faith at the moment, but would like to be. I want to give you an example prayer that you can pray to invite Jesus into your life and after saying it with sincerity you will know that you *have become a Christian!*

So, if you feel that you want to give your life to Jesus Christ, who is the only way to God, just repeat this prayer to God in Heaven and He will accept you into His family. Then let a mature Christian know what you have done, so that they can support you as you step out on a whole new life journey with God the Holy Spirit living inside of you.

"Dear Father in Heaven,

I acknowledge that I have many faults and I have not allowed you to be boss in my life. I have gone my own way. I see through the reading of this book that You are an all knowing God and Your Son on earth was a perfect reflection of Yourself, being full of love and compassion. I know that one day He's going to return to earth as King and Judge. I acknowledge Him to be all He said He was, the Son of God and the Redeemer of this world. I want to give my life to Him and serve Him from this day forth. Thank you for sending Jesus to be my Savior. Dear Jesus, I ask you to come into my life to be my Lord and my Savior. I ask that your Holy Spirit will guide my life from this day forward. I am eternally repentant for my sins. I am sorry for the things I've done in the past and from this day forth I will lean on your strength to show me a better way. I ask that you will direct my steps; that you cause me to hear Your promptings in my spirit and be my close friend until the day we meet in Heaven.

In Jesus' name, I ask all these things. Amen."

Now, for people who are Christians, there's a prayer that I'd like to encourage you to pray and I believe that Jesus will answer that prayer for you. This prayer is for a deeper commitment to God in order to live a more focused life that will fulfill your destiny. This is a prayer for new Christians and mature Christians who just want to go further with God.

"Dear Father,

Father, there is so much that I need to learn about You. Thank you for being so patient with me and for forgiving me when I don't measure up. Father I want to live a deeper life with You. I ask that you will lead me to the teachers of your choosing so that I will never be deceived with wrong teaching. Thank you for the Scriptures and for Your Holy Spirit who brings revelation. Cause me to be more open to Your leading in my life. I ask You, dear Father, that You'd lead me to the right spiritual gifts test so that I can acknowledge my spiritual gifts. I pray that You would also show me what I'm destined to become. Bring to my memory; use any resource You have so that I know what my purpose on earth is. Then, help me to achieve that purpose. Father, I want every day to bring You glory from now on.

Lead me to other writers who can expound Your truth to me in a simple way to make my life more honoring to You. Cause me to desire to praise you and thank you more and more. Help me to live a life that's worthy of You so that I might become a light to all those I meet. Help me to become a super Christian, someone who fulfills all these parables in their daily life and can live with a life full of joy. Send Your presence and send Your angels, and lead me into a totally fulfilled life here on earth.

In Jesus name I ask all these things, Amen."

Andrew Wommack shared his testimony how he was filled with the Holy Spirit. He said "I got down on my knees one evening in a field in Dallas, Texas, and said 'God I don't know about all this speaking in tongues and the baptism in the Holy Spirit that people are talking about, but if there's a way I can praise you, a way I can magnify you, a way I can go beyond my human English language, I want it.' I started worshiping God and as I did, the Holy Spirit gave me a language, an utterance that I hadn't known or learned."

Acts 2:4 says *"And they were all filled with the Holy Ghost, and began to speak with other tongues, as the Spirit gave them utterance."* Who did the speaking? They did. Who gave the utterance? The Holy Spirit!

A man called Don W Basham wrote a book called "Ministering the Baptism in the Holy Spirit." Here, he points out the steps of receiving this Baptism. Once you understand what is required of you, you will be able to speak in a heavenly prayer language. This ability means you are praying God's will over things and not your own thoughts.

This book explains that when Jesus summoned Peter to step out of the boat and walk on the water, that Peter only had to do what he had always done – to walk. When Peter began his walk of faith, God was right there to do His part. Peter walked: Jesus honored his faith and kept him from sinking. Physically it was no harder for Peter to walk, as it was if he was in shallow water. So the miracle was not in Peter walking but that he didn't sink. Peter by faith had to initiate the miracle and we have to initiate by faith the miracle of speaking in tongues. God always has a part for us to play by faith, before He will do His big part!

We must open our mouths and begin to speak "silly words" and expect that God will begin to speak through us. Forget you even know your native language because if you start speaking that, you will only have to stop and start over. Even the Holy Spirit can't make you speak two languages at the same time.

In Greek and Hebrew, the word for "breath" is the same as the word for "spirit." As you breathe in, believe that the Holy Spirit is coming into your life in a more powerful way. You must know that you will receive Him by faith not by "feelings." Most people don't feel anything! Believe you are breathing in the Holy Spirit and then as you release your breath: let strange words come out *with your breath.* The Holy Spirit will then take over. If you can say five words you can say five thousand words. Use this language each time you pray and you will grow stronger and stronger in the Lord.

"Father, I accept that part of Your perfect plan for me is that I ask Your Son to baptize me with the power of the Holy Spirit so that His gifts will manifest in my life. I need these gifts to be a witness to Your power, so that my life will be a testimony of Your glory. Father, please remove any obstacles in my mind. I release any conscious or subconscious defenses and I step out by faith to receive Your perfect will for me.

I surrender my tongue and my vocal chords to the Holy Spirit. As I take in a breath I will not only expel that breath but with that breath I will begin to speak strange words knowing that the Holy Spirit will then take over and speak His utterances through my mouth. I understand it is a work of faith and I believe that Jesus will baptize me as I do my part. Thank You Lord.

*In Jesus name I ask, Amen. "*Now put into practice what you have just said you would!

I encourage you to use this book as a manual. Put it in your bookshelf and take it out from time to time, and re-read the parables. Even though I am the author, I will still need to go back and read what it says, because so much of the truths that are shared didn't come from me; they came from the Holy Spirit. Therefore, I think that you, as someone who has read this book for the first time, might well do with revisiting it again.

I encourage you to obtain copies of this book for your friends and family. There are reviews on this book on Amazon.com that both you and they can read.

I want to give you some websites that you may want to visit and spend some time looking at. You can look up Andrew Wommack's Ministries whose website is listed below. He's one of the most dynamic and professional speakers of the Word of God. I highly recommend his book called "Sharper than a Two-Edged Sword". His teaching has totally transformed my life and as you've read in my book, I constantly refer to him. You can listen to all of his television broadcasts going back ten years on his website. So if you've got a broadband connection, I'd suggest you look at him.

Andrew's website is at http://www.awmi.net/

Joyce Meyer produces a half hour television show on her website that's listed below. Every day I suggest you tap into Joyce Meyer; she's one of the best Christian teachers in the whole world. She is one of my favorites and she has plenty of subjects to preach on and heaps of practical information for those of you who have just given your life to Jesus.

Joyce Meyer's website is at http://www.joycemeyer.org/

Joseph Prince is another good preacher who expounds God's grace. Visit his website that's listed below and tap into some of the teaching that he has on understanding the finished work of the Cross. His message called "Condemnation Kills but the Spirit Gives Life" is extremely powerful and I highly recommend it.

Joseph Prince's website is at http://www.josephprince.org/

I encourage you to visit my website that has my whole book published on it for free.

My website with this whole book on it is at http://www.parables-of-jesus-christ.net/

Once again, I encourage you to share this link with your Facebook friends. If you can't buy them a physical copy of a book, at least send them a link to this website where they can read this material. I pray that you will be blessed and I encourage any of you to write to me at my email address listed below. Write to me and ask me any questions that you'd like to ask about your Christian faith or things mentioned in this book.

My personal email is survivors.sanctuary@gmail.com

I encourage you to live a prosperous Christian life. I encourage you to find good teachers of the Word of God and simply apply the practical parables that are mentioned in this book. Look out for other books that I am going to write in the future.

God Bless You!

CLOSING THOUGHTS

Jesus by his work on the cross has done what the old Law could never do! This new system is meant for all people everywhere to enter into. No one can fully obey the Ten Commandments or other commandments in the Old Testament Law. It is impossible to fulfill the Law, because every time you break one commandment, you break them all, as it is said in the book of James 2:10 *"For whoever shall keep the whole law and yet stumble in one point, he is guilty of all."*

The whole world suffers and groans with the effects that sin has on people. We are not to be totally blamed for our sin. Our tendency to sin came from Adam, who was the first person to ever sin. That sin "disease" was passed down genetically to all people everywhere. The sin nature we have all inherited is like a disease and the effects of this disease are borne out in wars, genocide, criminal behavior, earthquakes, famines, calamities, starvation and sicknesses. All the suffering of the world comes from one man's original act of sin.

Some churches teach that, while a person has all their sins forgiven at salvation, they must maintain good works and keep themselves holy in order to be forgiven from that time onwards. That is an error! Jesus says if you are going to be part of the new Covenant: if you are going to receive "the new patch," representing God's grace: if you are covered with the patch of Jesus' grace" you can't mix that with the old garment – the old Covenant! If you try to mix the old and the new, it will make the tear worse!

God's laws are good for us, they protect us and they set boundaries which we all need, just like a parent is to love their children and to give them boundaries. But, if we focus on the Law and not on the Lawmaker Himself, we will come under condemnation and God does not want that. We are to place our trust in Jesus and His Holy Spirit in us, who will give us the power to live a God pleasing life.

God would prefer that you do not read your Bible at all, if you open it up with some sense of religion—that you have to do it to be a good Christian. God would prefer that you do not go to church, than for you to go for hypocritical reasons, coming from a legalistic mind-set. Jesus would be justified in feeling insulted, if you want to follow and practice a set of rules just to impress Him or to impress other people. Ask God to make His priorities your priorities - He will!

I am not saying here that Jesus wants you to disobey the Law or His precepts. Instead, I am saying that if you live in liberty, with the understanding that you are forgiven and you are already righteous and holy—if you understand that there is nothing further you need to do to make you more accepted—that God loves you fully for who you are and sees you holy and beautiful right now—if you understand this—you will do all the above things because you love God and for no other reason. Then, you will draw closer to God for all the right reasons. But if you try and mix a set of rules with the New Covenant Gospel of grace, you will end up with a big tear in your life.

I recommend that you check out the teaching of Andrew Wommack who has given me the reason for writing this book. I would never have been able to write as I have, except that he was used by God to correct my legalistic theology. For this I am forever thankful.

Printed in Great Britain
by Amazon